THE
CRITICAL RESPONSE
TO H. G. WELLS

Recent Titles in
Critical Responses in Arts and Letters

THE
CRITICAL RESPONSE
TO H. G. WELLS

Edited by
William J. Scheick

Critical Responses in Arts and Letters, Number 17
Cameron Northouse, Series Adviser

GREENWOOD PRESS
Westport, Connecticut • London

Library of Congress Cataloging-in-Publication Data

The critical response to H. G. Wells / edited by William J. Scheick.
      p.   cm.—(Critical responses in arts and letters, ISSN
1057–0993 ; no. 17)
    Includes bibliographical references and index.
    ISBN 0–313–28859–3 (alk. paper)
    1. Wells, H. G. (Herbert George), 1866–1946—Criticism and
interpretation. I. Scheick, William J. II. Series.
PR5777.C69   1995
823′.912—dc20   94–42119

British Library Cataloguing in Publication Data is available.

Library of Congress Catalog Card Number: 94–42119
ISBN: 0–313–28859–3
ISSN: 1057–0993

First published in 1995

Greenwood Press, 88 Post Road West, Westport, CT 06881
An imprint of Greenwood Publishing Group, Inc.

Printed in the United States of America

∞™

The paper used in this book complies with the
Permanent Paper Standard issued by the National
Information Standards Organization (Z39.48–1984).

10 9 8 7 6 5 4 3 2 1

Copyright Acknowledgments

The editor and the publisher gratefully acknowledge permission to use the following:

H. G. Wells, excerpts from *Experiment in Autobiography*, New York: Macmillan 1934. Reprinted by permission of A. P. Watt Ltd on behalf of The Royal Literary Fund.

"The Lounger," *Critic* (New York), 27 (9 November 1895): 305. Reprinted by permission of *The Atlantic Monthly*.

Bernard Bergonzi, excerpts from *The Early H. G. Wells* (Manchester University Press, 1961). Reprinted by permission of Manchester University Press.

"Literature" *Critic* [*The Atlantic Monthly*] (New York), 32 (22 January 1898): 56.

Excerpts from "Recent Novels," *The Spectator* 79 (25 September 1897): 408. Reprinted by permission of *The Spectator*.

[John St. Loe Strachey] excerpts from "The War of the Worlds," *The Spectator* 80 (29 January 1898): 168–69. Reprinted by permission of *The Spectator*.

Excerpts from *Mr. Sammler's Planet* by Saul Bellow. Copyright © 1969, 1970 by Saul Bellow. Used by permission of Viking Penguin, a division of Penguin Books USA Inc., and the Harriet Wasserman Literary Agency.

Excerpts from "The Ideas of H. G. Wells," *Quarterly Review*, 208 (April 1908): 472–90. Used with the permission of John Murray Publishers Ltd.

"History, Adventure, and School Stories," *Saturday Review* (London), Supplement, 92 (December 1901): x.

John R. Reed, excerpts from *The Natural History of H. G. Wells* (Athens: Ohio University Press, 1982). Reprinted by permission of Ohio University Press.

F.C.S.S., excerpts from "Sociological Speculations." Reprinted with permission from *Nature* 72 (10 August 1905): 337–38. Copyright 1905, Macmillan Magazines Limited.

F. G. Bettany, "Mr. Wells's *Kipps*," *Sunday Times* (London), 29 October 1905.

William Bellamy, excerpts from *The Novels of Wells, Bennett and Galsworthy: 1890–1910*. (London: Routledge & Kegan Paul, 1971). Reprinted by permission of International Thomson Publishing Services Ltd., on behalf of Routledge & Kegan Paul.

Catherine Rainwater, "Encounters with the 'White Sphinx': The Re-Vision of Poe in Wells's Early Fiction" *English Literature in Transition*, 26 (1983): 35–51. Reprinted with the permission of *English Literature in Transition* and the author.

W. H. Chesson, excerpts from "Mr. Wells's New Novel," *The Daily Chronicle* (London), 4 October 1909, p. 3. Reprinted by permission of United Newspapers.

H. L. Mencken, excerpts from "A Fictioneer of the Laboratory," *Smart Set*, 31 (July 1910): 153–55. Reprinted by permission of the Enoch Pratt Free Library in accordance with the terms of the will of H. L. Mencken.

Arnold Bennett, excerpts from *Books and Persons* (London: Chatto & Windus, 1917). Public domain, as per A.P. Watt Ltd.

John R. Reed, "H. G. Wells and Mrs. Humphry Ward," printed here for the first time.

Rebbecca West, excerpts from "The Novel of Ideas," *New Republic*, Supplement, 5 (20 November 1915): 3–5. Reprinted with permission of *New Republic*.

Catherine Rainwater, "Keeping the Game Going: The Re-Vision of Poe in Wells's Later Fiction." *English Literature in Transition,* 30 (1987): 423–36. Reprinted by permission of *English Literature in Transition* and the author.

Catherine Rainwater, "Ellen Glasgow's Outline of History *The Shadowy Third and Other Stories*," printed here for the first time.

E. B. Osborn, excerpts from "Mr. Wells's New Novel," *Morning Post* (London), 1 September 1926, pp. 9, 14. Reprinted by permission of Ewan MacNaughton Associates, Syndication Agents for *The Telegraph*.

Richard Jennings, excerpts from "Mr. H. G. Wells's Pamphlet Novel," *Daily Mirror* (London), 28 July 1927, p. 4. Reprinted by permission of *Daily Mirror*.

Janet Gabler-Hover, "H. G. Wells and Herny James's Two Ladies," printed here for the first time.

William J. Scheick, excerpts from *The Splintering Frame: The Later Fiction of H. G. Wells* (Victoria, B.C.: University of Victoria English Literary Series, 1985), pp. 88–98. Reprinted by permission of the ELS Monograph Series.

H. G. Wells, excerpts from *Meanwhile*. Copyright 1927. Reprinted by permission of A. P. Watt Ltd on behalf of The Literary Executors of the Estate of H. G. Wells.

H. G. Wells, excerpts from *Brynhild*. Copyright 1937. Reprinted by permission of A. P. Watt Ltd on behalf of The Royal Literary Fund.

The graphics in this book are from ClickArt® Images copyright © 1984–1994 by T/Maker Company. All rights reserved.

Every reasonable effort has been made to trace the owners of copyright materials in this book, but in some instances this has proven impossible. The editor and publisher will be glad to receive information leading to more complete acknowledgments in subsequent printings of the book and in the meantime extend their apologies for any omissions.

For
Soshi, Nikki, & Kodi

Contents

Series Foreword

Cameron Northouse

Critical Responses in Arts and Letters is designed to present a documentary history of highlights in the critical reception of the body of work of writers and artists and to individual works that are generally considered to be of major importance. The focus of each volume in this series is basically historical. The introductions to each volume are themselves brief histories of the critical response an author, artist, or individual work has received. This response is then further illustrated by reprinting a strong representation of the major critical reviews and articles that have collectively produced the author's, artist's, or work's critical reputation.

The scope of *Critical Responses in Arts and Letters* knows no chronological or geographical boundaries. Volumes under preparation include studies of individuals from around the world and in both contemporary and historical periods.

Each volume is the work of an individual editor, who surveys the entire body of criticism on a single author, artist, or work. The editor then selects the best material to depict the critical response received by an author or artist over his/her entire career. Documents produced by the author or artist may also be included when the editor finds that they are necessary to a full understanding of the materials at hand. In circumstances where previous, isolated volumes of criticism on a particular individual or work exist, the editor carefully selects material that better reflects the nature and directions of the critical response over time.

In addition to the introduction and the documentary section, the editor of each volume is free to solicit new essays on areas that may not have been adequately dealt with in previous criticism. Also, for volumes on living writers and artists, new interviews may be included, again at the discretion of the volume's editor. The volumes also provide a supplementary bibliography and are fully indexed.

While each volume in *Critical Responses in Arts and Letters* is unique, it is also hoped that in combination they form a useful, documentary history of the critical response to the arts, and one that can be easily and profitably employed by students and scholars.

Cameron Northouse

THE
CRITICAL RESPONSE
TO H. G. WELLS

Introduction: H. G. Wells and the Literate Subconscious

here is a character in Robertson Davies's *Murther & Walking Spirits* (1991) sportingly nicknamed the Sniffer by his newspaper colleagues. In his reviews of plays, the Sniffer delights in detecting influences. Convinced that no one can be original, at least not at this moment in time, he exposes whatever indications he can spot of a new writer's "leaning upon" or "dipping into" the work of established famous authors. Seeking to denigrate new artists, in short, the Sniffer reduces their work to some lowest common denominator of derivation. Several of his colleagues catch a whiff of sexual perversity in this manner.

Authors, confronted by this tendency in critics, likewise often suspect perversity. In an interview, for example, Shirley Hazzard responds to a query about literary influence by noting that the question strikes her "as an example of overstrained thinking from the academic point of view."[1] H. G. Wells would have agreed, but in less agreeable language. In a little-known passage in his autobiography, reprinted in this volume, Wells speaks of what he terms the "odd conventions" of *fin de siècle* literary criticism. In his opinion these conventions are replete with scholarly pretensions:

> It was dominated by the mediaeval assumption that whatever is worth knowing is already known and whatever is worth doing has already been done. Astonishment is unbecoming in scholarly men and their attitude to newcomers is best expressed by the word "recognition." Anybody fresh who turned up was treated as an aspirant Dalai Lama is treated, and scrutinized for evidence of his predecessor's soul. So it came about that every one of us who started writing in the nineties, was discovered to be "a second"—somebody or other.

The Sniffer in Davies's novel, accordingly, seems little more than a crude imitator of his own predecessors, the reviewers of Wells's day.

Wells, moreover, speaks of this perverse practice of reviewers as an influence in itself. He reports that as a result of this critical response to literature, publishers with an eye to reviews urged authors "to be new" without being too new or too strange. "A sheaf of secondhand tickets to literary distinction was thrust into our hands," Wells protests, "and hardly anyone could get a straight ticket on his own." He escaped the fate of nondistinction, he observes, by means of "the perplexing variety of [his] early attributions."

Today, the notion that authors, in whatever field, are self-contained individuals imaginatively separate or free from others is considered a fictional and specifically political representation of creativity. According to Raymond Williams, for instance, the idea of originality emerged during the industrial revolution, when artisans began to abandon their identification with service to a community. During the nineteenth century, Williams explains, the romantic idea of authorship surfaced, and it elevated the individual self over the community: "Under pressure, art became a symbolic abstraction for a whole range of general human experience . . . a general social activity was forced into the status of a department or province, and actual works of art were in part converted into a self-pleading ideology."[2]

Wells emerged as a writer at the time when this self-pleading ideology was on the verge of modernist apogee. And his reflections, apropos the practice of reviewers, suggests a personal tug-of-war between an author's communal and personal identity. There is a certain, typically Wellsian ambiguity in his observation that he had escaped the fate of nondistinction by means of "the perplexing variety of [his] early attributions." Did he escape this fate because of the confusing polyphony of his critics' attributions or because of the stymieing polymorphousness of his appropriations? The ambiguity here is informed by another, more fundamental tergiversation. While making these comments, he vacillates between denial and admission of literary influences. He presents himself as someone who has done something "actually new" even as he admits, in this passage as well as in others reprinted in this volume, the specific influence and his imitation of several "excellent masters."

This play of antitheses—paradoxically combining change and repetition, difference and sameness—is a characteristic of bricolage. Bricolage, Jacques Derrida explains, is an inherent condition of human expression: the art of "newly" combining discarded or prevalent fragments of "preceding" discourses. Creativity, accordingly, is not the production of someone who can "construct the totality of his language, syntax, and lexicon." In short, no artist, scientist, or engineer can claim "the absolute origin of his own discourse."[3]

This concept of bricolage furthers our understanding of the profound conflict lurking within Wells's desire to claim for himself the Romantic ideal— evident in some of the poetry he admired—of the lonely, rebellious, visionary artist revealing radical insights from the Parnassian height of his unique imagination. This conflict can be sensed not only in the claim itself, which is not new with him; this conflict can also be glimpsed when he advances his claim to originality while at the same time he admits his communal affiliation with precedent writers and advocates the development, with his readers, of a collective human consciousness.[4] Wells was, in this regard among others, a transitional figure. His comments simultaneously, if unwittingly, reflect previous notions and anticipate current reflections on authorship. He could not, in other words, escape "the melancholy of the creative mind's desperate insistence upon priority."

The implications of this emergent concept of creativity, it has been suggested, may inform socially unhealthy ideas, may possibly provide "motives for strange and destructive actions." One need not go this far, of course, nor necessarily prescribe that artists "be prepared to accept the guidance and supervision of their fellow citizens."[5] Nor need one necessarily subscribe to the new-historicist notion that there are no authors, only amanuenses unconsciously reinscribing the psychic and cultural patterns of their day.[6] The important point is that artists, whether or not they acknowledge it, are members of various extended communities, by which they are influenced and on which they in turn have an influence.

That no authors escape this circuit of influence is one of the significant insights of Harold Bloom's work. Bloom has shown that authors tend to correct some perceived errant movement in a predecessor's work (*clinamen*), to retain the terms but revise the perceived sense of a precursor's work (*tessera*), to break with or discard a predecessor's work (*kenosis*), to appeal to a power beyond and thereby diminish the uniqueness of a predecessor's work (*daemonization*), to purge human or imaginative features in an effort to truncate another writer's endowment (*askesis*), or to so open a production to an antecedent model as to suggest that what came before is in effect the creation of the present author (*apophrades*).[7] In short, no author ever creates in a vacuum; no author is totally emancipated from the ghosts of predecessors.

These various patterns, some transparent and some opaque, are addressed in the commentary collected in the present volume. This commentary collectively traces the history of Wells's reputation from 1895 to 1994 by featuring the theme of influence in the criticism of his work. If this book presents the reflections of various Sniffers, it does not seek to denigrate Wells's talent or to mitigate our experience of the novelty and strangeness of his work. This volume aims to integrate his achievement with that of his predecessors and his successors—to glimpse the innovation of an author's production as a kind of Phoenix always emerging from and returning to some communal identity. In short, the historical review of commentary on Wells's writings in this volume celebrates authors in communion with each other, in one way or another.

In the course of this record there is disagreement and agreement, disrespect and regard, among these communing authors. But the result is a fascinating dialogue, at once private and public, that we overhear like eavesdropping guests in someone else's living room. If, in the process, we too become Sniffers, we also potentially become Secret Sharers. Our position as outside observers can alternate with our position as inside witnesses if we speculate on this spectacle and if we detect in its speculum our own profound inclusion, as readers, in this community of concerned voices. In such a position we may witness the truth, as expressed by the narrator of William Boyd's *Brazzaville Beach* (1990), that our lives are not entirely the product of our direct choice any more than authored productions are entirely the product of independent creativity: "She often did this, she realized: she reshaped the haphazard inexplicable twists and turns of her life into an order that she approved of, where the controlling hand of her authorship could be read clearly, like a signature."[8]

The Early Career (1895-1905)

When Wells officially appeared upon the literary scene in 1895, he emerged with an overwhelming productivity. In that year alone, he published four books in various registers: *Select Conversations with an Uncle, The Time Machine, The Wonderful Visit,* and *The Stolen Bacillus, and Other Incidents.* Reviewers, suspicious of such prodigious productivity and uncertain of consistency in authorial point of view within such an array of writing, tended to express hesitant approval. Several spoke of Wells's potentiality, rather than accomplishment, as a satirist, allegorist, or romancer. They then set about the task of categorizing his work.

The earliest comments on Wells's writings mention his individual talent and imagination in the same breath as they report his indebtedness to predecessors. To praise him, as one anonymous reviewer did, for having written *The Wonderful Visit* better than perhaps would any other living author[9] leaves open the door to ghostly others. Contemporary novelist Grant Allen is mentioned in the passage reprinted in this collection, but the spirit most often evoked was that of Edgar Allan Poe. The shadow of Poe would relentlessly dog Wells's early career, and with cause; for, by his own later admission, Poe's example was indeed instructive to his early thinking about fiction. The problem was, however, that reviewers were inclined to speak too flatly to this Poe-esque inheritance. As Catherine Rainwater indicates in her revisionist essays reprinted in this collection, the subject of Poe's influence on *The Time Machine* and other Wellsian fiction warrants a subtle and sophisticated approach.

Not heeding his reviewers' concern with such rapid writing, Wells published two more, and very different, books during the following year: *The Island of Dr. Moreau* and *The Wheels of Chance.* As documented by Bernard Bergonzi in this collection, some of Wells's readers worried that his potentiality as an author seemed to be diminishing; three anonymous reviewers typically wondered whether Wells would ever live up to his talent.[10] Others gainsaid his talent by suggesting that, in the instance of *The Island of Dr. Moreau* at least, Wells's talent was wasted on degradation and the transgression of good taste.[11] A London *Times* reviewer asserted that *The Island of Dr. Moreau* exemplified the perverse commercial quest for something sensational.[12] And besides Poe, two new ghosts were glimpsed: Jonathan Swift in *Moreau* and Cervantes in *Chance.*

The following year, 1897, saw four more book by Wells: *Certain Personal Matters* ; *The Plattner Story, and Others* ; *The Invisible Man* ; and *Thirty Strange Stories.* The same complaints against his work of the previous two years resurfaced. There is praise, but always hesitant tribute—*Invisible Man,* for instance, was said to be less well done than it should have been, and Wells is admonished to write fewer books and take more time to perfect his craft.[13] Poe (as exemplified in the review reprinted in this volume) and especially Swift continued to hover. And two new figures were evoked to chastise Wells:

William Tyndale and Thomas Huxley. Huxley, Wells admitted and later critics
would emphasize, was indeed a profound influence on the Darwinian features of
Wells's art. At this early stage of his career, however, fellow author Edmund
Gosse indicated that Wells might have risen to the caliber of Tyndale and
Huxley, but had clearly chosen to "tell little horrible stories about monsters."[14]

A monster of another kind, at least from Wells's point of view, hatched
from the reviews of 1897—comparisons to Jules Verne that reduced him to the
status of an apostle. It was not flattering to be dubbed the Jules Verne of
England, especially since Wells, unlike Verne, had been trained as a scientist.
And in the offing was Rudyard Kipling, whose name by way of comparison was
mentioned in passing in at least one review, as it had been previously in 1895.

The extensive number of reviews responding to *The War of the Worlds*
(1898) indicates that whatever reservations previous reviewers had expressed
about his success, Wells had indeed emerged as a writer who could not be
ignored. There were, again, reservations about slipshod style, hasty plotting,
vulgar content and cheap effects; but these doubts were overrun by the general
verdict that this romance was one of the most ingenious stories of the year and
the best work to date of an author who was one of the most original of the
younger English novelists. Wells must have particularly appreciated the
observation that in this romance his management of scientific knowledge
outstripped the example of Verne, and (as evident in the passage presented in
this volume) that the humanity of his characters and density of detail surpassed
the example of Poe, Swift, and Defoe.

The romances Wells published from 1899 to 1905—*When the Sleeper
Wakes* (1899), *Tales of Space and Time* (1899), *The First Men in the Moon*
(1901), *The Sea Lady* (1902), *Twelve Stories and a Dream* (1903), *The Food of
the Gods* (1904), and *A Modern Utopia* (1905)—all received a similarly mixed
reception, with positive reactions predominating. Where once there was
uncertainty, now most reviewers were sure that Wells's work, whatever its
artistic merits and whatever its identity as fiction, had behind it a serious,
thought-provoking social program. The printing of his non-fictional
*Anticipations of the Reaction of Mechanical and Scientific Progress upon
Human Life and Thought* (1901), *The Discovery of the Future* (1902), and
Mankind in the Making (1903) left no doubt that Wells was in fact promoting a
socialist agenda in his work.

Ideas were not the only concern of the reviewers. *Men in the Moon*, for
instance, provoked a debate on whether Verne's inventions were more exciting
or less rich and mature than those of Wells. This controversy occurred in both
England and France, for by this time Wells's work was simultaneously published
in both countries. One can imagine Wells's irritation upon seeing the
controversy invade scientific journals such as *Nature*, and (even worse perhaps)
learning of Verne's own assertions that the Englishman's stories lack scientific
premises. The wraith of Swift, summoned (in commentary included in this
collection) specifically to displace the figure of Verne, was hardly consoling.
Wells's friend, Arnold Bennett entered the fray. Ventriloquizing Wells's own
views, Bennett denounced this controversy as absurd because Verne was usually
scientifically inaccurate and merely entertaining, whereas under the guise of

romance Wells presented a serious consideration of human existence.[15]

There were skeptics, nonetheless. A lengthy discussion in the conservative *Quarterly Review*, a portion of which is reprinted here, savaged Wells on both scientific and social grounds. And Gilbert K. Chesterton, whose antipathy to Wellsian thought would be long-lived, reduced *Food of the Gods* to the story of Jack the Giant-Killer, retold from the viewpoint of the giant.[16] Unwittingly Chesterton had come close to a very perceptive observation: that the inversion of previous narratives, with the intention of provoking a revisionary perspective, was a fundamental technique of Wells's artistic practice.

Revision is certainly at issue in *A Modern Utopia*, a book that revived the sort of reviewer interest that had been evident upon the publication of *The War of the Worlds*. Many of the responses to this hard-to-pin-down book were polarized in extreme political terms. Readers were quick to spot the vestiges of Platonic ideas in this book, a fact Wells encouraged rather than denied. From Wells's point of view, however, the issue was what he had done by way of refashioning Plato's thought in terms of, say, notions of progress. Very few reviewers, whether for or against the work, wrestled with Wells's revisionism, as did the author of the commentary included in this collection. Readers of one sociology journal were, more typically, told that *A Modern Utopia* was little more than a good-natured satire.[17]

In the midst of his fictional and non-fictional productions during these seven years, Wells published *Love and Mr. Lewisham* (1900). Critics, who hardly recalled the sparsely reviewed *Wheels of Chance*, were caught somewhat off guard by this humorous novel in the realistic mode—one more example of Wells's remarkable range. On the rebound, these reviewers overall declared this story in "the decadent school" to be a very promising sign of Wells's prospects as a contributor to the art of fiction.

Five years later Wells published *Kipps* (1905), another novel in the *Lewisham* mode. Like its two predecessors, *Kipps* received a very mixed reception, with finally more approving than disapproving commentary. F. G. Bettany, who appears in this collection, saw a resemblance between this novel and a contemporary farce, a suggestion no later critic has taken up. But it was the image of Charles Dickens that would become the haunt of choice among the Sniffers, a ghost who would rattle its chain in countless reviews to come. In a rare moment among such reductive comparisons, one anonymous reviewer ventured the opinion that in contrast to Dickens, Wells was more earnest than tender, more sociological than humane.[18]

The Middle Career (1906-1919)

By 1906, Wells's career was as firmly established as were the camps for and against him. His avid supporters looked forward to everything he would publish, and his equally avid detractors were sure they knew exactly what they would find before they opened the covers of any new book by him. Wells, however, was a man who entertained various ideas at various times of his life, a habit resulting in a corpus hardly consistent over time. His work would continue to surprise and to vex. Although, in a sense, the bloom was off during his mid-career, the plenitude and the boldness of his various undertakings continued to provoke intense debate.

During the fourteen years of his middle career Wells presented more than a score of non-fiction works. The best known of these works today are identical to the most extensively reviewed at the time of their appearance: *The Future in America* (1906), *New Worlds for Old* (1907), *First and Last Things* (1908), *God the Invisible King* (1917) and *The Way to a League of Nations* (1919).

God the Invisible King raised the hackles of a substantial number of readers, particularly given its insolent intolerance toward all established religious creeds. This book, it was even suggested, was plagiarized from the work of the early nineteenth-century positivist French philosopher Auguste Comte and also echoed features of the religious beliefs of contemporary playwright George Bernard Shaw. There were, as well, charges of inconsistencies, inaccuracies, and illogic in its alleged amateurish revival of Gnostic and Manichaean notions. And *The Soul of a Bishop* (1917), a novelistic treatment of the ideas in *God the Invisible King*, fared no better. When not dismissed as absurd propaganda for a feeble deity, *Bishop* was assailed as an incongruous journalistic jumble of humanitarian beliefs.

Controversy emerged as well over several of the other novels Wells published during this time. Adverse reaction to Wells's apparent allegiance to socialism, including his advocacy of free love, characterized a number of responses to *In the Days of the Comet* (1906). But the principal discontent with this romance concerned aesthetic dissatisfaction over the second part of the novel, when the comet arrives. It was not until William Bellamy, who appears in this collection, that this portion of the novel was defended. Although, in a minority report, the London *Times* critic F. G. Bettany approved of its dissemination of sociological ideas through the vehicle of fiction,[19] *Comet* struck most others as an instance of the Kiplingesque waste of talent whereby art is abandoned for sermon.

Wells's following two novels *Tono-Bungay* (1908) and *Ann Veronica* (1909) were likewise aesthetically faulted for structural amorphousness and authorial self-indulgence. Some readers noted the remarkableness of these two books, but by now reviewers were increasingly more engaged with the social implications of Wells's work than with his attitudes toward the art of fiction. And these implications were for many very provocative indeed. Several voices warned that the love story in *Tono-Bungay* was in bad taste because it reduced humans to animals without morals. Readers of the *Spectator* were told, in short, that this novel is "a strong, sincere, but in the main repellent work."[20]

The topic of repellent morality was certainly featured in a number of responses to *Ann Veronica*, the vulgarity of which (it was feared) may have a pernicious (that is, feminist) influence on young women. Under a pseudonym, Wilfred Witten warned that this book encourages women "to run amuck through life in the name of self-fulfillment."[21] Similar fears led to the banning of *Ann Veronica* by many libraries. While other readers thought it a remarkable book—for instance, W. H. Chesson's appreciation of its Thackerian satiric heritage, reprinted here—many rejected Wells's attempt to speak through a female persona. The protagonist is only Wells in petticoats, some suggested; as a mere prop for his social theories, they proclaimed, Ann fails to render a woman's sensibility.

The appearance of *The History of Mr. Polly* (1910) gave these guardians of society a respite, or so it seemed. *Polly* hearkened back to the manner of *Chance*, *Kipps*, and *Lewisham*, a fact that pleased as many reviewers as it disappointed. H. L. Mencken, who appears in this volume, not only was skeptical of this new book but also reassessed its alleged Dickensian features. *Polly*, with its charming idealism and humor, proved to be a lull, as it were, before the tempestuous storm of *The New Machiavelli* (1911), a *roman à clef* banned by some English libraries. Reviewers grudgingly admitted that this book caught the spirit of the time—the prevalence of social and moral discontent—but they backed away from what they sensed to be a dubious political and sociological philosophy. Once again, this time under a pseudonym, Wells's good friend entered the fracas; in an article reprinted in this collection, Arnold Bennett rebuked the animus of the reviewers of *Machiavelli*.

At this time, Bennett was a prominent figure in his own right. Reviewers, in fact, were quick to suggest similarities between Bennett and Wells, and not always approvingly for either of them. *Polly*, one person suggested, was not as accomplished as Bennett's *Old Wives' Tale* (1908). Others thought that the technique of *The New Machiavelli* and *Marriage* (1912) recalled Bennett's manner.

In an essay reprinted in this collection, Rebecca West (Cicely Fairfield) in effect suggests why *Marriage* was so tepidly received. This review, which approvingly situates Wells among continental realists and naturalists, occasioned the first meeting between West and Wells. Their subsequent liaison (1913-23) influenced his *The Passionate Friends* (1913), *The Wife of Sir Isaac Harmon* (1914), and *The Research Magnificent* (1915), novels of diarist impulse that were promptly faulted by reviewers: for unbelievable or underdeveloped characters; for poor plotting or disappointing conclusions; for belabored, hackneyed or confused thought; for unfocused, obscure, or contradictory viewpoint and intention. A few readers ventured the surmise that such facile arm-chair creations indicated that Wells had stalled as a writer.

There were, besides West's, two other particularly original observations about *Marriage*. One noted, unfortunately disapprovingly, that the technique of this narrative borrowed from scientific procedure.[22] The other described the novel as a transitional writing demarcating the movement of Wells's thought toward some sort of belief in a Bergsonain deity.[23] (Indeed *God the Invisible King* was in the offing.) That Henri Bergson's thought supported Wells's experimental method was likewise reported by a French critic.[24] Later critics have not pursued this contemporary influence on Wells, although they have observed the affect of Bergson's idea of *durée* on the narrative technique of the rising generation of novelists during the early twentieth century.[25]

At this time, other contemporaries with whom Wells was said to be communing, in one way or another, included George Gissing and Henry James. Whereas the characters in Gissing's fiction never succeed or even hope to succeed, one reader noted, Wells's protagonists discover their potentiality and struggle to prevail. Parts of *Machiavelli* reminded some of James. In *Boon*

(1915), a book which led one reviewer to refer to its author as a second Swift, Wells satirized James's method so harshly that he permanently ruptured their relationship. Several intricacies of the Wells-James relationship are revealed in Janet Gabler-Hover's innovative essay included in this volume.

Commentary on Wells continued to resurrect not just Swift but other standby ghosts, especially Dickens. To some reviewers, *Tono-Bungay* recalled *David Copperfield* ; the overview of *The New Machiavelli* was reminiscent of the artlessness of Dickens's manner; *The Wife of Sir Isaac Harmon* exhibited Dickensian flaws; and *The History of Mr. Polly* evidenced both similarities and differences between Wellsian and Dickensian technique.

Other haunts were spied as well. The specter of William Shakespeare was glimpsed in *Isaac Harmon*, which seemed to one reader to be a literal translation of *The Taming of the Shrew* without poetry, humor, or imagination. (Later, as the excerpt by Bergonzi in this volume reveals, Shakespeare's shadow would be seen in earlier Wellsian productions.) Whereas the vestige of Niccolò Machiavelli seemed to some to be conspicuously absent in Wells's *The New Machiavelli*, glimpses of an approving William Makepeace Thackeray were seen in the variety of this novel, as Chesson had seen in the satire of *Ann Veronica*.

Whereas Van Wyck Brooks reported shades of Mathew Arnold in Wells's corpus, Stuart P. Sherman saw spectral evidence of Percy Bysshe Shelley's self-willed, egotistic, anarchical imagination.[26] Although the influence of Eugène Fromentin's romantic psychological novel, *Dominique* (1863) was spied in *Passionate Friends*, in fact even today little has been written on the Romantic roots of Wells's fiction. This subject figures in Allan Chavkin's discussion, included in this volume.

Wells's romanticism, however frayed, weathered the years of the first world war, even in what one reviewer spoke of as the Hamlet-like tragedy of *Mr. Britling Sees It Through* (1916). Presenting various points of view, this novel was regarded at the time of its appearance more for what it recorded of English life at such a sensitive historical moment than for its disquisitional manner. This manner, however, became for Wells an *idée fixe*. Accordingly, his next two dialogue novels *Joan and Peter* (1918) and *The Undying Fire* (1919) predictably received a very ungracious reception.

Joan and Peter was faulted for lack of good writing, strong plot, deep characterization, and clarity of purpose. However much several reviewers thought its revisionary ideas about education were interesting, the majority dismissed this dialogue novel as repetitive, loquacious, and inchoate. *The Undying Fire*, a recasting of the Book of Job, struck many as another dubious sermon communicated through incessant talk. While one reader heard in this book strains of Alfred Tennyson's *In Memoriam* (1850), another anonymous voice barked: *Fire* "is called a contemporary novel. Heaven knows with what it is contemporary, and Hell knows that the thing is no novel."[27]

The Late Career (1920-1945)

Disenchantment with Wells was most pronounced toward the end of his career.

No longer was he considered as one of the rising generation. To the new crop of emerging authors he increasingly seemed to represent the pre-war old guard, those who had proffered the unfulfilled and unfulfillable promises of political pragmatism. His art, as well, struck many of this younger generation—such writers as Virginia Woolf—as passé; and H. L. Mencken pronounced the artist in Wells to be deceased.[28] Wells still commanded respect in some quarters, but he was also fair game for others expressing still more radical conceptions of art, society, and reality. Whether legitimate or *pro forma*, this adversarial posture toward Wells obscured the extent of his own aesthetic revisionism during his late career. With the exception of the highly controversial *Outline of History* (1920), Wells's late works were the least regarded of his writings during his lifetime and, inappropriately, remain so today.

The Outline of History, which saw numerous printings and editions, was a *cause célèbre*. With this massive attempt to interpret the course of mankind, Wells in effect placed all of his cards on the table in making a case for his idealistic vision of human potentiality. As might be expected, nit-picking preoccupied many reviewers; but appreciation of Wells's earnest contribution to humanity's self-awareness prevailed. During the remainder of his life, Wells would go on to write nearly fifty other contentious non-fiction books, including *The Open Conspiracy* (1928), *The Work, Wealth, and Happiness of Mankind* (1932), *World Brain* (1938), and *The Fate of Homo Sapiens* (1939)—all designed to advance mankind toward a greater realization of human perfection.

Wells's role as public spokesman in these works shifted attention away from artistic matters in his fiction during this time. There was, accordingly, decreased interest in his later novels generally, especially as *belles-lettres*. And, occasionally, reviewers wished Wells would return to his pre-1911 manner, particularly the manner of *Tono-Bungay* and *The History of Mr. Polly*.

Several expressions of approval of Wells's thought and his expansion of the novel of ideas notwithstanding, reviewers generally dashed *The Secret Places of the Heart* (1922) as dull, childish, and unconvincing; *Men Like Gods* (1923) as sophomoric, bureaucratic, and self-plagiarized; *The Dream* (1924) as boring, preachy, and undistinguished; *Christina Alberta's Father* (1925) as out-of-date, mechanical, and inconsistent; *The World of William Clissold* (1926) as unrealistic, vague, and stale; and *Meanwhile* (1927) as propagandistic, structureless, and undramatic. The sparsely reviewed *Mr. Blettsworthy on Rampole Island* (1928) received the most favorable responses during this decade, in part because this satiric and allegorical novel reminded a number of readers of an earlier stage of Wells's career.

In fact, the 1920s saw several attempts to review Wells's career, and all of them concluded that his early work was his best. The books most likely to endure, they mutually agreed, are *Kipps*, *Tono-Bungay*, and *The History of Mr. Polly*. Their precipitous consensus concluded that Wells's intellectual influence was not profound and his literary influence had been exhausted by 1915.[29] Of note, however, were two voices of dissent from this prevailing view. One declaimed that in spite of his bad press, Wells was one of the geniuses of the time; the other declared that although the younger generation had grown apart from him, this very disagreement indicated that Wells had been its ideal father.[30]

The keenest reassessment was offered by Stuart P. Sherman in a review of the Atlantic Edition of *The Works of H. G. Wells* (1924). Sherman acknowledges that whatever Wells's defects as a writer, there is much to appreciate, especially in the short fiction. Wells's short stories, Sherman reported, do not appear as purposeless as they originally did, but instead are burdened with moral meanings designed to urge new points of view.[31]

Of the ghosts that have been perennially seen by critics to haunt Wells's work, Dickens remained the most lively during the 1920s. He was spied not only in *Men Like Gods* but, as the assessments of Wells's work mounted, throughout his career. Wells, his reviewers agreed, was second only to Dickens in humorous characterization. Fellow novelist E. M. Forster added that, as humorists, Wells and Dickens mutually share the technique of cataloguing details of character, a technique without a sense of taste or beauty.[32] Besides Dickens, other specters were occasionally sited: Thomas Carlyle in *The Research Magnificent*, Isaiah and John Bunyan in *Men Like Gods*, a Quixotic Christ-figure and an older Ann Veronica in *Christina Alberta's Father*, Jonathan Swift and François Voltaire in *Mr. Blettsworthy on Rampole Island*, and Denis Diderot in Wells's belief in the interdependence of all beings. In comments by Richard Jennings and E. B. Osborn, both included in this volume, Karl Marx, George Bernard Shaw, and Noël Coward are mentioned. And whereas *Mr. Blettsworthy* was said to be influenced by the studies of Sir James Frazer, *The Dream* was said to respond to the reviewers of *Men Like Gods*. Wells's house of fiction was a crowded domicile, with even (according to John R. Reed's definitive essay in this anthology) Mrs. Humphry Ward arriving for an extended stay.

If through the next decade Wells continued to write exactly the kind of fiction he believed civilization needed, so likewise his critics continued to argue with him about his choice. But if Wells was as engaged as ever with the genre of fiction as a vehicle for social reform, his critics were increasingly withdrawing from their argument with him. During the 1930s and 1940's his novels received fewer and fewer reviews. And what reviews they received seemed as tired in their approach to his work as they accused Wells of being in his ideas and his attitude toward fiction. At present, one critic said mercilessly, Wells is "the sedulous ape of himself."[33] Much of Wells's creativity in this last phase of his career went undetected simply because reviewers, before reading a word of any new novel by him, were already sure no surprise or ingenuity could be found there.

The satire and characterization of *The Autocracy of Mr. Parham* (1930) received some praise, but this portrait of fascism was more often dismissed as tedious and outdated. (The illustrations for *Parham*, incidentally, presented only somewhat recognizable public figures so as to evade libel lawsuits.) Its clever flashes of insight notwithstanding, *The Bulpington of Blup* (1933) was commonly rejected as a myopic presentation of old exhibits that unwittingly included the author in its dwindling satire. Whereas some thought that Wells's repudiation of Robert Burton's *The Anatomy of Melancholy* (1621) offered a tonic for the times, others dismissed *The Anatomy of Frustration* (1936) as very irritating display of its author's mannerisms, including his mixture of balderdash and sagacity.

Seemingly reminiscent of his earliest romances, the allegorical novella *The Croquet Player* (1936) was praised as a symbolic thriller. *Star Begotten* (1937), a recasting of the birth of Jesus as a political allegory, fared somewhat less well—"a stick of lemon candy stuck in a dill pickle," as Fanny Butcher put it.[34] *Brynhild* (1937) fared much worse, deemed a disaster as art, propaganda, and entertainment. *Apropos of Dolores* (1938) received much more attention than *The Brothers* (1938), which struck many as a very thin fantastic melodrama. *Dolores* certainly had its detractors, including the reviewer who thought it accidentally read like the travesty of Wells in Max Beerbohm's *Christmas Garland* (1912).[35] But there was a substantial swell of voices who suggested that it might be the best novel Wells had written in years, a psychological study revealing creative energy and a mature mind. The down-stroke of this see-saw rhythm of critical reaction prevailed in the commentary on Wells's last four novels: *The Holy Terror* (1939), *Babes in the Darkling Wood* (1940), *All Aboard for Ararat* (1940), and *You Can't Be Too Careful* (1941).

As during the 1920s, so also during the 1930's *The History of Mr. Polly* remained the critical favorite of Wells's fiction, and Sinclair Lewis (who would later nominate Wells for the Nobel Prize) wrote an introduction for a new edition of it in 1942.[36] The Sniffers were still seeing Dickens not only in *Polly* but throughout Wells's fiction. A Dickensian presence was said (particularly in *You Can't Be Too Careful*) to leaven the spirit of Thomas Carlyle or (as observed by H. E. Bates)[37] to fuse with the spirit of Edgar Allan Poe. Surveys of Wells's literary corpus again spotted the example of Jonathan Swift, who was said to have inspired Wells to wed fantasy and social criticism. Other readers spied Charles Darwin and other Victorian predecessors, particularly Samuel Butler. Philosopher Georg Hegel was glimpsed in *The Holy Terror*, and both François Rabelais and Jean Jacques Rousseau were sighted in *Experiment in Autobiography* (1934). And a caricatured Gilbert K. Chesterton, who would die within three years of its publication, was spotted in *The Bulpington of Blup*. The company Wells was said to keep was certainly various from the beginning to the end of his career.

Perhaps Malcolm Cowley aptly summarized the ambiguous critical climate in which Wells found himself in the last years of his life. Cowley described Wells's autobiography, which received considerable commendation from reviewers, as "the best of his novels," as a miracle considering Wells's rapidly declining career. Cowley caught the ambivalence of the younger generation when he concluded that Wells was like "the survivor of a prehistoric time, a warm, ponderous, innocent creature ill adapted to the Ice Age in which we live, and yet overshadowing the smaller animals that shiver behind the rocks."[38] Cowley's implicit verdict on Wells was that while naively brave and defiant, the type he represented was doomed to extinction.

Wells Redivivus (1946-1994)

When Wells died in 1946, his fiction and message seemed dated to many commentators: a journalistic discursiveness deficient in artistic consciousness and evidencing a Victorian confidence in progress. Nevertheless, one obituary suggested that he was arguably the greatest journalist since Defoe. And, as time would reveal, the novels and short stories of this "new and livelier Plato," as Sinclair Lewis dubbed Wells, lived on not only as popular works but also as serious fiction.

This longevity was not particularly evident during the 1950s, when commentary on Wells experienced a lull. Dwindling regard prevailed, despite the appearance of several theatrical, television, and cinematic versions of his work. There was some recognition that writers had in effect dialogued with Wells through their work. Wells's presence or influence, in a sophisticated sense, was detected in George Bernard Shaw's *Man and Superman* (1905), Joseph Conrad's *Chance* (1914), Edgar Rice Burrough's *The Moon Maid* (1926), Aldous Huxley's *Brave New World* (1932), George Orwell's *Nineteen Eighty-Four* (1949), and Anthony West's *Heritage* (1955).

In turn, besides such customary figures as Darwin and Dickens, other influences on Wells's work were spotted. These ranged from Wells's revisionist response to the Fabian arguments of George Bernard Shaw and Beatrice Webb to (more speculatively) his possible knowledge of Francis Godwin's *Man in the Moone* (1638), Humphrey Davy's *Consolations in Travel* (1830), and Rudyard Kipling's "With the Night Mail: A Story of 2000 A. D." (1909).[39]

The 1960s were ushered in by both Richard Ellmann's *Edwardians and Late Victorians* (1960), which pronounced Wells's work to be less than expected, and Kingsley Amis's *New Maps of Hell: A Survey of Science-Fiction* (1960), which offered a favorable revaluation of Wells's achievement. There were several other positive reexaminations and the formation of an H. G. Wells Society, but the further decline of Wells's reputation was finally halted by Bernard Bergonzi's *The Early H. G. Wells: A Study of the Scientific Romances* (1961). Bergonzi's book, excerpted here, insisted upon Wells's successful integration of social and artistic consciousness. Bergonzi's study was reinforced by the serious consideration of Wellsian thought in W. Warren Wager's *H. G. Wells and the World State* (1961) and Mark L. Hillegas's *The Future as Nightmare: H. G. Wells and the Anti-Utopians* (1967).

As these two books indicate, major reconsiderations of Wells's work were now appearing not only in book-length studies but also under the impressive aegis of university presses. Indeed, the 1960s mark the transfer of interest in Wells to academia, where his legacy would generate countless publications until the present day. From the formalist interests of the 1960's (*e. g.*, Kenneth B. Newell's *Structure in Four Novels by H. G. Wells* [1968]), through the structuralist readings of the 1970s (*e. g.*, Darko Suvin's *Metamorphoses of Science Fiction: On the Poetics and History of a Literary Genre* [1979]), to the post-structuralist and post-Marxist considerations of the 1980s and 1990s (*e. g.*, John Huntington's *The Logic of Fantasy: Science Fiction and H. G. Wells* [1982]), Wells's fiction has proved a rich resource for academic critics.

Plato, Poe, and Dickens made their perennial appearance in later attempts to determine influences on Wells, but new possibilities included Johannes Kepler, John Milton (specifically in *Paradise Lost* [1667]), Nathaniel Hawthorne, Edward Bellamy, Olaf Stapledon, various French authors, and the socialistic and the scientific writings of his time. Much more prevalent were claims for Wells's influence upon the writings of others, an influence registered primarily in revision or repudiation of his ideas. Authors said to dialogue with Wells included Joseph Conrad (in *The Inheritors* [1903], with Ford Maddox Hueffer), Edwin Lester Arnold (in *Lieut. Gulliver Jones, His Vacation* [1905], Yevgenii Zamyatin, Dorothy Richardson (in *Pilgrimage* [1915-38]), Victor Rousseau Emmanuel, Rebecca West, Sinclair Lewis, Aldous Huxley (in *Crome Yellow* [1921] and *Island* [1962]), George Orwell, William Golding (in *The Inheritors* [1955] and *Pincher Martin* [1956]), and John Osborne. And during the 1960s, C. S. Lewis, Jorge Luis Borges, and Vladimir Nabokov publicly declared their special interest in Wells's writings, thereby opening the door later critical considerations of Wellsian influences on their own work.

In the 1970s, accordingly, critics sniffed the spirit of Wells in Borges's short fiction, Lewis's *Out of the Silent Planet* (1938), and Nabokov's *Invitation to a Beheading* (1938). Some of the similarly haunted sites of the preceding decade received still more attention, specifically works by Conrad (*The Secret Agent* [1907]), Zamyatin, Huxley, Orwell, and Golding. As if more active than ever, Wells's ghost was also seen in various traditions of modern science-fiction, especially in the work of John W. Campbell, Jr. and Isaac Asimov. Specific sightings were observed in George Gissing's *The Private Papers of Henry Ryecroft* (1903), E. M. Forster's *The Machine Shops* (1908), Ford Maddox Ford's *Mr. Apollo* (1908), Yuri Olesha's *Zavist* (1928), W. Somerset Maugham's *Cakes and Ale* (1930), Evelyn Waugh's *Love among the Ruins* (1953), L. P. Hartley's *Facial Justice* (1960), and V. S. Naipaul's *The House of Mr. Biswas* (1961).

Most of the specters previously seen in Wells's own work were likewise glimpsed during the 1970s. But there were, as well, other specters now lingering in his haunted house of fiction: John Bunyan, Voltaire, Henrik Ibsen, Arthur Schopenhauer, Friedrich Nietzsche, Oswald Spengler, Wilkie Collins, Sir James Frazer, Rebecca West, and Fritz Lang (by way of the film *Metroplis* [1928]). Wells's house of fiction became even more crowded in the 1980s with the apparitions of Suetonius, Petronius, the New Testament apostles, Maori priests, Robert Burton, Anthony Hope, various ghost-story authors, and Frank Challice Constable. The wraith of Poe made a particularly strong reappearance, from a post-structuralist angle, in two innovative essays by Catherine Rainwater, both reprinted in this anthology together with her new study of Ellen Glasgow's participation in the Poe-Wells connection. And John R. Reed's *The Natural History of H. G. Wells* (1982), also excerpted here, provided a rich mine for future scholars to explore influences upon Wells.

In turn, during the 1980s Wells's shadow was spied in Fedor Sologub's *Legend in Creation* (1907-12), Sinclair Lewis's *Our Mr. Wrenn* (1914), D. H. Lawrence's *Women in Love* (1921), F. Scott Fitzgerald's *The Great Gatsby* (1925), Adolfo Bioy Casares's *La invencion de Morel* (1953), J. R. R. Tolkien's *Lord of the Rings* (1954-55), and Arthur C. Clarke's and Jack Williamson's science-fiction. And in an essay commissioned for this book Allan Chavkin astutely detects Wells's spirit in Saul Bellow's *Mr. Sammler's Planet* (1970).

The 1960s through the 1980s saw efforts to define traditions in which Wells participated. Two especially noteworthy identifications pointed to the condition of England novel (David Lodge's *Language in Fiction* [1966]) and the modern therapeutic imagination (William Bellamy's *The Novels of Wells, Bennett and Galsworthy, 1890-1910* (1971). These decades also saw the publication of various valuable editions of Wells's previously uncollected writings, a substantial collection of commentary on Wells (Patrick Parrinder's *H. G. Wells: The Critical Heritage* [1972]), and a number of biographies (the most substantial being Norman and Jeanne MacKenzie's *The Time Traveller: The Life of H. G. Wells* [1973] and David C. Smith's *H. G. Wells, Desperately Mortal* [1986]).

Through all the decades of criticism, general readers and literary critics alike have preferred Wells's early fiction to his later novels. Two studies—one excerpted here—have specifically attempted to modify this feature of Wells's critical reception: Robert Bloom's *Anatomies of Egotism: A Reading of the Last Novels of H. G. Wells* (1977) and my *The Splintering Frame: The Later Fiction of H. G. Wells* (1984). Both studies suggest that Wells's late experimentation with the novel as a genre has been overlooked and underappreciated.

If Wells's fiction has been neglected, so have his short stories. This is most peculiar given his generally recognized mastery of this form and Stuart Sherman's specific valuation of them in 1925. Even today, critics routinely include Wells as a powerful influence on the development of the short story; yet there are very few considerations of any of his short fiction, certainly nothing comparable to the spate of commentary on his romances published at the same time as these tales. Two of these stories receive close readings in my *Fictional Structure and Ethics: The Turn of the Century English Novel* (1990) and *The Ethos of Romance at the Turn of the Century* (1994). Unfortunately, J. R. Hammond's *H. G. Wells and the Short Story* (1992), which contains a useful an annotated checklist of these tales, only flirts with the possibilities these tales offer the critic.

Aside from observing this preference for his early romances over his later fiction and the strangely tepid closure with his short stories, there are no easy generalizations to present at the conclusion of this overview of Wells's reputation during and after his life. At present, it is probably fair to say, he does not stand at the forefront of conscious critical concern. But he is still present, not only in such famous expressions as "the war to end all wars" and "the iron curtain," but also in such projects as the *Columbia History of the World*, which was inspired by Wells's *Outline of History*.[40] Especially in those of his books that have remained in print for decades, Wells is an abiding interest to a substantial number of general readers and academic critics. But he also figures, our survey suggests, as a ghostlike presence within the dialogic matrix of countless other writings currently more fashionable than his own. Culturally we inevitably encounter him directly or indirectly, and no critical exorcism has been able to rid our literary heritage of his lingering spirit. He is a permanent resident of the haunted house of both our fiction and our "literate subconscious."[41]

NOTES

1. Catherine Rainwater and William J. Scheick, "An Interview with Shirley Hazzard (Summer 1982)," *Texas Studies in Literature and Language* 25 (1983): 215.

2. Raymond Williams, *Culture and Society, 1780-1950* (New York: Columbia University Press, 1958), p. 47.

3. Jacques Derrida, "Structure, Sign, and Play in the Discourse of the Human Sciences," *Writing and Difference*, trans. Alan Bass (Chicago: University of Chicago Press, 1978), pp. 285-89.

4. The idea of a collective will is itself not original; see my *The Splintering Frame: The Later Fiction of H. G. Wells* (Victoria, B. C.: University of Victoria English Literary Studies, 1984), pp. 37-40.

5. Paul Feyerabend, "Creativity—A Dangerous Myth," *Critical Inquiry* 13 (1987): 700-11.

6. See, for example, Stephen Greenblatt, *Renaissance Self-Fashioning* (Chicago: University of Chicago Press, 1980).

7. Harold Bloom, *Anxiety of Influence: A Theory of Poetry* (New York: Oxford University Press, 1973).

8. William Boyd, *Brazzaville Beach* (New York: Avon, 1992), p. 113.

9. "Fiction," *Saturday Review* (London) 80 (26 October 1895): 554.

10. "Coming and Going," *Saturday Review* (London) 82 (12 December 1896): 630-31; "Novels," *Manchester Guardian* 14 April 1896, p. 4; Picaroon, "Mr. H. G. Wells," *Chap-Book* (Chicago) 5 (1896): 366-74.

11. "Fiction," *Speaker* 13 (18 April 1896): 429-30; P. Chalmers Mitchell, "The Island of Dr Moreau," *Saturday Review* (London) 81 (11 April 1896): 368-69.

12. "Recent Novels," *Times* (London) 17 June 1896, p. 17.

13. Claudius Clear, "The Fantastic Fiction; or, The Invisible Man," *Bookman* (New York) 6 (November 1897): 250-51.

14. Edmund Gosse, "Ten Years of English Literature," *North American Review* 165 (August 1897): 145.

15. Arnold E. Bennett, "Herbert George Wells and His Work," *Cosmopolitan* 33 (August 1902): 465-71.

16. G. K. Chesterton, "Mr. Wells and the Giants," *Bookman* (London) 27 (December 1904): 124.

17. A[bion] W. S[mall], "A Modern Utopia," *American Journal of Sociology* 11 (November 1905): 430-31.

18. "Comedy and Sociology," *Public Opinion* 39 (11 November 1905): 633.

19. F. G. Bettany, "The World of Books," *Sunday Times* (London) 30 September 1906, p. 2.

20. [Charles L. Graves], "Novels," *Spectator* (London) 102 (27 February 1909): 151-53.

21. John O'London, [Untitled column], *John O'London's Weekly* 14 (22 October 1909): 537-38.

22. Anonymous, "H. G. Wells, an Admirable Observer—Not Yet a Novelist," *New York Times Book Review* 6 October 1912, p. 548.

23. Edwin E. Slosson, "London and Labrador," *Independent* (New York) 73 (10 October 1912): 849-50.

24. René Seguy, "H. G. Wells et la pensée contemporaine," *Mercure de France* 95 (February 1912): 673-99.

25. See, for example, Shiv K. Kumar, *Bergson and the Stream of Consciousness Novel* (New York: New York University Press, 1963).

26. Van Wyck Brooks, *The World of H. G. Wells* (New York: Kennerley, 1915);

Stuart P. Sherman, *On Contemporary Literature* (New York: Henry Holt, 1917), pp. 50-84.

27. "Mr. Wells's Latest," *Saturday Review* (London) 127 (14 June 1919): 582-83.

28. [Virginia Woolf], "The Rights of Youth," *Times Literary Supplement* 19 September 1918, p. 439; "Modern Novels," *Times Literary Supplement* 10 April 1919, p. 189; H. L. Mencken, "The Late Mr. Wells," *Prejudices, First Series* (New York: Knopf, 1919), pp. 22-35.

29. See, for example, "Mr. Wells's Work," *Times Literary Supplement* 15 January 1925, p. 37; and Abel Chevalley, *The Modern English Novel* (New York: Knopf, 1925), pp. 156-66.

30. Simon Pure, "The Londoner," *Bookman* (New York) 58 (February 1924): 641-42; Freda Kirchwey, "A Private Letter to H. G. Wells," *Nation* (New York) 127 (28 November, 1928): 576.

31. Stuart P. Sherman, "Dreaming for the Future," *New York Tribune* 22 March 1925, pp. 1, 2.

32. E. M. Forster, *Aspects of the Novel* (New York: Harcourt, Brace, 1927), pp. 31-34.

33. David Ockham, "People of Importance in Their Day," *Saturday Review* (London) 151 (20 June 1932): 896.

34. Fanny Butcher, "Wells Develops Intriguing Idea in a New Novel," *Chicago Daily Tribune* 12 June 1937, p. 12.

35. "Voice of Reason, *Time* 48 (26 August 1946): 28.

36. Sinclair Lewis, "Our Friend, H. G.," *New York Herald Tribune* 20 October 1946, pp. 1-2.

37. H. E. Bates, *The Modern Short Story: A Critical Survey* (London: Nelson, 1941), pp. 106-11.

38. Malcolm Cowley, "Outline of Wells's History," *New Republic* 81 (14 November 1934): 244-47.

39. Marjorie Hope Nicolson, *Voyages to the Moon* (New York; Macmillan, 1948), p. 247-50; Roger Lancelyn Green, *Into Other Worlds: Space-Flight in Fiction* (London: Abelard-Schuman, 1958), p. 184; Reichard J. Davis, "Kipling and H. G. Wells," *Saturday Review* (London) 32 (18 June 1949): 22.

40. Alden Whitman, "A World History by 42 Professors," *New York Times* 18 July 1972, p. 23.

41. This phrase is appropriated from Godfrey Smith, "An Outline of H. G. Wells," *New York Times Magazine* 21 August 1966, pp. 30-44.

Experiment in Autobiography

H. G. Wells

ir Harry Fetherstonhaugh, like many of his class and time [the 1880s], had been a free-thinker, and the rooms downstairs abounded in bold and enlightening books. I was allowed to borrow volumes and carry them off to my room. Then or later, I cannot now recall when, I improved my halting French with Voltaire's lucid prose, I read such books as [William Beckford's] *Vathek* [1786] and [Samuel Johnson's *The History of*] *Rasselas* [1759], I nibbled at Tom Paine, I devoured an unexpurgated *Gulliver's Travels* [(1726) by Jonathan Swift] and I found Plato's *Republic*. That last was a very releasing book indeed for my mind. I had learnt the trick of mocking at law and custom from Uncle Williams and, if anything, I had improved upon it and added caricature to quaint words, but here was something to carry me beyond mockery. Here was the amazing and heartening suggestion that the whole fabric of law, custom and worship, which seemed so invincibly established, might be cast into the melting pot and made anew . . . .

[1884] Now under the stimulus of Plato's Utopianism and my quickening desires I began to ask my imagination what it was I desired in women . . . In the free lives and free loves of the guardians of the *Republic* I found the encouragement I needed to give my wishes a systematic form. Presently, I discovered a fresh support for these tentative projects in [Percy Bysshe] Shelley. Regardless of every visible reality about me, of law, custom, social usage, economic necessities and unexplored psychology of womanhood, I developed my adolescent fantasy of free, ambitious, self-reliant women who would mate with me and go their way, as I desired to go my way. I had never in fact seen or heard of any such women; I had evolved them from my inner consciousness . . . The women of the "Samurai" in my *Modern Utopia* (1905), the most Platonic of my books, are the embodiment of these Midhurst imaginings.

[1884-85] As I knew [Thomas Henry] Huxley he was a yellow-faced, square-faced old man, with bright little brown eyes, lurking as it were in caves under his heavy grey eyebrows, and a mane of grey hair brushed back from his

wall of forehead. He lectured [at the Royal College of Science] in a clear firm voice without hurry and without delay, turning to the blackboard behind him to sketch some diagram, and always dusting the chalk from his fingers rather fastidiously before he resumed. He fell ill presently, and after some delay, [G. B.] Howes, uneasy, irritable, brilliant, took his place, lecturing and drawing breathlessly and leaving the blackboard a smother of graceful coloured lines. At the back of the auditorium were curtains, giving upon a museum devoted to the invertebrata. I was told that while Huxley lectured Charles Darwin had been wont at times to come through those very curtains from the gallery behind and sit and listen until his friend and ally had done. In my time Darwin had been dead for only a year or so (he died in 1882).

These two were very great men. They thought boldly, carefully and simply, they spoke and wrote fearlessly and plainly, they lived modestly and decently; they were mighty intellectual liberators. It is a pity that so many of the younger scientific workers of to-day, ignorant of the conditions of mental life in the early nineteenth century and standing for the most part on the ground won, cleared and prepared for them by these giants, find a perverse pleasure in belittling them . . . Darwin and Huxley, in their place and measure, belong to the same aristocracy as Plato and Aristotle and Galileo, and they will ultimately dominate the priestly and orthodox mind as surely, because there is a response, however reluctant, masked and stifled, in every human soul to rightness and a firmly stated truth.

[1887] I was reading and reading poetry and imaginative work with an attention to language and style that I had never given these aspects of literature before. I was becoming conscious of the glib vacuity of the trash I had been writing hitherto. When I look back upon my life, there is nothing in it that seems quite so preposterous as the fact that I set about writing fiction for sale, after years of deliberate abstinence from novels or poetry. Now, belatedly, I began to observe and imitate. I read everything accessible. I ground out some sonnets. I struggled with Spenser; I read Shelley, [John] Keats, [Heinrich] Heine, [Walt] Whitman, [Charles] Lamb, [Oliver] Wendell Holmes, [Robert Louis] Stevenson, [Nathaniel] Hawthorne, and a number of popular novels . . . .

I projected a vast melodrama in the setting of the Five Towns, a sort of Staffordshire *Mysteries of Paris* [(1844) by Eugène Sue] conceived partly in burlesque, it was to be a grotesque with lovely and terrible passages. Of this a solitary fragment survives in my collected stories as *The Cone.* Moreover I began a romance, very much under the influence of Hawthorne, which was printed in the *Science Schools Journal,* the *Chronic Argonauts.* I broke this off after three installments because I could not go on with it. That I realized I could not go on with it marks a stage in my education in the art of fiction. It was the original draft of what later became the *Time Machine,* which first won me recognition as an imaginative writer. But the prose was over-elaborate . . . the story is clumsily invented, and loaded with irrelevant sham significance . . . And there is a lot of fuss about the hostility of a superstitious Welsh village . . . which was obviously just lifted into the tale from Hawthorne's *Scarlet Letter* [1850].

[1895-99] For a time the need to be actually new was not clearly realized.

Literary criticism in those days had some odd conventions. It was still either scholarly or with scholarly pretensions. It was dominated by the mediaeval assumption that whatever is worth knowing is already known and whatever is worth doing has already been done. Astonishment is unbecoming in scholarly men and their attitude to newcomers is best expressed by the word "recognition." Anybody fresh who turned up was treated as an aspirant Dalai Lama is treated, and scrutinized for evidence of his predecessor's soul. So it came about that every one of us who started writing in the nineties, was discovered to be "a second"—somebody or other. In the course of two or three years I was welcomed as a second [Charles] Dickens, a second [Edward] Bulwer Lytton and a second Jules Verne. But also I was a second [James] Barrie, though J. M. B. was hardly more than my contemporary, and, when I turned to short stories, I became a second [Rudyard] Kipling. I certainly, on occasion, imitated both these excellent masters. Later on I figured also as a second [Denis] Diderot, a second [Thomas] Carlyle and a second [Jean Jacques] Rousseau . . . .

Until recently this was the common lot. Literature "broadened down from precedent to precedent." The influence of the publisher who wanted us to be new but did not want us to be *strange*, worked in the same direction as educated criticism. A sheaf of secondhand tickets to literary distinction was thrust into our hands and hardly anyone could get a straight ticket on his own. These secondhand tickets were very convenient as admission tickets. It was however unwise to sit down in the vacant chairs, because if one did so, one rarely got up again. Pett Ridge for instance pinned himself down as a second Dickens to the end of his days. I was saved from a parallel fate by the perplexing variety of my early attributions.

The Wonderful Visit (1895)

The Lounger

Anonymous

wonder if anyone has noticed the similarity, in some respects only, between Mr. Wells's [*The*]*Wonderful Visit* and Mr. Grant Allen's *The British Barbarians* [1895]. In each of these stories a "being" from another world is the hero: in Mr. Wells's he appears as a bird, fluttering near to the earth, and is shot by a sporting person. He has wings, which he hardly conceals, under an all-fitting coat, and is unmistakably a visitor from "other worlds" than ours. Mr. Grant Allen's hero is an equally strange person, who appears suddenly in a London suburb; but he has no wings, and, as far as appearances go, is like any other man.

Both Mr. Wells and Mr. Allen use their heroes as mouthpieces for certain observations on the inconsistencies of civilization, and one incident is used by both: the bird and the man show special attention to a servant-girl—not from any particular taste for servant-girls, but because neither strange being can understand social differences. In the case of Mr. Wells's creature, there is a sort of love-affair with the servant-girl, but in Mr. Allen's story she merely serves to illustrate the "strange visitor's" democratic theories. Aside from these similarities there are none others. Mr. Wells's story is an allegory, entirely clean in the telling; Mr. Allen's is in the usual unclean vein of that extraordinary author.

The Island of Dr. Moreau
(1896)

The Early H. G. Wells

Bernard Bergonzi

ells had expected *The Island of Dr. Moreau* to be published in January 1896, three months after *The Wonderful Visit*, but in fact it did not appear until April of that year . . . The critical reception of the book was far less favourable than that given to Wells's previous books. Some reviewers were so horrified by what they considered the blatant sensationalism of the novel that they were quite unable to consider its literary merits. The *Times*, for instance, considered that "This novel is the strangest example we have met of the perverse quest after anything in any shape that is freshly sensational."[1] The *Athenaeum* devoted two-thirds of a column to horrified denunciation of Moreau, though without giving any idea of the subject or theme of the story: "The horrors described by Mr. Wells in his latest book very pertinently raises the question how far it is legitimate to create feelings of disgust in a work of art."[2]

There was a tendency to attack the book as though it were sexually offensive, even though this was not the case: "In the present instance he has achieved originality at the expense of decency (we do not use the word in its sexual significance) and common sense."[3] And Wells's colleague on the reviewing staff of the *Saturday Review*, Peter Chalmers Mitchell, who was himself a trained biologist, wrote a long notice of the novel headed "Mr Wells's 'Dr Moreau,'" which opened by admitting Wells's gifts—"We have all been saying that here is an author with the emotions of an artist and the intellectual imagination of a scientific investigator"—but went on to attack *Moreau*, more in sorrow than in anger, both for its failure in taste and sensibility, and for its propagating of various scientific impossibilities.[4] In particular, Mitchell argued that grafting operations could not be carried out on the scale shown in the book. After a delay of several months Wells replied to this particular criticism in a letter to the *Saturday Review* by referring to a recent article on grafting published in the *British Medical Journal*.[5]

Wells was irritated and perhaps surprised by these criticisms. In a magazine interview printed the following year he is reported as saying:

> I should say that *The Island of Dr Moreau*, although it was written in a great hurry and is marred by many faults, is the best work I have done. It has been stupidly dealt with—as a mere shocker—by people who ought to have known better. The *Guardian* critic seemed to be the only one who read it aright, and who therefore succeeded in giving a really intelligent notice of it.[6]

The review in the *Guardian* to which Wells referred was certainly more balanced than some of the others, though the writer was still uncertain about Wells's intentions:

> Sometimes one is inclined to think the intention of the author has been to satirize and rebuke the presumption of science; at other times his object seems to be to parody the work of the Creator of the human race, and cast contempt upon the dealings of God with His creatures. This is the suggestion of the exceedingly clever and realistic scenes in which the humanized beasts recite the Law their human maker has given them, and show very plainly how impossible it is to them to keep that law.[7]

This is a reasonably just account of the work, and in point of fact both alternative explanations are applicable. Wells implicitly acknowledged the truth of the latter interpretation when in 1924 he referred to *Moreau* as a "theological grotesque."[8]

Not all reviewers were shocked by the book, even though they may have had reservations of a literary kind. Richard Le Gallienne remarked, "Some have shuddered, and called the book 'revolting.' Perhaps it is; but a still more serious objection to it, from my point of view, is that it fails to convince,"[9] while Grant Richards wrote, "Only here and there do the means by which horror is attained transcend the legitimate. The truth is, Mr Wells has an unusually vivid imagination, which sometimes runs away with him."[10] But read over sixty years after its publication, *The Island of Dr. Moreau* can still affect the nerves in an unpleasantly direct fashion, which is in itself evidence of its power. Whatever his stated intentions may have been, one cannot acquit Wells of a certain desire to *épater le bourgeois*, which proved in the event to be eminently successful. In fact the horrified reaction of many readers can be seen as not merely a response to passages of bad taste in the book, but, more significantly, as an unconscious recognition of the implications of its symbolism.

Whereas Wells's other novel-length romances draw to some extent on his own experiences for their setting and background (this is true even of *The Time Machine*, where the world of the Eloi is superimposed on the still faintly familiar topography of the Thames valley), *The Island of Dr. Moreau* does not, for at the time he wrote it he had never been out of England, still less made a voyage to a remote Pacific Island. It is composed of extremely literary materials, and is, in fact, an example of what a Swiss critic, Richard Gerber, has recently described as "the English Island" myth:

> Even for the continental imagination, the concept of the island beyond the sea has always had a positive mythical aspect: Atlantis, Ultima Thule, Elysium.

> While such island myths are probably not more frequent in English than in continental poetry—and even if this were so they have not succeeded in affecting the continental imagination—in prose fiction English writers, being nearer island reality, have been able, as no others have done, to stamp the island myth indelibly on the continental mind: in [Daniel Defoe's] *Robinson Crusoe* [1719], in [Jonathan Swift's] *Gulliver's Travels* [1726], in [Thomas More's] *Utopia* [1515]. They are all of them "world-books" and living myths for almost everybody. Of what other prose fiction in English literature can we safely say the same? And what other literature has produced anything similar, not only in the mere concept, but in general imaginative force and validity?[11]

The tradition has continued in the nineteenth century by certain immensely popular and influential boys' books, such as [R. M. Ballantyne's] *Coral Island* [1858] and [Robert Louis Stevenson's] *Treasure Island* [1883]. . . .

It is in this tradition that *The Island of Dr. Moreau* takes its place; it may even be a demonic parody of another and older island story, [William Shakespeare's] *The Tempest* [1611], for Moreau as king of the island, seems to be a perverted image of Prospero, while his drunken assistant, Montgomery, stands for Ariel, and the humanized bear, M'ling, for Caliban. But if Wells's novel takes its place in a long and venerable line of "island myths," the myth, in this particular instance, is given vitality by the meaning which it conveys. And the meaning of the novel is to be found, I think, in one of the profoundest intellectual preoccupations of the second half of the nineteenth century: the implications of Darwinism.

For the popular mind, at least, Evolution had substituted blind Chance, as a force governing the universe, for the beneficent attentions of a Deity. And Chance makes an appearance in the very first chapter of *The Island of Dr. Moreau*: Edward Prendick, shipwrecked whilst crossing the Pacific, is drifting in a dinghy with two other men; after eight days they are almost dying for want of food and water. One of the two men proposes that they draw lots to determine which of the three will be killed and eaten by the other two (Wells's source for this incident may have been Poe's *Narrative of Arthur Gordon Pym* [1838]); for a long time Prendick resists this proposal, but he finally assents to it. Lots are drawn, and the victim is one of the other two men, who violently resists; there is a struggle[,] and both men fall overboard, leaving Prendick alone in the dinghy. The incident has nothing to do with the narrative that is to follow, but it sets the emotional tone of the whole work, by demonstrating the savagery of nature, even—or especially—human nature, and by showing that survival can depend on pure chance. . . .

Moreau is not only a nightmarish caricature of the Almighty: he can also be seen as a hypostatized image of the pretensions of science, already foreshadowed by the surgically-minded Dr. Crump in *The Wonderful Visit*, despite the great differences in tone and treatment between the books. Yet he is also contrasted with the orthodox and humane scientist, Prendick, the former pupil of [Thomas] Huxley. Moreau is both a traditional and a contemporary figure, and his most obvious literary progenitors are Mary Shelley's *Frankenstein* [1817] and Stevenson's Jekyll-Hyde [1886]. (In 1914 Thomas Seccombe remarked of *The Island of Dr. Moreau*, "*Membra disjecta* from

"Gulliver's Fourth Voyage," could perhaps be detected in it.)[12]　Prendick's association with Huxley is not, I think, purely arbitrary: three years before *The Island of Dr. Moreau* appeared, Huxley had delivered at Oxford his Romanes lecture, *Evolution and Ethics* [1893], a powerful summary of the moral dilemmas with which the theory and practice of Evolution confronted the late-Victorian world.　For Huxley, Nature, as manifested in evolutionary processes, was cruel and arbitrary, and ethical progress could only be made in opposition to it. . . .

Wells's own attitude, as not infrequently in his early fiction and essays, was calculatedly ambiguous.　Moreau is shown, in effect, as a monster who meets the fate he deserves, but at the same time Wells seems to make out as good a case for him as he can.

But there is no doubt that *The Island of Dr. Moreau* is a deeply pessimistic book, and its Swiftian view of human nature is not a mere literary exercise. Anthony West has remarked, "What the book in fact expresses is a profound mistrust of human nature, and a doubt about the intellect's ability to contain it."[13]　When we compare this with the relative complacency of Wells's later utopian constructions, we have a measure of the change of attitude he was to undergo in the next few years.　In *Evolution and Ethics*, Huxley had observed that Man had kept his ascendancy by the qualities of the ape and the tiger, but that in civilized society these were seen as defects.[14]　*The Island of Dr. Moreau* is a dramatization of the dilemma implicit in this statement.

NOTES

1. *The Times* (London), 17 June 1896, p. 17.
2. *Athenaeum*, 9 May 1896, p. 615.
3. *Speaker*, 18 April 1896, p. 430.
4. *Saturday Review* [London], 11 April 1896, p. 368.
5. *Saturday Review* [London], 7 November 1896, p. 497.
6. *The Young Man*, August 1897, p. 256.
7. *Guardian*, 3 June 1896, p. 871.
8. *Works* (Atlantic Edition, 1924), 2: ix.
9. *Idler*, June 1896, p. 724.
10. *Academy*, 30 May 1896, p. 444.
11. *Critical Quarterly*, 1 (1959): 37.
12. *Bookman*, 46 (1914): 16.
13. *Principles and Persuasions* (1958), p. 10.
14. *Romanes Lectures 1892-1900* (1900), pp. 95-96.

The Invisible Man (1897)

Literature

Anonymous

f the people one meets on the street, and talks with, and walks with, were half as real as the Invisible Man, the world would be an entertaining place. He arrives one wintry day "early in February through a biting wind and a driving snow," "carrying a little black portmanteau in his thickly-gloved hand." In the third chapter, to be sure, Mr. Wells sees fit to change it to "the twenty-ninth day of February, at the beginning of the thaw." But one does not expect consistency in either invisible men or their creators. For artistic purposes, early February and a driving snow storm harmonize better with the little black portmanteau than the beginning of the thaw. We elect to believe that the stranger arrived in early February. We feel sure that Mr. Wells—except for a slip of the pen—would have held to the more artistic date, even at the expense of truth.

Invisible Man bristles with art. On his first appearance[,] "He was wrapped up from head to foot[,] and the brim of his soft felt hat hid every inch of his face but the shiny tip of his nose." Even the dullest reader must have a suspicion of that shining tip of a nose, even though he does not at first glance know it for a false one. Mr. Wells takes care that the reader shall, at every step, know just enough and not too much to hold his attention unflagging up to the last pages of the last chapter when "there lay, naked and pitiful on the ground, the bruised and broken body of a young man about thirty. 'Cover his face!' said a man. 'For Gawd's sake, cover that face!' And three children pushing forward through the crowd were suddenly twisted round and sent packing off again."

If Poe had never written "The Facts in the Case of M. Valdemar" [1845], or "The Fall of the House of Usher" [1839], or "The Masque of the Red Death" [1842], Mr. Wells's work might rank him higher as an artist than it is likely to do now. Dr. [Arthur] Conan Doyle has made a fortune from his stories, we understand, which is only another way of saying that his versions of the detective stories of Edgar Allan Poe have been very popular. It is more than possible that like good fortune may attend Mr. Wells's efforts, and that he will glean from the supernatural side of Poe's work as rich a harvest as Dr. Doyle has gathered from the analytic. It only remains for some discerning critic to make a fortune out of his [Poe's] critical method.

As for Poe himself, he could easily have given odds to any three men of talent. There is little doubt that he was something of a rascal. He died a pauper, in a public hospital. But first, last and always, he knew himself for an artist of the first rank, an original man.

The War of the Worlds (1898)

The War of the Worlds

[John St. Loe Strachey]

n *The War of the Worlds* Mr. Wells has achieved a very notable
success in that special field of fiction which he has chosen for the exercise of his
very remarkable gift of narration. As a writer of scientific romances he has
never been surpassed. Poe was a man of rare genius, and his art was perhaps
greater than Mr. Wells's, though Mr. Wells has a well-cultivated instinct for
style. But in Poe there is a certain vein of pedantry which makes much of even
his best work tame and mechanical. The logical method he invented, or at any
rate perfected, is too clearly visible in his stories, and appears to cramp his
imagination. Besides, in Poe there is always a stifling hothouse feeling which is
absent from Mr. Wells's work. Even when Mr. Wells is most awful and most
eccentric, there is something human about his characters. The Invisible Man is
in many ways like one of Poe's creations; but yet we feel that Poe would have
stiffened the invisible man into a splendidly ingenious automaton, not left him a
disagreeable, but still possible, medical student. Both Poe and Mr. Wells are, of
course, conscious or unconscious followers of Swift, but Mr. Wells keeps
nearest to the human side of the author of *Gulliver*.

In manner, however, as in scheme and incident, Mr. Wells is singularly
original, and if he suggests any one in externals it is [Daniel] Defoe. There are
several pages in *The War of the Worlds* which seem to recall the *History of the
Plague* [1722]. Nevertheless, we should not be surprised to hear that Mr. Wells
had never read Defoe's immortal book. In any case, the resemblance comes, we
are certain, not from imitation, but from the parallel action of two very acute and
sincere intelligences. Each had to get into something like the same mental
attitude towards the things to be related, and hence the two narrations are
sometimes akin. We say "sincere intelligences" advisedly. We feel that in spite
of the wildness of Mr. Wells's story it is in no sort of sense a "fake." He has not
written haphazard, but has imagined, and then followed his imagination with the
utmost niceness and sincerity. To this niceness and sincerity Mr. Wells adds an
ingenuity and inventiveness in the matter of detail which is beyond praise. Any

man can be original if he may be also vague and inexpressive. Mr. Wells[,] when he is most giving wings to his imagination[,] is careful to be concrete and specific. Some sleights of chiaroscuro, some tricks of perspective, some hiding of difficult pieces of drawing with convenient shadows—these there must be in every picture, but Mr. Wells relies as little as possible on such effects. He is not perpetually telling us that such-and-such things could not be described by mortal pen.

Mr. Wells's main design is most original. As a rule, those who pass beyond the poles and deal with non-terrestrial matters take their readers to the planets or the moon. Mr. Wells does not "err so greatly" in the art of securing the sympathy of his readers. He brings the awful creatures of another sphere to Woking Junction, and places them, with all their abhorred dexterity, in the most homely and familiar surroundings. A Martian dropped in the centre of Africa would be comparatively endurable. One feels, with the grave-digger in *Hamlet* [1601], that they are all mad and bad and awful there, or, if not, it is no great matter. When the Martians come flying through the vast and dreadful expanses of interplanetary space hid in the fiery womb of their infernal cylinders, and land on a peaceful Surrey common, we come to close quarters at once with the full horror of the earth's invasion. Those who know the valleys of the Wey and the Themes, and to whom Shepperton and Laleham are familiar placccs, will follow the advance of the Martians upon London with breathless interest. The vividness of the local touches, and the accuracy of the geographical details, enormously enhance the horror of the picture. When everything else is so true and exact, the mind finds it difficult to be always rebelling against the impossible Martians.

We shall not attempt here—it would not be fair to Mr. Wells's thrilling book—to tell the story of the Martian war. We may, however, mention one point of detail. Many readers will be annoyed with Mr. Wells for not having made his Martians rather more human, and so more able to receive our sympathy of comprehension, if not of approbation. A little reflection will, we think, show that this was impossible. This is the age of scientific speculation, and scientific speculation, rightly or wrongly, has declared that if there are living and sentient creatures on Mars they will be very different from men. Mr. Wells, whose knowledge of such speculations is obviously great, has followed the prevailing scientific opinion, and hence his appalling Martian monster—a mere brain surrounded by a kind of brown jelly, with tentacles for hands—a creature which, by relying upon machinery, has been able to dispense with almost everything connected with the body but the brain. Mr. Wells has made his Martians semi-globular and bisexual. Had he, we wonder, in his mind the passage in Plato's *Symposium* which describes how man was once two sexes in one, and had a round body? If he was not relying upon Plato's legend, it is curious to note how the scientific imagination has twice produced a similar result.

Mr. Sammler's War of the Planets

Allan Chavkin

> There are no parallels to life in the concentration camps. Its horror can never be fully embraced by the imagination for the very reason that it stands outside of life and death. It can never be fully reported for the very reason that the survivor returns to the world of the living which makes it impossible for him to believe fully in his own past experience. It's as though he had a story to tell of another planet.
>
> Hannah Arendt

> We have learned now that we cannot regard this planet as being fenced in and a secure abiding-place for Man.
>
> H. G. Wells

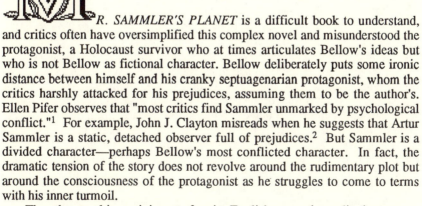*R. SAMMLER'S PLANET* is a difficult book to understand, and critics often have oversimplified this complex novel and misunderstood the protagonist, a Holocaust survivor who at times articulates Bellow's ideas but who is not Bellow as fictional character. Bellow deliberately puts some ironic distance between himself and his cranky septuagenarian protagonist, whom the critics harshly attacked for his prejudices, assuming them to be the author's. Ellen Pifer observes that "most critics find Sammler unmarked by psychological conflict."[1] For example, John J. Clayton misreads when he suggests that Artur Sammler is a static, detached observer full of prejudices.[2] But Sammler is a divided character—perhaps Bellow's most conflicted character. In fact, the dramatic tension of the story does not revolve around the rudimentary plot but around the consciousness of the protagonist as he struggles to come to terms with his inner turmoil.

Thus the novel is reminiscent of major English romantic meditative poems, such as Wordsworth's "Ode: Intimations of Immortality from Recollections of Early Childhood," Shelley's "Ode to the West Wind," and Keats's "Ode to a Nightingale." As M. H. Abrams and Harold Bloom have observed, the English romantics created a new genre in which the speaker attempts in the course of his discursive meditation to overcome some kind of crisis.[3] Though its shifting tone full of irony and sardonic humor contrasts to the solemn tone of the romantic poems, *Mr. Sammler's Planet* should be considered as an elaborate variation of the discursive crisis meditation, the genre initiated by Wordsworth that presents the gradual process of the mind's coming to terms with what is tormenting it.

Irvin Stock has suggested that this meditative novel owes a debt to the English romantics, especially to Wordsworth: "Bellow has a gift, reminiscent of Wordsworth, for evoking in his sentence rhythms, as well as in his words, the experience of thought, the drama of its emergence out of the life of the whole man."[4] In his nonfiction Bellow has at times seen the modern writer as a kind of twentieth-century Wordsworth in a modern crisis in which the mind confronting distraction, irrationality, and madness has a similar but much more arduous task than the English romantic poet had.[5] In this novel, which might have the same subtitle as Wordsworth's *The Prelude*, "the growth of a poet's mind," Sammler suffers from a profound sense of alienation as he confronts a society in the throes of radical change, a society that is both capable of astonishing technological progress (symbolized by the space program) and also self-destruction. As Malcolm Bradbury observes, "*Mr. Sammler's Planet* is evidently a crisis book for a crisis year, 1969, the year of high radical passions and moonshot."[6] Bradbury and other critics have not recognized that the key figure in Sammler's crisis meditation is H. G. Wells.

1

Supported by his benefactor Elya Gruner and brought to the United States after World War II, Sammler is supposed to be writing an important memoir of H. G. Wells, with whom he had extensive discussions when he was part of Wells's circle in the pre-War period. Sammler's daughter Shula is convinced that her brilliant father's book on Wells will be a monumental work.

In Shula's version, her father had enjoyed conversations with H. G. Wells lasting several years. He took his notes to Poland in 1939, expecting to have spare time for the memoir. Just then the country exploded. In the geyser that rose a mile or two into the skies were Papa's notes. But (with his memory!) he knew it all by heart, and all you had to do was ask what Wells had said to him about Lenin, Stalin, Mussolini, Hitler, world peace, atomic energy, the open conspiracy, the colonization of the planets. Whole passages came back to Papa. He had to concentrate of course. Thus she converted his moving in with Margotte into her own idea: he had moved there to concentrate better. He said he did not have much time left. But obviously he exaggerated. He looked so well. He was such a handsome person. Elderly widows were always asking her about him. The mother of Rabbi Ipsheimer. The grandmother of Ipsheimer, more likely. Anyway (Angela still reporting here), Wells had communicated things to Sammler that the world did not know. When finally published, they would astonish everyone. The book would take the form of dialogues, like those with A. N. Whitehead that Sammler admired so much.[7]

When with a hint of mockery Angela remarks that Shula's "Wells routine is so great" and wonders if Sammler was really "that close to H. G.," he states they were "well acquainted" but also remarks that what the "graphomaniac" Englishman said to him he eventually also found in "written form" (30). Wells possessed an unusually active mind, Sammler observes, and expressed himself very well, such as when he said that "science is the mind of the race" (30). Sammler tells Angela that "on the whole he [Wells] was a sensible intelligent person, certainly on the right side of many questions." Angela reveals that she knows Sammler has lost interest in the Wells memoir, for she says, laughing, "but she [Shula] says you're composing that great work a mile a minute" (30). Even though Shula exaggerates, there is little doubt that Sammler is capable of writing the kind of important work Shula envisions, although in fact he is not. The question that needs to be posed and answered is: why?

Although *Mr. Sammler's Planet* has prompted much critical analysis, little attention has been focused on the extensive references to H. G. Wells.[8] While Sammler also alludes to other writers, he pays the most attention to Wells, which is not surprising since until he was in his forties Wells was the center of his life. One should note, too, that Wells is at the heart of the plot in which Shula steals Dr. Govinda Lal's manuscript about colonizing the moon. In short, understanding what Wells meant to Sammler before World War II and what he means to Sammler in 1969 provides a key to unlocking the meaning of the work. During the course of his crisis meditation in which Sammler remembers the past, ponders the present, and speculates about the future, his attitude toward Wells shifts as he tries to decide what he really thinks about the man and his work. Focusing on the allusions to Wells will clarify the source of Sammler's crisis and its resolution.

2

Sammler's spiritual crisis is evoked in the opening of the work. "The soul wanted what it wanted. It had its own natural knowledge. It sat unhappily on superstructures of explanation, poor bird, not knowing which way to fly" (3-4). Sammler knows that there are plenty of theories, but these intellectual explanations do not constitute wisdom; they merely add to the mass of distracting facts, sensations, and ideas threatening to overwhelm the soul. Believing that he should devote himself to the spiritual life only, Sammler's desires to be a soul detached from the turbulence of contemporary reality, "released from Nature, from impressions, and from everyday life" (117). As a survivor, who had been buried in a mass grave from which he escaped over bodies of the dead and dying, he feels he should be "perfectly disinterested," but as a reader of thirteenth-century mystics he is drawn back to ordinary reality when he witnesses in fascination and horror a majestic African-American pickpocket victimizing the old and the helpless.

Sammler tries to reconcile three radically different worlds (or "planets," to borrow Arendt's metaphor)[9] that are at war within himself: his "British world" when he resided in England as part of Wells's circle; his "Polish world" when he suffered during the Holocaust and witnessed the murder of his wife Antonina; and his "American world," now seemingly on the verge of collapse, with the threat of ubiquitous barbarism just below the civilized surface. ("You opened a jeweled door into degradation, from hypercivilized Byzantine luxury straight into the state of nature, the barbarous world of color erupting from beneath" [7]). His "British world" was civilized, idealistic, optimistic, and complacent. It was a heady time for the Sammlers when they had "the most distinguished intimacy with the finest people in Britain," as Sammler's wife Antonina saw it. Even young Shula could sense her parents' "pride in high connections, their snobbery, how contented they were with the cultural best of England" (28). In dramatic contrast was Sammler's unearthly experience in the world of the concentration camps and genocide, that "other planet." In this alien world, where he was separated from his daughter and suffered great physical and mental agony, he witnessed a nihilistic barbarism that he never before imagined. Now, in 1969, he tries to understand a civilization that can make plans to explore and ultimately colonize outer space, and is capable of marvelous technological achievements, but that also seems to be at a crisis point, a society on the verge of breaking apart, collapsing. New York City is the representative chaotic metropolis that symbolizes this society; it is "crime-ridden, over-populated, lost, sexually barren; only evil appears to invigorate."[10] "New York makes one think about the collapse of civilization, about Sodom and Gomorrah, the end of the world," Sammler says to his niece (304). Witnessing the breakdown of civilization in World War II and suffering its horrors make this cultural crisis in 1969 a personal one for him.

When Sammler recalls his idyllic days with Wells in pre-War England, his attitude is ambivalent. Despite the fact that he claims to remember Wells "always with respect" and not to judge him, his recollection suggests otherwise:

> Sammler knew that he [Wells] had been a horny man of labyrinthine extraordinary sensuality. As a biologist, as a social thinker concerned with power and world projects, the molding of a universal order, as a furnisher of interpretation and opinion to the educated masses—as all of these he appeared to need a great amount of copulation. Nowadays Sammler would recall him as a little lower-class Limey, and as an aging man of declining ability and appeal. And in the agony of parting with the breasts, the mouths, and the precious sexual fluids of women, poor Wells, the natural teacher, the sex emancipator, the explainer, the humane blesser of mankind, could in the end only blast and curse everyone. Of course he wrote such things in his final sickness, horribly depressed by World War II. (28)

Sammler's hostility is evident in his snobbish reference to the British writer's humble origins and in his pejorative references to Wells's nationality and age. The chaste Sammler finds the sexually active Wells repugnant.

Later he juxtaposes a recollection of one of Angela's wild sexual escapades with a recollection of Wells's view of sexual passion. He is surprised to find "a superior individual" such as Wells, a man in his seventies, obsessed with women. He had expected Wells's views to be "more in line with those of

Sophocles in old age, "who said that he was glad to have escaped from "the hands of a mad and furious master" (71). To Sammler, Wells made elaborate arguments for a complete revision of sexual attitudes to conform to the increased life span. He implies that Wells was not able to accept the aging process and finds the Utopian thinker guilty of not foreseeing the unfortunate consequences of his views on sexuality—that is, "excess, pornography, sexual abnormality" (72).

Sammler is preoccupied with sex throughout his crisis meditation, during which the sexual antics of Angela, Wallace, Feffer, Bruch, and others are described. He sees the sexual revolution as sexual madness and symptomatic of the breakdown of civilization. According to the Holocaust survivor, criminality and sex are romanticized. It is not an accident that the princely African-American pickpocket intimidates Sammler by cornering him and exhibiting his penis, for in this society where youth is worshipped and the old have little value, sexual potency is the ultimate authority. He reflects on the meaning of the pickpocket's intimidation with his "huge piece of sex flesh, half-tumescent in its pride and shown in its own right, a prominent and separate object intended to communicate authority." Sammler then thinks, "It was a symbol of superlegitimacy or sovereignty. It was a mystery. It was unanswerable" (55). Sammler suggests that by making nature your God, by elevating sexuality to such heights, one can "count on gross results," though perhaps gross results are inevitable under any circumstances (55). This new sexual madness has so overwhelmed Western civilization that a currently circulating story reports the American President exhibited himself in the manner of the pickpocket to representatives of the press to validate his leadership qualifications, the assumption being that certainly a man "so well hung" could be trusted to lead his nation (66). Although Sammler knows that the story is apocryphal, he suggests that it is evidence of the sexual insanity that corrupts civilization.

Instead of sexual liberation, he believes, the sexual revolution has created a kind of sexual slavery from which even a Holocaust survivor who wants to remain detached from everyday reality to devote himself completely to the spiritual is not immune. In fact, we see his morbid preoccupation with sex throughout his meditation. Even when he ruminates on his idyllic days in pre-War Britain, he notes the social-erotic influence of Wells on Antonina ("plumper between the legs," Sammler thinks). Echoing Blake, he reflects that "great cities are whores" (163), and decries the lack of restraint by millions of civilized people who have lost patience and become puerile in their demands for immediate gratification. People, he is sure, are ruled by their primitive passions.

Sammler's sexual attitudes have been determined to a large degree by the Old Testament, though he is not always a champion of monogamy. He hopes that Gruner found a mistress to compensate for his cold wife. While Sammler politely listens to Angela's confessions of her sexual experimentation, he doubts "the fitness of these Jews for this erotic Roman voodoo primitivism. He questione[s] whether release from long Jewish mental discipline, hereditary training in lawful control, [is] obtainable upon individual application" (72-73).

While Wells did not have this Jewish mental discipline that might have curtailed his powerful sexual drive, it is also likely that Sammler's view of

Wells's sexual behavior is distorted, perhaps as a result of his repugnance for the sexual excesses that he sees in 1969 and associates with Wells. David C. Smith observes that one can easily misinterpret Wells's sexual behavior and see him as "simply an aging roué and libertine," and his wife Jane, who consented to Wells's affairs, a weak, compliant person; actually, the sexual relationship between Wells and his wife "diminished fairly quickly," and "by 1906 or so," with the acquiescence of Jane, he began to look for sexual satisfaction outside his marriage.[11]   Although Somerset Maugham remarked that Wells was a highly-sexed individual who saw sex as a purely physiological matter separate from love, Norman and Jeanne MacKenzie argue that Wells regarded sex as "a vital anodyne for despair"; when Wells became severely depressed as a result of overwork, lovemaking followed by sleep would enable him to return to his writing with fresh exuberance the next morning.[12]

In contrast to Wells, Sammler seems to have no sexual drive, and in fact sex seems distasteful to him and is invariably described in a negative way. His misogynistic tendency can be seen throughout this meditative novel (e.g., "Females were naturally more prone to grossness, had more smells, needed more washing" [36]) and probably has its origin in his revulsion against the sexual revolution.   When he describes the activist youth of the radical movement, some of whom have been student-readers in his employment, he indicates his dislike of them—for their ignorance, lack of self-esteem, and disrespect—by endowing them with a gross animalistic sexuality: "He no longer wanted these readers with the big dirty boots and the helpless vital pathos of young dogs with their first red erections" (37).

His association of these radical activists with animalistic sexuality is reinforced during his lecture at Columbia University on the British Scene in the Thirties.   He is interrupted by a man who illogically concludes that as an old man Sammler "can't come" and thus has worthless ideas.   Lionel Feffer, an ingenious promoter, has persuaded Sammler to talk to a seminar for a student project to help disadvantaged African-American students with reading problems. Actually, Feffer has deceived him, for the one-eyed Holocaust survivor finds himself addressing a mass meeting; only later is he informed that the audience had expected a lecture on Sorel and violence.   Instead, he talks about intellectual life before World War II.   With Gerald Heard and Olaf Stapledon, Sammler, "handsomely acknowledged by H. G. Wells," had been part of the *Cosmopolis* project and had written articles for *News of Progress* and *The World Citizen*.   He describes Wells's Utopian vision in some detail for half an hour, "feeling what a kind-hearted, ingenuous, stupid scheme it had been" (41).   At that point his lecture comes to a sudden conclusion when it is interrupted by an angry activist youth who objects to Sammler's reference to George Orwell, "a sick counterrevolutionary" according to the young man (42).[13]

Judie Newman suggests that "Sammler's account of the Open Conspiracy incorporates within it Orwell's pessimistic attack on Wells."[14]   She argues that the novel is about two opposing views of history, history-as-progress and history-as-nightmare, with Wells's ideas representing the former and Orwell's views the latter.   In his essay "Wells, Hitler and the World State," Orwell harshly attacked Wells, whom he saw as an uncritical champion of scientific progress and a naive intellectual who did not anticipate the coming of a new Dark Age. Newman seems to accept completely Orwell's criticism of Wells, and she assumes Sammler does, too. Actually, Orwell's charges here are simply not accurate. Moreover, I think that Sammler, while skeptical of Wells's Utopian outlook, would not agree with all of Orwell's conclusions, such as his claim that Wells believed science can solve all of man's ills. Wells himself felt that Orwell was distorting his work, and when Orwell repeated some of the charges from "Wells, Hitler and the World State" in March, 1942, on the BBC, including the charge that Wells believed science could eliminate all of man's troubles, Wells wrote Orwell an abusive note, insisting, "I don't say that at all. Read my early works, you shit."[15] In short, Newman oversimplifies Sammler's attitude toward Wells.

That Sammler is ambivalent about Wells is indicated when, for a moment at least, he reflects on the future of civilization and he entertains the notion that perhaps Wells was correct after all. Sammler speculates that perhaps there is no alternative for civilization but to continue in the direction it has been heading and wait for the spirituality that has been left behind by technological progress to regain the importance it once had: "Perhaps by a growing agreement among the best minds, not unlike the Open Conspiracy of H. G. Wells. Maybe the old boy (Sammler, himself an old boy, considering this) was right after all" (54).

But the Wells to whom Sammler is most attracted is the Wells of *The Time Machine* and *The War of the Worlds*. As Sammler contemplates the grim urban landscape, indicative of a civilization in decline, he reflects that the youth of the so-called "counter-culture" is similar to the Eloi of *The Time Machine*: "Lovely young human cattle herded by the cannibalistic Morlocks who lived a subterranean life and feared light and fire. Yes, that tough brave little old fellow Wells had had prophetic visions after all. Shula wasn't altogether wrong to campaign for a memoir. A memoir should be written" (106). But then he observes that there is little time left for him to investigate curious but complicated subjects such as Wells's attempts to be accepted as a Fellow to the Royal Society, he has "higher priorities" (107).

When Sammler writes a letter to Dr. Lal to reassure him that his manuscript (stolen by Shula) is safe, he minimizes the significance of his book on Wells, suggesting it is an "imaginary project that obsesses" his daughter. Sammler recounts matter-of-factly that he was a friend of Wells, "whose moon-fantasy you undoubtedly know—Selenites, subterranean moon-ocean, and all of that" (129). Although he downplays his interest in Wells here, he does spend much time contemplating the meaning of space exploration and reads with real attention Dr. Lal's manuscript about "colonizing the moon and the planets." He ponders mankind's desire to travel to other planets and reflects that Dr. Lal's manuscript reveals that the Indian professor is not just another inhuman scientist interested only in the technological aspects of space travel. Rather Dr. Lal is concerned about the human implications of space exploration, as is Sammler, who reflects that new worlds and fresh beginnings are not such simple matters as many people assume. Sammler recalls that Wells's Time Traveler "fell in square love with a beautiful Eloi maiden" when he journeyed thousands of years into the future (136). One cannot escape the past so easily, Sammler implies.

He also remembers that on the ocean bottom Captain Nemo of *20,000 Leagues Under the Sea* played Bach and Handel, not Wagner, who in Verne's day was considered avant-garde among the symbolists. In his associative meditation, Sammler notes that for him "Wagner was background music for a pogrom" (136).

For his part, Sammler, unlike so many others, does not have a strong desire to escape from the earth, and he speculates why others do. "The planet was our mother and our burial ground" (182), and the human spirit desires to leave this immense belly, which is also one vast grave. "Passion for the infinite caused by the terror, by *timor mortis*," he reflects, "needed material appeasement" (182). When Wallace, who has already made reservations with the airlines for a hypothetical trip to the moon, questions him about his space-travel plans, the Holocaust survivor responds by observing that he does not "care for the illimitable" and will be content to remain in New York City and to admire the "gorgeous Faustian departures for the other worlds" (184). The implication is that while civilized society, having ravaged this planet, is now ready to escape to another, Sammler's planet remains "this death-burdened, rotting, spoiled, sullied, exasperating, sinful earth" (278).

He implies that as a Jew, he is suspicious of boundlessness and vulgarized Faustian strivings for the infinite. He associates the Nazis with the kind of bad or apocalyptic romanticism of Wagner and of Faustian thinkers who refuse to acknowledge limits and can sacrifice the human in their quest for absolutes. He believes that civilization is in trouble because people are willing to turn traditional morality on its head and justify any action if it is done for a "higher purpose." In this view, the criminal who breaks the laws of society becomes a romantic hero. He implies that Angela's sexual wildness may in part be the result of her "bad education" in French literature, with such bad role models as Genet, Sartre, Rousseau, and other anti-civilization writers of whom he disapproves. Even Shula seems to have been infected with this new ideology because she defends her theft of Dr. Lal's manuscript by claiming, much to his chagrin, that "for the creative there are no crimes" (199). Shula wonders if her father is truly a creative person, capable of bold theft for his work on Wells. "Could he risk all for H. G.?" (199).

Sammler is disgusted with this kind of justification for bad behavior and the romance of the criminal. At this point he also forces the Wells-obsessed Shula to admit that she has not read the British writer's work. In fact, she confesses that she only tried to read one of his books, *God the Invisible King*, which she did not finish. Sammler admits that he also did not complete this book: "I just couldn't read it. Human evolution with God as Intelligence. I soon saw the point, then the rest was tedious, garrulous" (199-200). Shula insists that her father is more important than Dr. Lal and that she stole the manuscript so that he could complete "his life work." Despite Sammler's open skepticism, Shula does not seem discouraged about her father's completion of the Wells's memoir.

At this point, their conversation is interrupted by the entrance of Margotte who (on Sammler's directions) has brought Dr. Lal to meet him. In the most important section of the novel (201-237), he and Lal converse; but the "dialogue" is closer to a monologue, for the Holocaust survivor seems to be in the process of pondering the subjects under discussion and deciding what he really thinks about them as he is talking to the Indian scientist. This lengthy climactic "conversation" includes his most detailed meditation on Wells, a figure whom he considers very seriously.

3

In this "conversation," the Holocaust survivor discusses Wells in some detail, trying, it appears, to decide exactly what his attitude toward the author should be. He explains that he took walks with Wells, then an old man, and listened to his ideas on "scientific humanism, faith in an emancipated future, in active benevolence, in reason, in civilization." These were ideas which Sammler was enthusiastic about at the time but which seemed irrelevant a short time later in World War II Poland. And today, he reflects, civilization is also "disliked" (210).

He observes that Arthur Schopenhauer, who "didn't care for Jews" and called them "vulgar optimists," would not have said that of Wells because the British writer "had many dark thoughts" (209-10). Sammler suggests that in *The War of the Worlds* the Martians intend "to get rid of mankind"; "they treat our species as Americans treated the bison and other animals, or for that matter the American Indians. Extermination" (210). He deliberately seems to universalize his Holocaust experience, suggesting that it was not unique to the Jews or a mere aberration in history. The narrator of *The War of the Worlds* also reminds the reader "what ruthless and utter destruction our own species has wrought not only upon animals, such as the vanished bison and dodo, but upon its own inferior races."[16] During "the great Calcutta Killing" of 1947, Dr. Lal has also witnessed firsthand hatred that resulted in genocidal attacks by "homicidal maniacs."

Sammler implies that this Holocaust experience is not a "theoretical matter" for him or Dr. Lal, although it is for "excellent goodhearted gentlemen" such as Arnold Bennett and Wells, "Olympians of lowerclass origin" (211). Since his wartime experience, Sammler explains, his "judgments are different," and he confesses to Dr. Lal that he has "grave doubts" about the worth of Wells's writing (211-12).

Sammler discusses a troubling paradox about a new social type—the poor man who becomes rich and influential because of his radical ideas. "If you wrote for an elite, like Proust, you did not become rich," but if your "ideas were radical," you became wealthy and powerful. Shaw presented his Marxism to the public and became a millionaire. Moreover, often these "Olympians of lower class origin" who started out with only "mental capital" but achieved "immense influence" also became dissatisfied with words and then lusted for violent action. Sammler gives Jean Paul Sartre as an example of a writer who, having become an aristocrat through his skill with language, felt obligated to act. (In his nonfiction Bellow has attacked Sartre for romanticizing revolutionary violence and murder.)[17] To his credit, Sammler remarks, Wells did not follow the pattern of these radical Olympians and call for "the sacrifice of civilization. He did not become a cult-figure, a royal personality, a grand art-hero or activist leader. He did not feel disgraced by words" (213).

But if Wells at least was not as irresponsible as were these blood-thirsty writers, "soaring from their slums or their little petit-bourgeois parlors" to lead us into revolutionary violence, he was guilty of other sins. In his desire to determine world history, he may have become much more popular and wealthy than Proust yet did not produce works with the Frenchman's high art.

Here in his conversation with Dr. Lal and earlier in the novel in his conversation with Shula about *God the Invisible King*, Sammler implies that Wells wrote too much. In his view, Wells's work suffered because he was too prolific and sacrificed quality for quantity. Bernard Bergonzi pertinently observes that "as a young man in the 1890's, Wells had taken the art of fiction very seriously, both as a critic and a practising writer," whereas "by 1914 he had ceased to regard it as an art at all"; in fact, in 1915, at the end of his famous dispute on the art of the novel with Henry James, he wrote: "I had rather be called a journalist than an artist, that is the essence of it."[18] Wells had concluded that the presentation of his ideas, especially the ones that he hoped would serve to reconstruct the world, must be the overriding concern of his fiction. Apparently, Sammler's conclusion is the same as that of Norman and Jeanne Mackenzie: Wells's "fiction became simply a vehicle for his evangelism, and his imagination began to wither in the pulpit" (279).

Sammler even dislikes "The Country of the Blind," usually considered one of Wells's best stories. In fact, Richard Hauer Costa states that it "is more than Wells's finest achievement as a writer of short fiction. Of all his vast array of works, this story best states H. G. Wells's philosophical position in terms of the techniques of the literary artist."[19] Sammler would disagree with this conclusion. "Not a good story," he remarks tersely (211). Passages in the unpublished manuscripts of *Mr. Sammler's Planet* make the reason for his disapproval clearer: "He labored it ["The Country of the Blind"]. A good story does not grow from a thesis." Elsewhere in the manuscripts, he laments Wells's development as a writer: "A man like Wells did not choose the way of art. He preferred to be a spokesman or explainer, or encyclopedaist."[20] Although we might argue, as Fuchs does, that Sammler does not seem to be suitable as a logical champion of "the way of art" because he is so involved in ideas, actually Bellow's intellectual protagonist, unlike Wells, does not have a position to present. In fact, Bellow apparently intends to present the associative process of Sammler's mind struggling to find what will suffice to end its crisis.

Sammler knows that he does not want his crisis to culminate the way Wells's did. When World War II made clear that his Utopian plans for the transformation of civilization were not possible, Wells despaired and became misanthropic: "He compared humankind to rats in a sack, desperately struggling and biting" (214). At this point in their conversation, Sammler tells Dr. Lal that he has "exhausted" his interest in Wells and, he hopes, Dr. Lal's interest too. The Indian scientist responds, "Ah, you did know the man well," and compliments him for his lucid analysis. Although Sammler does not consider Wells worthless (he admires *The War of the Worlds* and Wells's refusal to become a social type of the kind Sammler abhors), the Utopian thinker no longer has the attraction for the Holocaust survivor that he once had.

4

In the last scene in which Wells is discussed, Sammler holds out the possibility that he may yet try to write the memoir, but this might be a way of momentarily appeasing his daughter and therefore not a serious declaration of intention. Shula's position is clear, however:

> "I'm glad you understand that I took the moon thing for you. You aren't going to give up the project, are you? It would be a sin. You were made to write the Wells book, and it would be a masterpiece. Something terrible will happen if you don't. Bad luck. I feel it inside."
> "I may try again."
> "You must."
> "To find a place for it among my preoccupations."
> "You should have no other preoccupations. Only creative ones." (265)

His concession to Shula here, that he "may try again" to write the book on Wells, reveals a change of attitude in which he sees the need for commitment instead of "perfect disinterest." Despite his aversion to his daughter's behavior and her eccentricities, he recognizes his paternal obligation to her and says, "Shula, we must take care of each other. As you look after me on the H. G. Wells side, I think about your happiness" (264). Sensing another potential disaster for his daughter, he persuades her to forget the idea of marrying Dr. Lal. He even refers, for support, to the authority who most impresses her when he seems to remember Wells saying that "people in scientific research made poor husbands" (265).

If he does some day write his book on Wells, one can be certain that it will be a different book from the one he planned to write in the 1930s, when he was a "relatively useless" assimilationist "Anglophile intellectual Polish Jew" (303) smitten with the Utopian ideas of the optimistic apostle of progress. This older Sammler died in the Holocaust, and another Sammler was reborn when a one-eyed persecuted Jew crawled out of a mass grave and took a new look at Wells. The Wells whom he sees is, of course, the product of his own making.

As in Freud's view of the Oedipal relationship between father and son, the younger writer's relationship to his literary "father" is ambivalent, a mixture of love, trust, respect, hate, jealousy, and disdain. Like many other literary "sons," Sammler views his "father" defensively, unconsciously oversimplifying and distorting as he does so. Sammler's critical eye focuses on a flawed Wells now. He finds Wells's Utopian views and schemes, such as Cosmopolis, humane but naive. He objects to Wells's idea of "free love" and his sexual behavior, both of which he associates with the sexual excesses of the 1960s. He disapproves of the despairing misanthropy of Wells's final years. Like Henry James, he faults Wells for his didactic aesthetic, which resulted in too much writing with too little art.

Yet there is another major reason why Sammler finds Wells an unattractive figure now. He never explicitly states this reason because he himself may not be fully aware of it. Sammler has returned to his Jewish roots, an action that Wells would have found distressing. Despite his horror of war and his advanced age and poor health, this septuagenarian in 1967 flies to Israel where, he fears, Jews are once again being threatened with mass extermination during the Six-Day War. By the end of his crisis meditation, he concludes that the person whom he especially admires is Elya Gruner, "an *Ostjude* immigrant" (77), who is "on an old system"—that is, Gruner adheres to traditional Eastern European Jewish values. Although Gruner is not free from the corruption of American life, he possesses such basic qualities as "feeling, outgoingness, expressiveness, kindness, heart" (303), and Sammler sees this dignified, decent person as a model worth imitating and as an alternative to the ubiquitous role-playing, the degraded clowning, and the circus of emotions that plague modern society.

The assimilationist Jewish self that Sammler now finds distasteful was the self that Wells found admirable. Sammler's strong support for Israel would have been repugnant to Wells. Wells's *The Anatomy of Frustration* includes his indictment of Zionism and his rebuttal to charges that he is anti-Semitic. The best one can say for Wells on this subject is that while he claims to despise the Nazi persecution of the Jews, his attack on Zionism contains insensitive remarks in which he blames the victims for their persecution. (Some of Wells's friends suggested that his remarks gave aid to the fascists.) According to Wells, Jews are responsible for bringing on their own troubles by seeing themselves as the chosen people, thereby making themselves an obvious target. Norman and Jeanne Mackenzie paraphrase Wells's position: "Nazism, indeed, was simply 'inverted Judaism', the effect upon the Germans of centuries of teaching from the Old Testament" (402). Wells can be even blunter. In a 11 November 1933 letter, he declines an invitation to join a committee against anti-Semitism, which he considers "a natural reaction to the intense nationalism of the Jews and to the very distinctive role they play in the world of art and business . . . A careful study of anti-Semitic prejudice and accusations might be of very great value to many Jews who do not adequately realize the irritations they inflict."[21] Sammler knows, however, that even a highly-assimilated Anglophile Jew without any interest in a Jewish homeland can end up the target of the anti-Semites.

In short, if Sammler can criticize Churchill and Roosevelt for failing to take action to curtail the slaughter in the concentration camps, it is likely that he now finds Wells's view of anti-Semitism perverse. He would probably find appropriate Bertrand Russell's speculation that only Wells's incarceration in a place like Buchenwald would have resulted in Wells's loss of faith in the unlimited power of reason.[22]

5

While Sammler now finds the man he once revered unappealing in a number of ways, it would be wrong to conclude that Wells's work does not have any continuing influence on the Holocaust survivor's sensibility. One of the major influences that shapes his sensibility is English romanticism. Sammler's Wordsworthian imagination enables him to feel intimations of immortality at times, and Wells's version of English romanticism influences Sammler's outlook. As I have argued elsewhere, the most important allusions in

Henderson the Rain King (1959) and *Humboldt's Gift* (1975) are to Wordsworth's "Ode: Intimations of Immortality from Recollections of Early Childhood," for in these two novels Bellow reveals how man achieves a "soul" according to the conception of spiritual growth delineated in this poem. Moreover, one sees the influence of Wordsworth throughout Bellow's canon, especially in his belief that the imagination has the power to discover the miraculous in ordinary reality and liberate the individual's mind from the mortmain of custom and the slavery of routine perception.[23] While the Wordsworthian imagination is important in *Mr. Sammler's Planet*, Sammler's romanticism also comes by way of Wells.

With his scientific point of view, Wells is not usually seen in the nineteenth-century English romantic tradition. However, as Samuel L. Hynes and Frank D. McConnell make clear, this is a profitable way to see Wells. They suggest that while science and romanticism are often perceived as antithetical, they should be regarded "as parallel and complementary developments." Scientists "from Laplace through Darwin to Einstein" have demonstrated that the external world is "irretrievably *other*, unrelated to our own innate ideas of rational proportion or causality," while writers "from Wordsworth through Conrad to Joyce" have demonstrated how isolated our internal world, the human mind, is from external "Nature" that "might putatively support or illustrate its passions or its deepest longings."[24]

As a young man, Wells read the work of Shelley, one of his favorite poets. In his *Hymn to Intellectual Beauty*, Shelley questions why nature is unable to sustain a person's view of his own dignity or moral value and suggests that such questions are self-destructive because the cosmos is indifferent to human myth-making:

No voice from some sublimer world hath ever
　　To sage or poet these responses given—
　　Therefore the names of Demon, Ghost, and Heaven,
Remain the records of their vain endeavour,
Frail spells—whose uttered charm might not avail to sever,
　　From all we hear and all we see,
　　Doubt, chance, and mutability.

Shelley suggests Nature's indifference to man's struggle to create "parabolic value systems" with three powerful negatives: "Doubt, chance, and mutability." Chance and mutability became the unconscious "mainspring forces" in "the most anti-mythic work of nineteenth-century thought" and "the most formative single influence on all of Wells's thought," Charles Darwin's *Origin of Species*.

Hynes and McConnell further argue that Darwin should be considered as "one of the most important romantic poets of the century" who completed "the destructuring of Nature as the grounds of human mythmaking." The conventional view of English romanticism, which modern scholars such as Hynes and McConnell have shown is flawed, presents the romantic writers as celebrating nature for its "healing powers." On the contrary, "the romantic obsession with 'Nature' is not the expression of a passionate at-homeness in the natural world, but quite the reverse: a profound nostalgia, at first loving but very rapidly becoming bitter, for a 'Nature' that once seemed to support the imposition of moral values, but that resists more and more such imposition."[25]

Wells's romanticism is most evident in his early period, especially in *The War of the Worlds*, before there was a change in his attitude, before the apostle of progress and technology would dominate the writer of dark romances who questioned and criticized optimistic faith in the inevitable development of civilization. The Wells that Sammler identifies with is the Wells of *The War of the Worlds*, the dark Wells who, like Sammler, is anxious about the survival of the species and ponders whether evolution will lead toward progress or extinction. Both Sammler and the author of *War of the Worlds* are concerned with the complacent assumption that mankind will continue to dominate his planet. In a passage in which Olaf Stapledon, Wells's friend and disciple, is mentioned, Sammler considers the evolution of man: "What will become of us? Of the other species, yes, and of us? How will we ever make it?" (190).

Wells was influenced by Thomas H. Huxley's cosmic pessimism, in which evolution is seen not as inevitable progress but as regression ending in destruction. He was also affected by Lord Kelvin and others who argued that "the law of entropy would eventually lead to a cooling of the sun and the reduction of the planets to a system of dead matter whirling in the nothingness of space."[26] The narrator of *The War of the Worlds* speculates that mankind may be able to colonize "our sister planet" Venus "when the slow cooling of the sun makes the earth uninhabitable as at last it must do."[27]

Sammler also assumes the eventual destruction of the sun: "Another six billion years before the sun explodes" (190). Like Wells, Sammler's reflection on the future of mankind varies from wondering if human civilization will survive in some form on another planet to fear that mankind will become extinct. Sammler's Wellsian cosmic speculations often seem based on the assumption that humans are planning "to bolt to other worlds" because the earth, "a glorious planet," is becoming ravaged by "madness and poison":

> Men would set their watches by other suns than this. Or time would vanish. We would need no personal names of the old sort in the sidereal future, nothing being fixed. We would be designated by other nouns. Days and nights would belong to the museums. The earth a memorial park, a merry-go-round cemetery. (134-35)

Daniel Fuchs observes that Sammler's final words, the repetition of "we know, we know," are perhaps an unconscious echoing of another Holocaust survivor, the narrator's wife in *The War of the Worlds*, who says "I knew—knew" when she is reunited with her husband; the similar expressions suggest a "last-ditch affirmation."[28] In fact, there are some other important similarities between the two works.

In both works, an idealistic, complacent character realizes, after surviving a genocidal attack, that he was naive and must revise his most basic assumptions about the world. When the narrator of *The War of the Worlds* returns to his desolate home after surviving the Martian Holocaust, he looks at the manuscript that he had interrupted to investigate the first Martian cylinder. "It was a paper on the probable development of Moral Ideas with the development of the civilizing process; and the last sentence was the opening of a prophecy: 'In about two hundred years,' I had written, `we may expect—.'"[29] The optimistic future that the narrator had originally envisioned has been undermined by the Martian attack. Similarly, Sammler was about to write a book on Wells that also would have been full of optimistic predictions, a project is also subverted by a genocidal attack. With a romantic faith in the basic worth of everyday existence but no longer complacent, both characters realize that they cannot consider this planet as a secure place for human beings, whom they now recognize as simply a small part of the vast cosmos.

6

At the very end of the novel, in the work's final lines in which he says a prayer for Elya Gruner, Sammler resolves his crisis, having been "drawn back to human conditions" despite his goal to be "free from the bondage of the ordinary and the finite" (117-18). In a civilization poised, paradoxically, for space exploration and colonization yet threatened with collapse on its own planet, Sammler recollects, evaluates, speculates, and judges as he tries to reconcile the three different "worlds" warring within his soul. In his crisis meditation, he continually ponders H. G. Wells, who is at the center of his pre-World War II world and whose presence is also felt in the worlds of Holocaust Poland and contemporary America. Though not explicitly stated, the reason why Sammler has not been able to make progress on his book is evident by the end of the crisis meditation: Sammler feels ambivalent toward the man who was the center of his universe until this assimilated Jewish intellectual was caught in the Holocaust and his outlook was fundamentally transformed. Although Sammler finally decides that he has grave doubts about Wells, his speculations on mankind's position in the cosmos, and his concerns for the survival of the species reveal Wells's influence. When Sammler abandons the Utopian Wells and jettisons his naive assimilated Jewish Anglophile self, he is influenced by Wells's dark romanticism of *The War of the Worlds* period.

One should be careful not to overstate this influence, however, for others help shape Sammler's outlook. The most important is his discovery of his Jewishness, which accounts for his moral code and the particular kind of comedy that pervades this somber meditation. Dorothy Seidman Bilik has shown that Bellow's revision of the early published version of the novel in *Atlantic* reveals his intention to enlarge the Jewish material for the final published version of the book. For example, Bellow substantially developed the Rumkowski material for the final published version. It is also worth noting that while Sammler after the Holocaust never does publish on Wells or the mystic writers who intrigue him, he does publish articles on the Six-Day War, suggesting "how important the specifically Jewish past and future have become" to him.[30]

Although it echoes a similar line at the end of *The War of the Worlds*, Sammler's "last-ditch affirmation"—when he asserts "we know"—owes a large debt to his Jewish background. Here he affirms our ancient covenant with God and with our fellows. This covenant cannot be scientifically proven but only can be known intuitively by the power of the imagination. Sammler, who at times seemed to be a prophet from another planet, has come to recognize that his planet is the earth and that there are different forms of escape from one's responsibility to this world, all of which one must avoid. He abandons his goal of being "perfectly disinterested" and uncontaminated; now he demonstrates a commitment to Shula and expresses his admiration for Elya Gruner, who could not completely avoid the corruption of American society but who met his everyday obligations and acted humanely, if not always strictly legally. The novel concludes with the implication that, inspired by Elya Gruner, Sammler has ended his "war of the planets" with the decision to forsake his goal of mystic detachment and, instead, to commit himself to everyday life on Earth, where "doubt, change, and mutability" are inevitable.

NOTES

1. *Saul Bellow: Against the Grain* (Philadelphia: University of Pennsylvania Press, 1990), p. 11.

2. *Saul Bellow: In Defense of Man* (Bloomington: Indiana University Press, 1979), pp. 230-50.

3. Abrams, "Structure and Style in the Greater Romantic Lyric," *Sensibility to Romanticism: Essays Presented to Frederick A. Pottle*, ed. Frederick W. Hilles and Harold Bloom (New York: Oxford University Press, 1965), pp. 527-60; and Bloom, *The Ringers in the Tower: Studies in Romantic Tradition* (Chicago: University of Chicago Press, 1971), pp. 323-337.

4. *Fiction as Wisdom: From Goethe to Bellow* (University Park: The Pennsylvania State University Press, 1980), p. 219.

5. Gordon Lloyd Harper, "Saul Bellow—The Art of Fiction: An Interview," *Paris Review* 9 (Winter 1965):65-66; and Saul Bellow, "A World Too Much With Us," *Critical Inquiry* 2.1 (1975):9.

6. Bradbury, *Saul Bellow* (London: Methuen, 1982), p. 78.

7. Saul Bellow, *Mr. Sammler's Planet* (New York: Viking, 1970), p. 29. Subsequent references will be given parenthetically in the text.

8. Judie Newman, *Saul Bellow and History* (New York: St. Martin's, 1984), pp. 133-156, is the only critic who has recognized the importance of Wells in the novel, though her view is different from mine, as I explain in section 2 of this essay.

9. Edward Alexander, "Imagining the Holocaust: Mr. Sammler's Planet and Others," *Judaism* 22 (1972):300, quotes the passage, with this metaphor, from Arendt's *The Origins of Totalitarianism* to support his view that Mr. Sammler's planet is that other world of the Holocaust.

10. Bradbury, p. 78.

11. *H.G. Wells, Desperately Mortal: A Biography* (New Haven: Yale University Press, 1986), pp. 197-199.

12. Mackenzie, *H.G. Wells: A Biography* (New York: Simon and Schuster, 1973), pp. 387.

13. William J. Scheick, "Circle Sailing in Bellow's *Mr. Sammler's Planet*," *Essays in Literature* 5.1 (1978):97, suggests that "Sammler detects an irony in the revolutionary posture (in a political, cultural sense) of contemporary youth because it is merely a somewhat shabbier demonstration of the same impulse expressed in his 'revolutionary' youth during the Thirties, when he knew H. G. Wells and Olaf Stapledon, and especially

because it evinces merely one extreme in the revolutionary (circular, cyclic) nature of human life, in which future and past never separate."

14. Newman, p. 135.

15. Mackenzie, pp. 430-31.

16. *The Time Machine, The War of the Worlds: A Critical Edition*, ed. Frank D. McConnell (New York: Oxford University Press, 1977), p. 125.

17. Bellow, "A World Too Much With Us," p. 5.

18. "Introduction," *H.G. Wells: A Collection of Critical Essays* (Englewood Cliffs, N. J.: Prentice-Hall, 1976), p. 6. In *The Splintering Frame: The Later Fiction of H. G. Wells* (Victoria, B. C.: University of Victoria English Literary Studies, 1984) William J. Scheick counters this general assessment of Wells's career, and in *The Ethos of Romance at the Turn of the Century* (Austin: University of Texas Press, 1994) he provides an alternative interpretation of the terms *journalist* and *journalism* as used by Wells and others.

19. Costa, *H. G. Wells.* (Boston: Twayne, 1985), p. 36.

20. Daniel Fuchs, *Saul Bellow: Vision and Revision* (Durham, N. C.: Duke University Press, 1984), p. 221.

21. Mackenzie, p. 402.

22. Costa, p. 148.

23. "Humboldt's Gift and the Romantic Imagination," *Philological Quarterly* 62 (1983):1-19, and "Bellow and English Romanticism," *Studies in the Literary Imagination* 17.2 (1984):7-18, rpt. in *Saul Bellow in the 1980s: A Collection of Critical Essays*, ed. Gloria L. Cronin and L. H. Goldman (East Lansing, MI: Michigan State University Press, 1989), pp. 67-79.

24. Hynes and McConnell, "The Time Machine and The War of the Worlds: Parable and Possibility in H. G. Wells," *H. G. Wells, The Time Machine, The War of the Worlds: A Critical Edition*, p. 356. Scheick, in *The Splintering Frame*, comments on Wells's romanticism, including his "Romantic affirmation of the human self," an affirmation at the foundation of Bellow's fiction.

25. Hynes and McConnell, pp. 357-58.

26. Mackenzie, p. 120.

27. *War of the Worlds*, p. 299.

28. *War of the Worlds*, p. 296; Fuchs, p. 222.

29. *War of the Worlds*, p. 296.

30. Bilik, Dorothy Seidman. *Immigrant Survivors: Post-Holocaust Consciousness in Recent Jewish-American Fiction* (Middletown, Conn.: Wesleyan University Press, 1981), pp. 148-52, 164-65.

When the Sleeper Wakes
(1899)

The Ideas of H. G. Wells

Anonymous

emarkable as Mr. Wells is as an individual author, he is still more remarkable as a representative figure. He exhibits in a striking manner the virtues and defects of a new and increasing class in the English *bourgeoisie*. He is a revolutionary fanatic with that doctrinaire cast of mind which, as it used to be more common in France than in England, is sometimes regarded as a mark of race, but which, in matter of fact, is merely the product of a certain kind of intellectual atmosphere and a certain kind of training. He is the child of an age of *schwärmerei* [fanaticism], with the qualities of that age enhanced by a scientific education of a peculiar sort. No inconsiderable part of his originality is due to the fact that he happened to appear in a period of unsettlement, when the English mind was, for the first time, losing hold of the world of experience and groping wildly in a world of theory.

From the epidemic of frantic sciolism produced by the eighteenth century movement of enlightenment, the English middle classes escaped somewhat lightly. Their knowledge was the fruit of experiment rather than of deduction; and a happy play of circumstances enabled them to elaborate, out of their own affairs, the principles of modern industrial civilisation. But their exemption from the general disease of thought of their age was purchased at a heavy price. Having initiated, as a matter of practice, the movement of illumination which the spokesmen of the French *bourgeoisie* adopted as a matter of theory, they acquired a dangerous contempt for mere ideas. Their placidity of mind soon degenerated into lethargy. They stilled the growing-pains of their intellect by drugging themselves with work; and the result was that they not only ceased to grow, but became, in regard to the things of the mind, childish.

In the age of Matthew Arnold and [Thomas] Huxley, however, the soporific commended by [Thomas] Carlyle began to lose somewhat of its efficacy. The more blindly the English middle classes threw themselves into all kinds of mechanic labour[,] the more ample were the means of leisure and luxury which they thereby accumulated. At last, about 1890, the temptation to acquire a taste [for] and [to] display culture grew irresistible; the results were soon to be seen in all the circulating libraries in the kingdom. Grant Allen's novel, *The Woman Who Did* [1895] is, in its extravagance of sentiment and its ineptitude of thought, a typical example of the literature of this period. The errant sons and daughters of the Philistines tried in vain to assure their emancipation by masquerading, in bacchanalia of nonsense, as the children of light. Their notions were both trite and belated.

Emerging from a fabric of conventions erected in the eighteenth century, they accepted the order of ideas contained in the prose of [William] Godwin and the poetry of [Percy] Shelley as a novel, daring, and profound philosophy of life and society. Of the works of the men of science and learning who, in the later part of the nineteenth century, had overthrown that philosophy, they were as ignorant as the average socialist. Many of them, indeed, were socialists, and especially socialists of the school of thought which found expression in Edward Bellamy's romance, *Looking Backward* [1888]. In fact, the revival of general interest in socialism was the pregnant event of the movement in its first stage. That compound—in its cruder forms—of antiquated theory and unenlightened humanitarianism then began to acquire the vogue which seems now to have made it the most popular of political nostrums.

In fine, the intellectual atmosphere in certain circles in London when Mr. Wells came from the country to study at the Normal School of Science [later the Royal College of Science] was similar to the intellectual atmosphere in certain circles in Paris just before the establishment of the Second Empire. And the description of student life in the Normal School in 1890, given by Mr. Wells in his novel, *Love and Mr. Lewisham*, resembles the description of student life in the École Normale in 1850, given by [Charles] Sainte-Beuve in his article on [Hippolyte] Taine. There is a similar ferment of thought on matters of science and socialism among a similar group of young men, selected from the middle classes, and converted by the training they receive into vigorous but narrow-minded doctrinaires. The student lives in these intellectual furnaces in a state of perpetual excitation and ardent discussion. His intelligence, formed in solitude on science and books, has to discover everything anew for itself, and refashion everything in its own way. Hence[,] he naturally contracts a certain violence and overweeningness of mind, together with a taste for exaggeration. His judgments are trenchant and uncompromising, owing to his lack of those finer shades and correctives of knowledge which are a matter of long experience and unbroken tradition. . . .

In his genius for framing vast and picturesque generalisations on a very narrow ground of fact, Mr. Wells, who was a pupil of Huxley, exhibits in a striking way the strange defects of an education based on the study of science. His extraordinary disregard for facts would have astonished his master. But Huxley failed to see, in his famous controversy with Matthew Arnold, that, while science in the making is partly concerned with facts, science in the learning is wholly concerned with generalisations. To the man of science[,] an hypothesis is serviceable only as a means of illustrating some matter of observation or experiment; to the student of science, on the other hand, a matter of observation or experiment is serviceable only as a means of illustrating some current hypothesis. Since the question of the value of science, as the supreme instrument of education, retains all its importance at the present day, it is worthy of remark that Mr. Wells himself confesses to a passion for mere speculation and an extreme impatience of facts. The result of his severe training at the Normal School of Science has been to make him only an amateur of the architectural beauty of science. . . .

Like certain etchers of Gothic cathedrals, he has studied his subject so well from the point of view of his own art that he can now invent all the material which he requires for his pictures. Indeed[,] he finds this so facile a way of obtaining effects that he inclines to contemn the laborious means which the men he imitates use to an end entirely different. In a recent romance, *The Food of the Gods*, he goes so far as to express an arrogant surprise that the minds of "the little scientists" who are building up the temple of modern knowledge should be concentrated on small matters of actual fact. He compares Bensington, a character in the story who is represented as a man of Darwin's calibre, to the reef-building coral insects which do not realise the things they are doing. . . .

[Moreover,] how could a writer of no mean intellectual power, who in 1901, in his *Anticipations*, fiercely attacked socialism as a vain theory long since discredited by [Thomas] Malthus and Darwin, and who in 1903, in his *Mankind in the Making*, defended the institution of monogamy, have found in 1906 [*In the Days of the Comet*] salvation in socialism and a glimpse of heaven in a wild dream of a new earth peopled by polyandrous houris and polygamous demi-gods? As a matter of fact, Mr. Wells is a Frankenstein who has been frightened out of his senses by a horde of spectral monsters which he invented in the irresponsible days of his youth, when he indulged his genius for "fantastic exaggerations, fantastic inversions of all recognised things."

As works of fantasy some of these monsters are admirable. They possess something of the decorative ugliness of the demons of Japanese art. In his excursions in sociology Mr. Wells exhibits the talent of a brilliant and suggestive, but narrow-minded and one-sided critic. This talent, directed by a deep but indiscriminate sense of wrong, and enhanced by an uncommon power of imagination, made him in his younger, wilder days, a satirist of no little force. The inveterate urbanity of his style prevents us from comparing him in a general way with [Jonathan] Swift. He never addresses the reader as an equal, in a quite, simple, and persuasive manner . . . The affectations of diction, the awkward gestures, the air of uneasy superiority, the loud voice and the magic lantern, by means of which lecturers of a certain sort try to command the attention of an uncultivated audience—these things Mr. Wells'[s] way of expressing himself only too often calls to our mind.

Through all this uncouthness, however, the passion and the power of the writer still shine; and on some points the comparison between him and Swift does not seem to us to be inept. *When the Sleeper Wakes* and *The Time Machine* are good examples of his satirical genius. These two tales are based upon one of those ideas which the amateur of science, anxious to startle an indifferent public, is tempted to catch up from current scientific literature and develop in an extravagant manner.

When Mr. Wells was studying science and discussing socialism at South Kensington, [George] Romanes succeeded in exciting considerable interest in a new theory of the origin of species. Its author, Mr. J. T. Gulich, having observed that the form and colour of the shells of snails in the Sandwich Islands varied according to the locality, concluded that the diversity of species was the result of in-breeding produced by segregation. Men with cautious minds, however, held to the ideas of Darwin; and at the present day the theory of the regulative action of natural selection on mutations, or sudden and important "sports" which are secured against decadence by prepotence, is conceived to be sufficient to account for the facts of the evolution of life.

Naturally, Mr. Wells was not among the men with cautious minds. His eyes were fixed upon the future; and Darwinism, an old, orthodox and complex doctrine bearing on matters of the past, was of little use to him. The hypothesis of segregation, on the other hand, was a novel, heretical, and simple notion, which, as it seemed to permit the speculator to neglect the incalculable, disconcerting factor of "sports," reduced prophecy to an affair of slight and facile generalisation. Mr. Wells had only to glance at modern conditions of life in order to divine the disastrous event to which the process of segregation was working. Mankind was rapidly splitting up into two new species. On the one side was the pleasure-loving, witty and graceful type; on the other, the sombre, mechanically-industrious, inartistic type. "The gradual widening of the present merely temporary and social difference between the capitalist and the labourer was the key to the whole position" (*The Time Machine*, p. 82).

This idea is of course the grand fallacy in the literature of socialism from [Charles] Fourier to [Karl] Marx; but Mr. Wells redeemed it from commonplaceness by the ingenuity and impartiality with which he worked it out. As an amateur of socialism he pitied the imaginary inferior race; as an amateur of science he foresaw the triumph of the *Übermensch*; and this he depicts in wild lights and lurid shadows in *When the Sleeper Wakes*. Instead of framing, out of the best elements of contemporary life, the idea of an earthly paradise, in the manner of [Thomas] More, he fashions out of its worst elements the idea of a terrestrial inferno in the manner of Swift.

The sleeper of the story is a modern socialist, who awakes out of a trance of two hundred years, in a London of titanic edifices roofed in from the weather and inhabited by thirty-two million people. All the sinister forces of a purely industrial civilisation have been allowed to expand unchecked. The result is a vivid caricature of those ideals of Chicago which were set out some time ago in the *Letters from a Self-Made Merchant to His Son* [by George Horace Lorimer]. There are some acute observations on the same subject in Mr. Wells'[s] later work, *The Future in America*, wherein socialism is preached as the only solution of the tremendous questions which the great Republic has to face. But in this work, it is needless to say, the criticism is not so fine and subtle as that contained in Mr. Henry James'[s] impressions of travel[,] *The American Scene* [1907]; and moreover, the value of the more recent book is diminished by the extravagantly socialistic attitude therein adopted. Mr. Wells is more brilliant, while, at the same time, he is more impartial, in his earlier satire, *When the Sleeper Wakes.* . . .

In accordance with the theory invented by Fourier and appropriated by Marx, the development of an individualistic policy is traced from the rise of a network of monopolies to the establishment of a tyrannical plutocracy. A French or a German writer would probably have concluded the tale at this point; and Mr. Wells, with a fine touch of irony, had provided the machinery for this purpose. The sleeper is a modern socialist and heir to the immense accumulated wealth on which the power of the oligarchy rests. The populace was waiting for him to arise and bring in the millennium. A tyrant appears, organises the mob, and awakens the sleeper; and a revolution takes place in which the oligarchy is routed. The socialist and tyrant afterwards fight out, single-handed, the question as to the future mode of [the] government of the world. And the socialist of course wins?

No. That is the dramatic surprise which Mr. Wells skilfully engineers. He had read Carlyle on "Heroes" [*On Heroes, Hero-Worship, and the Heroic in History* (1841)] before he studied Marx on "Capital" [*Das Kapital*], and, in spite of his sympathy with certain socialistic ideas, he still admired, above all others, the capable, masterful individual whose creative and organising genius is the great instrument of progress in civilisation. The tyrant in *When the Sleeper Wakes* is a philosopher of the Nietzschean school; and some of his sayings are worth citing by way of illustrating one phase of Mr. Wells'[s] thought.

> The day of the common man is passed . . . The common man now is a helpless unit. In these days we have an organisation complex beyond his understanding . . . There is no liberty, save wisdom and self-control. Liberty is within, not without. It is each man's own affair.
>
> Suppose . . . that these swarming, yelping fools get the upper hand of us, what then? They will only fall to other masters . . . Let them revolt, let them win and kill me and my like. Others will arise—other masters. The end will be the same . . . What right have they to hope? The hope of mankind, what is it? That some day the Over-man may come; that some day the inferior, the weak and the bestial may be subdued or eliminated. Their duty—it's a fine duty too!—is to die. The death of the failure! That is the path by which the beast rose to manhood, by which man goes on to higher things. (pp. 235-39)

If that were Mr. Wells'[s] first idea of the manner in which the theory of natural selection ought to be reduced to practice, no wonder he inclined to a gentler hypothesis of the origin of species by segregation! Mere elimination serves at best only to maintain a race at a certain level. It does not provoke the mutations which are the prime factor in evolution. These, we fancy, are most likely to occur in the order of men with rather unstable temperaments which ranks lowest in Mr. Wells'[s] scale of efficacy. But in any event neither elimination nor segregation avail much if we believe in the tales of the traveler in *The Time Machine. . . .*

After a voyage of eight hundred thousand years[,] the traveler alighted, expecting to be amazed at the development of mankind. The earth was a tangled waste of strange, beautiful bushes and flowers, a neglected and yet a weedless garden. It was peopled by a race of pretty, graceful creatures, only four feet high and indescribably frail, whose days were spent in eating fruit and sleeping and love-making. In the matter of intelligence they were on the level of children five years of age. This was what the victory of the "Over-man" had ended in! The serfs had been subdued and driven back into their underground factories, and the aristocracy had obtained one triumph after another over nature until all diseases had been stamped out, and all the hard, invigorating conditions of life removed. Then, *vaincue par sa conquête* [that is, defeated by themselves], the higher race had degenerated in the paradise from which it had exorcised the spirit of evil which had provoked its strength.

And the same dehumanisation which too easy a life had effected the lords of the upper world, had been produced in the slaves of the nether earth by too brutal and empty a way of existence. The artisans, reduced at last to mechanical tenders of intricate machinery, the principle of which they were not required, or allowed, to understand, had gradually lost in their subterranean factories vigour and intelligence, and become noisome beasts of prey with nocturnal habits. What they preyed on is a thing best left to the imagination.

Mr. Wells, however, is, without the excuse of madness, as explicit in the matter as Swift was in his *Modest Proposal for Preventing the Children of Poor People Being a Burden* [1729]. One is at times inclined to agree with Taine and other French critics, that English literature, for all its magnificence, is the work of a race of barbarians. Mr. Wells seems to have at least one trait of the barbaric mind—superstitiousness. As we have remarked, he is now haunted by the gruesome creatures of his imagination. Some of the ways in which he has tried to lay these spectres are as curious as those adopted in similar cases by African witch-doctors. He has endeavoured to transform a few of the phantoms into gracious and noble giants by feeding them on *The Food of the Gods*, hoping to slay, with the help of these giants, all the other bugbears. Then he has fled in despair to a remote star and entrenched himself there behind the walls of *A Modern Utopia*. And, finally, he has returned to earth, *In the Days of the Comet*, with a magical green vapour[,] by means of which he now expects to change all the children of men, from whom the monsters which harass his prophetic soul are fated to descend, into a race of divinities with the beauty of person and the laxity of manners of the gods and goddesses of Homer. . . .

In regard to the most brilliant notion in *A Modern Utopia*, in which the idea of the army of the giants of modern science in *The Food of the Gods* is developed into a scheme for the establishment of an order of "Samurai," or lay priests of ascetic habits of life, devoted to the furtherance of the general mundane interests of humanity, Mr. Wells candidly admits his indebtedness to Plato. But, as his training in history has not been so thorough as his training in science, he does not seem to know how often the idea of the guardians in the *Republic* has been acted on, and how often it has been proved impracticable. The story of every famous monastic order shows what too rigid and complete an organisation of the moral and spiritual energies of any age inevitably ends in. The stronger, the more efficient the machinery of regimentation, the sooner does a sort of fossilisation, if not a sort of decay, set in. . . .

Happily, Mr. Wells is a man of varying moods. On the one hand, he is the artificial creature of an education based on abstract science, to whose cold, unmoved intelligence the life of humanity is a colourless spectacle which interests him as a kind of problem merely by reason of its possible developments . . . This is the mood in which he inclines to become a meddlesome, hasty, impatient fanatic, with an aggressive creed of Calvinistic socialism in which there is neither help and pity for the weak, nor scope and liberty for the strong.

On the other hand, there is in him a child of nature who is as little concerned as Charles Dickens was with the frigid, logical, scientific study of mankind. In this mood he is a fine novelist, the idiosyncrasy of whose genius resides in the power of quick and winning sympathy with which he irradiates every petty, commonplace detail in the life of the lower-middle classes. Far from despising those whom the stern socialists of the vegetarian school account dull and base, he exerts all the might of his imagination in an endeavour to exalt the humble and put down the mighty. Like Dickens, with whom he has much more in common than [George] Gissing had, he shows a happier touch in revealing the merits of the meek and lowly than in exposing the failings of the rich and noble. Vivid as is the gift of satire which he exhibits in other directions, he cannot get a scantling of truth and sharpness into his caricatures of overbearing squires and supercilious ladies of the manner.

But how fresh and clear, on the other hand, is the picture of the poor rustic scholar in *Love and Mr. Lewisham*! How tender the humour, and how light and telling the touch with which the story of his struggle between love and ambition is depicted! It is, we think, the cheeriest biographical novel in recent English literature, and the most interesting. Without any of the cumbrous apparatus employed by the writers of the psychological school, Mr. Wells succeeds in conveying a very definite impression of the vacillations of mind of the younger generation of the English middle classes between 1890 and 1895.

Probably *Love and Mr. Lewisham* is not so popular a novel as *Kipps*, but to our mind it is the more finished work. It is more of a piece, a tissue of exquisite realism in which the actual colours of life are subdued by being blended. The first part of *Kipps*, however, is better than anything else Wells has written. Kipps himself strikes us as one of the most life-like personages in modern fiction. Few of even the best of our novelists of the younger generation are able to create a character of this kind, which lives and moves with an energy of its own in the memory of the reader.

In regard to the conduct of the action, Mr. Wells is less fortunate. A striking, original plot which does not exceed the bounds of verisimilitude is as rare a thing in modern fiction as is a striking, original character. The touch of the magic wand which lifts Kipps from the position of a draper's assistant to the rank of a man of wealth and leisure, changes the story of his struggles into the only kind of fairy-tale which does not entertain us. The narrative loses its close relation to life just at that point at which the relation becomes very interesting. And what makes the use of this primitive machinery for effecting a revolution in the plot especially irritating is the fact that it is quite unnecessary. In the precarious existence of the drifting part of our lower-middle-classes there is sufficient of the genuine stuff of romance to enable a writer with Mr. Wells'[s] gifts to make a novel of manners dealing with that existence as full, if so he wished, of hazard, variety, and sudden change as is an ordinary novel of adventure.

At present, we are afraid, Mr. Wells wishes only to make his novels the vehicle for the exposition of certain socialistic theories. It is a great pity that a novelist with so lively a sense of the picturesque, so impressive an imagination, and so gracious a power of sympathetic insight, should have been drawn into a frothy movement of enlightenment in which his natural genius is dwarfed and distorted. We do not think he will become the "Luther of Socialism," of whom he speaks in *Love and Mr. Lewisham*. He lacks the soul of iron and the colour-blindness of the systematiser. The stream of his feelings does not run in the same direction as that in which the current of his thoughts has, unhappily, been turned. Hence his continual alterations of opinion.

His polemical works are written with a view to convincing himself. But he cannot make up his mind. He is not, like Mr. G[eorge] B[ernard] Shaw, a gay and curious sceptic of nature, who has taken up socialism as the latest and most perverse form of intellectual dilettantism. Mr. Wells is in earnest, but he is not certain what he is in earnest about. He wants to reduce everything to some formula which he can swear by; but whenever he rises into the cold, grey world of misty abstractions in which the makers of rigid systems dwell, he is enticed down to the warm, green earth by the sounds, the stir, the hues, and the fullness of real life. So he vacillates in a strange, spiritual unrest; being, on the one hand, an anarchist, who would destroy, out of wild, personal discontent, a civilisation on which rests everything that he loves and admires; and, on the other hand, a troubled, anxious, questioning spirit, seeking vainly amid the shows of time for the eternal foundations of religious faith.

The First Men in the Moon
(1901)

History, Adventure, and School Stories

Anonymous

t is safe to say that no growing lad with a taste for science who gets hold of Mr. Wells'[s] story [*The First Men in the Moon*] will readily put it down. To some elder readers it will appeal with the force of a splendidly contrived nightmare. Not the least of its merits is its natural beginning[,] and this is equaled by its plausible ending. The idea of elastic brains, the conception of a race of intellectual fungi nourished on mushrooms and mooncalves[,] and bred in sections to each one of which is allotted one special task—these are flights of imagination that have about them somewhat more of the satire of a Jonathan Swift than the frank inventions of a Jules Verne. But such a consideration will not disturb the pleasure of many readers. The book, it is worthy of note, has already made its appearance in French.

The Sea Lady (1902)

The Natural History of H. G. Wells

John R. Reed

ells was not so candid about a more eligible source for
this novel [*The Sea Lady*] that "stressed the harsh incompatibility of wide public
interests with the high, swift rush of imaginative passion."[1] I am not thinking of
[Baron F. H. K.] la Motte Fouque's classic tale, *Undine* [1811], which Wells
does mention pointedly and which had appeared in a handsome new edition in
1896, but of Henrik Ibsen's play *The Lady from the Sea* (1888), which was
translated into English as early as 1891 and was performed in England in that
same year. It was presented in a better production in May of 1892, when it
received reviews in such notable journals as the *Athenaeum* (10 May 1902) and
the *Westminster Review* (July 1892).[2]

In Ibsen's play Ellida Wangel is haunted by memories of a love she once
felt for a mysterious sailor. For her, the sea represents romance and "a craving
for the unattainable . . . for the limitless, for the infinite."[3] The sea both awes
and attracts her, and the men who love her recognize that she is herself like the
sea. Early in the play Ellida says, "I think if only man had learnt to live on the
sea from the very first . . . perhaps even in the sea . . . we might have developed
better than we have, and differently. Better and happier" (act 3). She is,
however, reconciled to the fact that "we've taken the wrong track and become
people of the land instead of the sea," with no way of putting things right again
(act 3). Ellida fears the return of her sailor lover, who, when he reappears,
demands that she join him on his new sea voyage. When her husband yields to
Ellida's request that she be permitted to make her choice in complete freedom,
she decides to banish the romantic Stranger and remain with her dependable
husband. Although she is associated with heathen, dangerous, and mysterious
qualities of the sea, she decides to become a land creature, turning from the
wildness of the imagination to the calmer certainty of reason.

Ellida's case is framed by a pair of references that establish metaphorical
dimensions for her behavior. At the opening of the play, Ballested, an amateur

artist, explains that at Ellida's suggestion he is adding a dying mermaid to the seascape that he is painting. "She has strayed in from the sea and can't find her way out again. So here she lies dying in the brackish water, you see" (act 1). At the end of the play, Ellida remarks that "once a creature has settled on dry land, there's no going back to the sea"; and Ballested exclaims, "Why, that's just like the case of my mermaid!" but adds that the mermaid dies, whereas men and women can acclimatize themselves. Yes, says Ellida, if they are free (act 5).

Wells was apparently not happy with this resolution to Ellida's or the mermaid's dilemma, and in *The Sea Lady* he arranged a different outcome. His lady from the sea, Miss Doris Thalassia Waters, not only is beautiful and mysterious like Ellida Wangel but also is a genuine mermaid. Moreover, although she has apparently come to land by accident—she is found in a condition strangely resembling that of Ballested's mermaid—we soon learn that she has a determined plan to win the love of Chatteris, a promising young journalist and aspiring politician. Before long, the stuffy society of Folkestone recognizes the threat that the mermaid represents. Melville, a sort of intermediary between the sea lady and the conventional world of which he is a part, explains that she is attractive to Chatteris because she represents openness and naturalness as opposed to duty; she stands for what he is constantly seeking and never understands. The sea lady informs Melville that she comes from the elements, which are nothing more than the imagination. The limited conventional life with all of its trivial cares, its extraordinary little duties and hypnotic limitations, is, she says, "a fancy that has taken hold of you too strongly for you to shake off." She tells Melville, "You are in a dream, a fantastic, unwholesome little dream," and promises "there are better dreams."[4] Although he did not alter the essential opposition in Ibsen's play, Wells did reverse the conclusion, for Chatteris rejects his Marcella-like fiancée and, in a chapter entitled "Moonshine Triumphant," returns with Miss Waters to the sea and its mystery and romance.[5]

Wells later declared that he had "considerable sympathy for the passion," beauty, and imagination that Chatteris elected in favor of a life of order, duty, and service, but he did not imitate his character[6] . . . Wells rejected the artistic-aesthetic position in favor of a role governed by the principle that all of his "art" should serve the larger purpose of promoting human welfare and bringing about a new world order. At the same time he rejected the codification of the rules that put limits upon what the novel could do and how it could do it.

NOTES

1. H. G. Wells, *Experiment in Autobiography* (New York: Macmillan, 1934), p. 398.

2. Miriam Alice Franc, *Ibsen in England* (Boston: Four Seas, 1919), pp. 66, 90-91.

3. Henrik Ibsen, *The Lady from the Sea*, trans. James Walter McFarlane in the Oxford Ibsen, Volume VII, ed. James Walter MacFarlane (London: Oxford University Press, 1966), p. 120 (act 5). Subsequent indications of acts appear in the text.

4. *The Sea Lady* , *The Works of H. G. Wells* (New York: Scribner's Sons, 1925), 5:399-418.

5. The chapter had been titled "Moonshine" and "Moonshine In Excelsis" before "Moonshine Triumphant" was selected (Illinois). On my allusion to Marcella, see my other essay in this volume.

6. Wells, *Experiment*, p. 398.

A Modern Utopia (1905)

Sociological Speculations

F.C.S.S.

t is instructive to watch the growth, both in power and in hopefulness, of Mr. Wells's criticism of life. In the *Time Machine* his forecast of the future of humanity was frankly appalling; in *When the Sleeper Wakes*, [his forecast was] more lucid (albeit far more probable) than the worst imaginings of "reforming" socialists. *Anticipations* was a most stimulating book, but so deliberately confined itself to exalting and exaggerating the prospects of a single aspect of life, so exclusively devoted itself to glorifying mechanical and material progress, that those sensitive to our spiritual and aesthetic possibilities might be pardoned for regarding the present order, with all its cruelty, waste, sordidness, and grotesqueness, as a golden age in comparison with Mr. Wells's world. *Mankind in the Making* contained much vigorous criticism and many sensible and practical suggestions. In the present book [*A Modern Utopia*] Mr. Wells has become still more moderate and practicable and hopeful, without in the least derogating from his ingenuity and originality. We sincerely hope, therefore, he will not, as he threatens, stick henceforth to his "art or trade of imaginative writing," but will continue from time to time to regale and stimulate us with sociological speculations.

Stripping off the romantic form—in which Mr. Wells dreams himself and a companion, a botanist suffering from a chronic affair of the heart, into a distant planet which is an exact duplicate of our earth, save that it has realised all the good which is attainable with our present resources—his main argument may be condensed as follows.

As the philosophic foundation of his whole enterprise, Mr. Wells assumes what he calls the "metaphysical heresy" (though it is rapidly forcing itself upon the notice even of the most stagnantly "orthodox" philosophers) that all classifications, though convenient, are crude, and that whatever is real and valuable in the world is individual, a thesis he had expounded in the brilliant contribution to *Mind* [13 (July 1904): 379-93] entitled the "Scepticism of the Instrument," which he has now reprinted as an appendix to his book. From this philosophy he infers that progress depends on individual initiative and variation, leading to successful experiment. Hence, the infinite preciousness of freedom, which the Utopian World-State must restrict only when and in so far as it would oppose the freedom of others. Hence, too, there will be extensive toleration of "cranks," while even criminals would merely be segregated as failures and condemned to work out their ideas of a good life in a society of their likes, after a fashion charmingly described in the account of the arrival of involuntary immigrants at the "Island of Incorrigible Cheats." But although Utopia is strangely kind to the cranky, the criminal and the inefficient, because it regards their occurrence as the measure of the State's failure, it does not allow them to reproduce their kind. Parentage is a privilege, and the production of superior offspring a service to the community for which a wise State will handsomely reward its women.

But the efficiency and prosperity of the Utopian order ultimately depend on the ruling class, which Mr. Wells seems to have taken bodily out of the Platonic Republic, and, with a fine compliment to the unparalleled rise of Japan, entitled the "Samurai." The Samurai are conceived as a "voluntary nobility" which (like the mediaeval Church) all may enter who are able and willing to lead the strenuous and somewhat ascetic life prescribed by the rules of the Order. Among these obligations to buy and read every month at least one book published in the last five years, and every year to go out into the wilderness and to travel through it in silence and solitude for at least seven days, are perhaps the most noticeable, together with the prohibition of acting, singing and reciting, and the playing of games in public.

It is remarkable how Platonic is the general spirit of their institutions in all save the high appreciation of individual freedom, to the value of which Plato showed such singular blindness. Nor is their general aim hard to discover. At several points, however, a critic will be disposed to doubt whether Mr. Well's's means are adequate to his ends. He has seen, indeed, what never seems to have occurred to Plato, that if wisdom is to control the State, elaborate precautions must be taken to keep learning progressive, and to prevent it from fossilising into pedantry. The Platonic State, if it could ever have come into existence, would systematically have suppressed originality, and simply have stereotyped the condition of science and art prevailing at the date of its institution. If it could be conceived as surviving to the present day, it would still be sending its heroic hoplites against quick-firing guns, and still be punishing a belief in evolution or metageometry as heresies worthy of death. Mr. Wells seeks to guard against the universal tendency to fix in rigid forms whatever man admires. But though he insists on the importance of preserving the "poetic," *i. e.* originative, types of man and endowing their researches, it may be doubted whether even under his laws they would not be overpowered by the "kinetic," *i. e.* the efficient administrators, who everywhere conserve the established order. For these latter would control the Order of the Samurai.

Again, Mr. Wells's distrust of eugenics, justified as no doubt it is by the present state of our knowledge, seems unduly to disparage the prospects of scientific discovery in the future. It does not follow that because now we know too little to entrust the State with the function of controlling the reproduction of the race, this will continue to be unsafe, and it is easy to imagine circumstances in which such control would become almost inevitable. For example, if one of the many attempts to discover what determines the sex of an embryo should chance to be crowned with success, the numerical equality of the sexes would in all probability be gravely imperiled, and the State would almost certainly have to intervene.

Again, while Mr. Wells is doubtless within his rights in scoffing at the racial prejudices of the time, in his scorn of popular notions of "superior" races, "including such types as the Sussex farm labourer, the Bowery tough, the London hooligan, and the Paris apache," and in his contention that "no race is so superior as to be trusted with human charges," his anticipation of wholesale racial fusions seems to involve a serious underestimate of the aesthetic instincts.

Lastly, although Mr. Wells has keenly perceived the spiritual value of a temporary retreat from society, it may be doubted whether he does not purchase its advantages at too high a cost. The solitary voyages of his Samurai would assuredly lead to a high death-rate among them, and though one type of mind was thereby strengthened, another would be unhinged. The rule, in short, seems too rigid for the variety, and too cramping for the freedom, of man, both of which Mr. Wells is elsewhere anxious to appreciate.

But Mr. Wells, on the whole, shows a wisdom far superior to that of former Utopianists in not seeking to construct out of the imperfect materials[,] which alone the actual can furnish[,] a state order which shall be, and if possible remain eternally, perfect. He aims rather at laying down the principles of an order which shall be capable of progressively growing towards perfection; and so it may well be that in his ideal society men will be less reluctant than now to learn from experience.

Kipps (1905)

Mr. Wells's Kipps

F. G. Bettany

t is a pleasure to find Mr. H. G. Wells turning aside occasionally from his "anticipations," whether prognostic or fantastic, to that humane form of realistic fiction, of which his *Wheels of Chance* and now his story of *Kipps* are such charming examples. For even the most commonplace features of this our everyday world, even the most inarticulate and down-trodden types of mankind, gain dignity and interest as viewed from the angle of his kindly vision. Mr. Wells, indeed, has a positive genius for discovering what is pitiful and gracious in sordid and even vulgar lives. Give him a world to play with, and his imagination runs to ruthless lengths; set before him some despised slave of industr[y] and tyranny, and he will prove that his philosophy counts nothing which is human, common, or unclean.

Take his *Kipps*. What could be a less promising hero of fiction than an aitchless, unpresentable shop-assistant? As a laughing-stock of farce, of course, we know what Mr. [R. C.] Carton [pseudonym of Richard Claude Critchett] has made of his sort [of hero] in *Mr. Hopkinson* [published in book form in 1908]. Curiously enough, the scheme of Mr. Wells's tale rather closely resembles that of the play. Kipps, like "Hoppy," comes into a fortune, is lifted into a higher social environment, and becomes engaged to a girl of superior rank.

But the two authors' treatment of their subject is altogether different. Certainly the novelist spares us none of the vile clipped speech, the odious mispronunciations, the social banalities, the poverty and confusion of thought, which would necessarily characterise a youth a Kipps's sorry up-bringing. But Kipps is a modest, sensitive, and, as Mr. Wells styles him, 'simple' soul, who though pathetically incapable of self-expression, is only too anxious to learn—painfully anxious to learn the convenances—and suffers agonies from his mistakes, from the routine of society, from his "chaperon's" rebukes, and from the ridicule, real or imaginary, of his betters. As far, then, as Kipps is concerned, Mr. Wells's story, though told with unrelaxing comic zest and yet with infinite tenderness, is a very piteous affair.

But there is another side of the novel, for it is also a most ferocious satire on the Briton's instinctive snobbery and worship of social distinctions. All the greater irony, then, is there in the fact that Mr. Wells himself has to sacrifice at the shrine of his countrymen in concluding his tale, and can only secure happiness for his hero by reducing his income to small proportions and making him choose a wife of his own class, a servant-girl who is his "proper" mate.

In the Days of the Comet
(1906)

The Novels of Wells, Bennett and Galsworthy

William Bellamy

n the Days of the Comet is divided into two parts: in the first[,] the lower-class Leadford is driven to desperation when his beloved Nettie has a love affair with the upper-class Verrall. He sets out to murder them both. At the very climax of the murder-hunt, the apocalyptic comet effects a global "Change" in human psychology, and a new sense of "well-being" and rationality descends upon all the characters of the novel. A Wellsian *ménage à trois*, rationally managed, is the outcome. The new triumph of the rational ego is associated with a widespread communalization of society.

In the Days of the Comet is thus radically different from the science-fiction novels of the 1890s. It might be seen as a way of talking about the transition from pressurized *fin-de-siècle* time to the post-1900 experience of "redeemed" time. Its time-structure is interestingly similar, in fact, to [Shakespeare's] *The Winter's Tale* [1610] (which may also, of course, relate to the experience of living through the turning of an important century).

In this novel of 1906[,] a para-Freudian analytic therapy is set up as the cure for cultural crisis. Frank Wells has drawn attention to the existence of the characters in the book *Beyond Culture*: "This novel is . . . a touchpaper to set off a rocket of discussion, ideas and argument. The characters are not inhabitants of the Five Towns, as are the living characters of Arnold Bennett[;] they are "world" characters—strangely English. "[1] This [observation] usefully emphasizes H. G. Wells's sense of the incongruousness of the residual cultural characteristics of his post-cultural characters; but only in the second half of the book is Frank Wells's second sentence strictly applicable. In the first half of the book[,] the murderous intensity with which Leadford pursues his class-hatred is depicted strictly—though, indeed, crudely—in a specifically English milieu, with the social divisions which Wells saw characterizing that milieu depicted in some "cultural" detail. Seen in this light, Leadford is initially an *alter ego* of Kipps's. Only after the comet has effected its change does the "citizen of the World" character of Leadford emerge.

Wells's depiction of Leadford in a pre-apocalyptic state of cultural repression, driven into an irrational murderous rage by the exigencies of contemporary society, may bear resemblances to the state of Wells's mind before 1900 and indeed to the psychic condition of the late-Victorian period as a whole. Leadford, writing of an imminent fictional war with Germany from his post-apocalyptic vantage-point, defines himself in much the same way as the symptomatics of the 1890s unconsciously defined themselves:

> It was like one of a flood of disease germs that have invaded a body, that paper [the *New Paper*]. There I was, one corpuscle in the big amorphous body of the English community, one of forty-one million such corpuscles; and, for all my preoccupations, these potent headlines, this paper ferment, caught me and swung me about. And all over the country that day, millions read as I read, and came into line with me, under the same magnetic spell, came round—how did we say it?—Ah!—"to face the foe." [2]

Here Wells is defining *fin-de-siècle* crisis in terms of a disease of society, and relating the sense of apocalypse to a synthesis of war-feeling.

As in much of the pre-1900 writing of Wells, Bennett and Galsworthy, Leadford's translation here of the *fin-de-siècle* experience gives the impression that men felt themselves to be under the influence of magic, as if afflicted by a voodoo charm. The words, "magnetic spell," are suggestive of the very heavily "determined" state of Western thinking in the years just before calendar apocalypse. In this novel of 1906 (which perhaps reflects the apocalyptic "disconfirmation" provided to a degree by the outcome of the Boer War), news of the coming war results in the comet's being "driven into obscurity overleaf" (94), just as information about the coming freeing to be derived from passing through the year 1900 was hidden by the "disease germs" of *fin de sièclism*.

Again, the state of Leadford after the comet has passed seems exactly to match Wells's consciousness after 1900; the transition is made in Wells's fiction from a preoccupation with isolated individuals in desperate states to a speculative concern for the quality of individual life within society as a whole. As soon as Leadford wakes up from the short sleep induced by the comet, he meets Melmount, one of the fifteen men who are supposed to have been controlling the Empire and thus have been responsible for the German war. Leadford is thus, by coincidence, introduced to the first sane (i.e. Wellsian) meeting between the statesmen: "And what a strange unprecedented thing it was that cabinet council at which I was present, the council that was held two days later in Melmount's bungalow, and which convened the conference to frame the constitution of the World State" (188). Nothing could be more naïvely the projection of a writer's own personal wishes than this, and the lack of artistic tact with which Wells frames this section is analogous to (though not simultaneous with) the general movement in Wells's own development from artist to therapist impatient of art.

It would be easy to accuse the second section of the novel of being mere discursive polemic, even less patiently "realized" than the first half. But if there is niaïveté in Wells's account of the changes wrought by the comet (and indeed of the initial "spell" upon Leadford, the naïve . . . apocalypse of the 1890s and a sense of a beginning in the 1900s *were* absurdly, childishly, structured out of the gullibility of men projecting, as [Frank] Kermode would say,[3] their existential anxieties upon a cultural ending. Thus, although Wells's novel is objective enough to depict the turning into a new era with some justice, it partakes of some of the simple-mindedness of the immediately post-1900 period. It [the novel] positively takes simple-mindedness to be a sign of health. . . .

The primary strength of the work as [a] model of centurial apocalypse is its principal weakness as a conventional novel. It has no simple sequential structure. The first half has close affinities with the ordinary suspense novel of the Victorian world, but just at the climax of the action, when the reader expects Leadford to murder Nettie and Verrall, the green mist falls. The speeded-up time of the murder-hunt makes the strongest possible contrast with the new order of time which follows the change. . . .

The transition from a hysterically rapid process of uncontrolled violence to the redeemed springtime of a pastoral world is also the pattern of *The Winter's Tale*, whose structure is similarly split and "flawed." In each work an apocalyptic pastoralization occurs which provides the formal opportunity for measured discourse. In the second half of *In the Days of the Comet* a form of therapeutic society is constructed out of the ruins of the old order. This is typically Wellsian, of course, but in this particular novel[,] the discursive element is presented in satisfying formal contrast to the strict sequentiality of the first section of the narrative.

In the Days of the Comet is, then, an interesting attempt to render the transition to . . . a Rieffian universe.[4] The breakdown in linear, sequential narrative, and the breakthrough into a non-sequential narrative universe, reflects a general movement towards analytic activism. Wells uses an image strikingly similar to the "nihilistic" vision of the end of *Tono-Bungay*:

> We sat silently for a time before our vivisected passions.
> "Gods!" I cried, "and there was our poor little top-hamper of intelligence on all these waves of instinct and wordless desire, these foaming things of touch and sight and feeling, like—like a coop of hens washed overboard and clucking amidst the seas."
> Verrall laughed approval of the image I had struck out.
> "A week ago," he said, trying it further, "we were clinging to our chicken coops and going with the heave and pour. That was true enough a week ago. But today—?"
> "Today," I said, " the wind has fallen. The world storm is over. And each chicken coop has changed by a miracle to a vehicle that makes head against the sea." (211)

This concept of post-cultural man who escapes a purposeless clucking through cognitive control of himself and his environment is akin to [Philip] Rieff's idea of a Freudian analytic therapy-for-therapy's sake, in which the aim is to "keep going."

In his para-Freudian assertion of the power of the ego and a concomitant passing beyond culture[,] Wells deliberately undermines the "cultural" content of his writing by using an image which is both banal and absurd. There is a built-in safeguard against the critic who might read such a passage and claim it to comprise a "myth of centurial apocalypse," say. By writing in this way[,] Wells sets out to reverse the appeal being made to the reader as he reads the first part of the book. At first, such is the physiology of reading, the reader is bodily following Leadford on his murder-hunt; then Wells devalues all the emotional involvement of the reader by offering an absurd fiction of chickens and chicken coops. The reader is forced into an analytic mode in the very act of processing his own "literary" reactions, his fictional disappointments.

The reader's vertigo is not least among the elements which come under cure when Wells deliberately destroys the cultural "integrity" of the novel, leaves the initial action unfinished, and proceeds to analyse the sexual relations between the characters with a patience which is unwittingly Freudian. Cultural ordering, which to Wells involves conforming to an evolved state of disinheritance and existing in perpetual crisis, is replaced by therapeutic community, involvement in the ongoing activist creation of a psychomorphous universe.

NOTES

1. Frank Wells, *Beyond Culture* (London, 1954), p. 15.
2. H. G. Wells, *In the Days of the Comet* (London, 1906), p. 94.
3. Frank Kermode, *The Sense of an Ending* (New York, 1967).
4. Philip Rieff, *The Triumph of the Therapeutic* (London, 1966).

Tono-Bungay (1908)

Encounters with the "White Sphinx": The Re-Vision of Poe in Wells's Early Fiction

Catherine Rainwater

n "Popularising Science" (1894), H. G. Wells cites Edgar Allan Poe as one of his literary precursors: "the fundamental principles of construction that underlie such stories as Poe's 'Murders in the Rue Morgue,' or Conan Doyle's 'Sherlock Holmes' series," he says, "are precisely those that should guide a scientific writer."[1] Moreover, according to Wells, Poe's "fundamental principles of construction" underlie several of his own science-fiction works.[2] Throughout Wells's lengthy career, his fiction develops a fascinating intertextual relationship to Poe's, as well as to a number of works by other authors in an ever-widening, Poe-inscribed textual network that, to date, has received little critical attention.[3]

Many of Wells's works contain both overt and indirect intertextual references to Poe's fiction—up through the turn of the century, especially to "Ms. Found in a Bottle" (1833), "Ligeia" (1838), "The Fall of the House of Usher" (1839), "A Descent into the Maelstrom" (1841), and *The Narrative of Arthur Gordon Pym* (1838). Among Wells's early works that feature a Poe-inscribed intertext are his short story, "The Red Room" (1896), three of his scientific romances—*The Time Machine* (1895), *The Island of Dr. Moreau* (1896), and *The First Men in the Moon* (1901)—and his 1908 social novel, *Tono-Bungay.*

These early works establish three basic intertextual sites that Wells seems self-consciously to contemplate and develop more complexly over the years. At these sites, a reader observes (1) Poe-esque tropes for psychological terrain in the form of symbolic settings and spatial metaphors; (2) spatially disoriented or otherwise unreliable narrators, such as those inhabiting Poe's fiction, whose discourse undermines conventional notions of objective reality and individual identity; and (3) metafictional "scenes of writing," similar and often directly allusive to those in Poe's texts, emphasizing the dual creative-destructive capacities of language. Iconizing these intertextual phenomena, the "white sphinx" in *The Time Machine* recalls the "white god" at the end of Poe's *Pym*; like the "white god," it signifies much about mind and its relation to the external world, and about representational practices that attempt to span the gap between these interior and exterior realms.

In several works appearing between 1895 and 1901, Wells devises Poe-esque settings that obscure traditional boundaries between the phenomenal world and human imagination. Like Poe's texts, Wells's challenge Enlightenment notions of objectivity and underscore the constitutive role of mind in making and sustaining what is called reality. Through an elaborate intertextual matrix of tropes—dreams, drugs, art, intense emotions and encounters with strange beings in outlandish environments—Wells's texts incorporate Poe's, together with the latter's warning about the permanent effects of extraordinary states of mind upon self and semiosis.

Wells's "The Red Room" might in some ways be easily mistaken for a story written by Poe himself. The narrator of the story spends the night in a haunted room, a Poe-esque spatial metaphor for a terror-stricken human mind. Initially skeptical about haunted rooms and somewhat boastful of his own rationality, he follows the confusing directions of Lorraine Castle's "grotesque custodians"—down a shadowy hallway, up a spiral staircase, and through a "long, draughty subterranean passage" lit only by a few flickering candles. Like the narrator of "The Fall of the House of Usher," he admits being "affected" by the environment as he proceeds through this Gothic labyrinth of an edifice, in which a "subterranean passage" may, despite logic, exist at the top of a stairway that begins, presumably, on the ground floor of the castle. The narrator tries hard to maintain a "matter-of-fact" attitude, despite intimations of a sinister, animate quality in the furniture and statuary of the castle. During the night, he burns seventeen candles against his fear of the dark, but hysteria grows as a shadowy presence seems bent on extinguishing them. Perhaps a victim only of his own state of mind, the narrator huddles in a remote and claustrophobic chamber where terror "seal[s his] vision" and "crush[es] the last vestiges of reason from [his] brain."[4] Trying to escape the room, he stumbles over a piece of furniture, has a "horrible sensation of falling," and lies unconscious until dawn. Later, he declares the room haunted, not by a ghost but by "the worst of all things that haunt poor mortal man . . . *Fear!* " (*Works* 10: 335).

Wells could not have devised a more Poe-like haunting nor a more Poe-esque setting. "FEAR" debilitates Roderick Usher and several other Poe characters who emerge, after all, primarily the victims of their own imaginations. Their emotions preside over rational judgment, and their subsequent actions often cause permanent changes in their external worlds. Along with Usher, consider as well Poe's narrator in "The Tell-Tale Heart" (1843). Paranoid delusions about an old man's supposed "evil eye" dominate his thoughts until he finally commits murder; fear and anxiety, in part, drive him to reveal himself to the police. A similar psychological state develops in the narrator of Wells's "The Red Room" and accounts for his panic, self-inflicted head wound, and near self-destruction.

Like Poe, Wells in "The Red Room" contrives a psychological horror story in which a narrator's external environment seems to cause his mental breakdown, but instead this environment perhaps merely conforms to his increasingly deranged perceptions. Furthermore, echoing Poe's narrators in works such as "The Fall of the House of Usher," "A Descent into the Maelstrom," and "The Tell-Tale Heart," the narrator of "The Red Room" insists he is lucid even as he outlines bizarre, indescribable experiences and admits that language fails him. Like so many of Poe's narrators, Wells's narrator cannot gauge the extent of his own mental deterioration within an environment "too stimulating for the imagination" and only partially illuminated by firelight and candlelight. He proclaims his objectivity while stating, contradictorily, that he "fancies" he hears noises. "I was in a state of considerable nervous tension," he concedes, "although to my reason there was no adequate cause for the condition. My mind, however, was perfectly clear" (*Works* 10: 329-30).

This passage reveals a well-documented Poe-esque conception of the human psyche.[5] In "The Cask of Amontillado" (1846), for example, Fortunato and Montresor represent rational and nonrational aspects of mind at war with one another; so do the two Wilsons in "William Wilson" (1839), and Roderick and the narrator in "The Fall of the House of Usher." "The Red Room" strongly implies Wells's primary indebtedness in his early works to Poe for his ideas about human psychology (ideas that Wells's knowledge of Freud reinforces after 1914).

Like the speaker in "The Red Room," the narrator of Wells's *The Time Machine*, remains confident of his objectivity in the face of fantastic events. The wary reader, however, quickly suspects his naiveté. Indeed, neither the narrator nor the Time Traveller, whose story the narrator relates, inspires reader confidence in his objectivity. Though the Traveller warns his audience that they will hear only his own interpretations of incomprehensible experiences in the eighty-third century, the narrator makes strong claims about the truth of his own narrative. He distrusts the Time Traveller owing to some deceptive quality perceived beneath the latter's "lucid frankness," yet after the fashion of Poe's deluded, self-proclaimed paragons of rationality, this same narrator flatly denies that he, himself, could be tricked or deceived.

The narrator hears the Traveller's story and sees a miniature model of the time machine in a firelit parlor after dinner when, he admits, "thought runs gracefully free of the trammels of precision."[6] Agreeing that people are more credulous by night than by day, he nevertheless insists—in Poe-esque self-contradictory language[7]—"It appears incredible to me that any kind of trick . . . could have been played upon us under these conditions" (*TM* 19). Belying the objective certainty implied in the narrator's emphatic statement are the subjectivity and hesitancy he reveals through the words "appeared . . . to me." (It is interesting that this same phrase occurs in Poe's "Usher" under nearly the same narrational circumstances. After he is already "infected" with Roderick's hysteria, Poe's narrator announces that "it appeared" to him that strange noises, such as those described in the "Ethelred" tale, came from some remote region of the house.) In this passage from *The Time Machine,* Wells's narrator unwittingly reiterates what the Time Traveller openly admits, that a reporter is limited to descriptions of mere appearances. Furthermore, the "conditions" the narrator finds conducive to objectivity are, in fact, quite the opposite; when the

Traveller shows his guest the miniature time machine and later the full-scale apparatus, the demonstration takes place by candlelight and lamplight, to which the narrator refers contradictorily as "brilliant" and "shadowy."

Within the framework of the narrator's less-than-reliable report lies the Time Traveller's presumably verbatim account of his adventures among the Eloi, a dubious account by the Traveller's own admission. Besides acknowledging that he imposes nineteenth-century interpretations upon the phenomena he observes in the distant future, the Traveller describes his extreme psychological disorientation prior to arriving among the Eloi. Moving through time, he has a "nightmare sensation of falling . . . an eddying murmur filled my ears, and a strange, dumb confusedness descended on my mind" (*TM* 29-30). All of these "peculiar sensations . . . merged at last into a kind of hysterical exhilaration, characterized by "a certain curiosity" and "a certain dread," which "at last . . . took complete possession of me" (*TM* 31). His account, ostensibly an effort at objective reporting, actually serves further to obscure the "truth."

Wells's Time Traveller resembles many of Poe's narrators who are adversely affected psychologically even before they begin to undergo the series of events comprising the substance of their narratives. In fact, the Time Traveller's "peculiar sensations" are quite similar to those reported by the old man in Poe's "A Descent into the Maelstrom" and by the narrator of "Ms. Found in a Bottle," both of whom fall through a vortex of ocean, feel terror, hysteria, paralysis, dread, and finally a calm curiosity enabling them to make a self-proclaimed "objective" account of their surroundings and feelings. Their objectivity, however, becomes increasingly dubious as the details of their narratives unfold. For Poe and for Wells, a powerful interior force may tyrannize over exterior forms and appearances, just as the subterranean dwellers, the Morlocks, in *The Time Machine* prevail over the docile surface inhabitants, the Eloi.

In *The Time Machine*, Wells's Poe-inspired image of the white sphinx illustrates how appearances may intimate but never disclose the "unseen" forces informing them. The white sphinx, like the white figure at the conclusion of Poe's *Pym*, challenges the observer to discover its meaning, its hidden interior. For the Traveller, the sphinx is a key to the mysteries of the strange world into which he has ventured. A look inside, he hopes, might also help him find his lost time machine. Like the image Pym confronts, however, the white sphinx forces the Traveller to explore his own interior, to discover the extent to which the human mind projects meanings onto the exterior world. Pym's narrative discloses no ultimate knowledge derived from contemplation of a white god; instead, the narrative traces the processes of mind in search of ultimate knowledge that presumably exists independently of mind.[8] Likewise, the hermetically sealed white sphinx finally discloses nothing; instead, it forces the Traveller to suspect that exterior phenomena are without meaning beyond that imposed by mind. Thus the Traveller warns his dinner guests that his narrative consists mainly of his own interpretations of experience. But the naive narrator, insisting upon his own ability to report "objective" truth, fails to hear this message even as he reports it.

Like the "editors" of *Pym*, this narrator argues for the "veracity" of a report that challenges all traditional notions of narrative veracity. Moreover, the blank "whiteness" of Poe's god and Wells's sphinx suggests the whiteness of the uninscribed page onto which narrative is recorded. Both icons mark the "scene of writing," to which both writers repeatedly return throughout their works, as well shall presently see.

The same intertextual features occur in *The Island of Dr. Moreau* and in *The First Men in the Moon*. Prendick in *Moreau* is another narrator who filters his story through a Poe-esque subjective haze obscuring the boundaries between mind and phenomena. Feverish and delirious from alcohol for many months, he calls himself in the end "an outcast from civilization"; his perceptions of himself, humanity and the world are irrevocably altered.

Prendick's experiences on Moreau's island recall those of Pym on Tsalal. Just as Pym attempts to identify forms of life on Tsalal,[9] including the peculiar white, scarlet-clawed animal at which the natives call out, "Tekeli-li," Prendick tries to assign names and meanings to the strange but, he assumes, natural sights and sounds he witnesses. However, on Moreau's island, which is soporifically warm and suspends Prendick in a trance-like state, the expected "laws of nature" do not apply, for they have been humanly altered by Moreau. Furthermore, Moreau's attempts to keep his vivisectionist activities secret from Prendick help confuse Prendick's perceptions of the events going on about him. His memories of inexplicable sights and sounds intermingle with the contents of his dreams, and in turn the island environment becomes "altered to [his] imagination" (*Works* 2: 49).

Prendick's subsequent account of the ordeal acknowledges language as the primary tool for wresting meaning out of a chaos of memories. Before he can logically organize and interpret his experiences for the reader, he faces the difficult task of finding serviceable language to describe them. Like the narrator of *The Time Machine*, Prendick struggles with language because he believes in objective "truth." Repeatedly, Prendick's experiences teach him what the Time Traveller learns from the white sphinx—the meanings we attribute to exterior phenomena actually arise within us; narrative is never the objective report of "truth" but is instead the subjective record of the human mind's interactions with the "white sphinx" of outward form.

As in *Moreau*, Wells in *First Men* contrives a narrator who suffers increasing difficulties in the use of language and, owing to the strange character of his actual experiences, in distinguishing between "real" and dreamed events. Prior to landing on the moon with Cavor, his visionary scientist companion, Bedford undergoes a series of bizarre experiences sufficiently dream-like to be confused with actual dreams he has later.

Anticipating the voyage to the moon, Bedford dreams that he "fell and fell and fell for evermore into the abyss of the sky" (*Works* 6: 42). When he finally leaves the earth, he remarks several times that the experience is "like the beginning of a dream" (*Works* 6: 49); later he reports that enroute to the moon both he and Cavor were "in a sort of quiescence that was neither waking nor slumber" as they "fell through a space of time that had neither night nor day in it, silently, softly and swiftly down towards the moon" (*Works* 6: 56). Already disoriented when they step onto the moon's surface, Bedford and Cavor complicate their conditions by drinking the latter's "sickly tasting" concoction to prevent moonsickness and by eating "fleshy red" moon flora which renders them totally incoherent. Later, very aware of his previous intoxication, Bedford wonders if some of his experiences were dreamt owing to the fungus they had eaten. Like Prendick, Bedford is profoundly different when he returns home. He develops an irrational grudge against Cavor, whom he leaves stranded on the moon among the Selenites and who telegraphs fragmentary messages to earth.

Cavor's messages emanate not from the surface of the moon, but from its interior, a subterranean labyrinth where the controlling lunar beings reside. (Like the Morlocks in *The Time Machine*, the Selenites dwell beneath the surface of their world and feed on surface life.) Cavor's telegraphed messages describe the interior of the moon as a type of supernal region reached by traveling in a diminishing spiral direction through huge lunar caverns, the environment growing "less and less material" all the time. Recalling Poe's Tsalal in *Pym*, this lunar supernal region is a labyrinth of chasms illuminated by phosphorescent rocks and water. At the lowest point in the Grand Lunar chamber lies "a lake of heatless fire, the waters of the Central Sea, glowing and eddying in strange perturbation, 'like luminous blue milk that is about to boil'" (*Works* 6: 220). In this innermost cavern resides the Grand Lunar, a god-like being which Wells develops emblematically to coalesce cosmos (exterior) and mind (interior) in the same fashion as Poe coalesces the mind of Roderick with the House of Usher. The chamber is a cavernous rocky enclosure suggestive of a skull and housing the Grand Lunar whose form is that of a luminous disembodied brain. However, owing to the vastness of the cavern and to its indistinct, dimly lit boundaries (a chamber calling to mind a similar one in Poe's "Usher," where the narrator struggles to see the "remoter" parts of the "large and lofty" room),[10] the Grand Lunar also reminds Cavor of a star floating in a "blaze of incandescent blue" (*Works* 6: 220).

Such presumably are the "facts" about the moon. Before stumbling into a well-prepared Poe-esque trap of textual veracity, however, a reader should pause to observe the vague origins of ostensibly factual data. Wells's narrative is a Poe-esque baroque, a highly detailed body of information arising out of and encircling an indistinct, unfathomable center composed of a series of complex interiors. The narrator of the opening chapters of *First Men* is a man whose mind has been affected first by an "implosion," then by intoxicating drink, and overall by the exotic lunar atmosphere. Following his return to earth, Bedford's narrative, now completely unreliable owing to the grudge he bears Cavor, becomes an amalgam of his own and his former companion's distorted points of view. Because Bedford believes Cavor maligns him in the telegraphed communications from the moon, Bedford edits Cavor's messages to his own advantage. All narrative information emanates first from the mind of Bedford, then from the mind of Cavor, and finally from the interior of the moon, a region emblematically suggesting a vast, cosmic mind. Thus, as in a Poe text, any careful reader attempting to distinguish between reliable and unreliable narrative data must suddenly realize that narrative reflects no "truth" at all, but the processes of the mind confronting phenomena and pursuing certainty which is not forthcoming.[11]

Ultimately the reader shares the dilemma of Bedford when, in a passage evoking an episode in Poe's *Pym*, he receives from Cavor a partially intelligible message scribbled in blood. Just as Bedford must decipher this fragmentary note, the reader must deal with the many disjunctions occurring within Bedford's text which, conflated with Cavor's telegraphed communications, finally degenerates into silence as the Selenites deliberately scramble the already feeble signals; containing their forever inaccessible "secret," these signals drift out into the "impenetrably dark" expanse of the universe.

Although *The Time Machine*, *Moreau* and other works deal tangentially with such questions of language and text, *First Men* represents Wells's earliest scientific romance to evince sustained, complex concern with these matters. (A social novel, *Love and Mr. Lewisham*, published only a year later in 1900, also exhibits a pervasive interest in language.) Cavor's language floating through the dark silence of space possesses a "secret" which it will never render up. This "secret" at the heart of language gradually becomes the focus of Wells's preoccupation with the "unseen." Perhaps because of this interest in language, from about 1900 on Wells's works rely less and less upon conventionally Gothic or fantastic accouterments to embody "the unseen." Instead they begin to explore language itself as the most profound revealer and concealer of the mysteries of existence. In *Tono-Bungay*, when Wells's narrator resigns himself at last to ultimate inarticulateness after a sustained effort to state "something" (a word he and other characters repeat in frustration) which remains ineffable, he expresses Wells's own most consistently maintained attitude toward language as a powerful force forever seeking a forever-elusive mystery "at the heart of life." Such a notion of language comprises a fundamental affinity between Wells and his predecessor Poe.

After 1900, Wells's texts begin to incorporate many of Poe's notions about language and logos-power that are stated in various ways throughout Poe's works. Poe's narrators become increasingly inarticulate, for example, as they enter into nonordinary modes of consciousness. In such works as "The Conversation of Eiros and Charmion" (1839), "The Colloquy of Monos and Una" (1841), and "The Power of Words" (1845), we learn that beyond the earthly realm human language as we know it actually ceases to exist. Much of the time, Poe considers language inadequate to express ethereal, exalted feelings and impressions. In the *Marginalia*, he also expresses his fears about the dangerous illusions created by "mere words." However, alternating with these periods of cynicism about language are Poe's highly idealistic phases when he entertains more optimistic notions.

Eureka (1848) and the previously mentioned cosmic dialogues contain some of Poe's most definitive remarks on language, revealing much about his ambivalent attitude toward the potentiality of language. In *Eureka* Poe describes the human word not as the "expression of an idea, but of an effort at one" (*Works* 16: 200). That is, the human mind intuitively senses much beyond what it can fully comprehend and articulate. For example, Poe explains that a word such as "infinity" does not describe any quality of the universe so much as it represents a collective human effort to name the ineffable. As the expression of an effort at an idea, words for Poe are certainly "vague things" (*Works* 4:

206). Despite this vagueness, however, language evinces a formidable "physical power." In "The Power of Words," for instance, Agathos (a celestial being whose creative powers exceed but parallel those of humans) "speaks" a star into existence much as God in the beginning spoke the universe into existence.[12] Furthermore, Poe's "Drake-Halleck" review (1836) notes the power of poetry to awaken the "poetic faculty" in others—to awaken the sentiment which inspires the highest of human aspirations. Finally, in "The Philosophy of Composition" (1846) Poe proclaims the power of language to achieve various "effects" which provide glimpses of supernal "Beauty." Thus, according to Poe, although language may be inadequate to express much of what lies within the ken of human awareness, it nevertheless possesses great inherent power to alter the conditions of human existence.

From Poe's viewpoint, language at its best can favorably affect existence. The skeptical side of Poe's nature usually prevailed, though, and in his works we see the failure of human beings to achieve supernal states of being. Indeed, his characters most often create their own nightmarish situations. In these situations, the dissolution of familiar notions about self and reality characteristically precedes the diminishment of linguistic ability.

Thus for Poe, and for Wells prior to *Lewisham* and *Tono-Bungay*, the failure of language is usually a result, not a cause, of the breakdown of some other order.[13] Still, as Wells begins to place primary emphasis upon language, he suggests that its relative force or failure may determine the difference between satisfactory order and catastrophic disorder in the universe. Subsequent works entertain such a notion until it emerges fully articulated in *Men Like Gods* (1923), where the success of utopian aspirations depends largely upon the human use of language as an instrument in the construction of a desirable reality. This shift away from a focus upon language as a reflector or creator of illusions to a focus upon language as a maker of utopias marks the end of a phase in Wells's career when his Darwin-influenced notions of human evolution coexist most sympathetically with Poe's notion of devolution.[14] Although Poe sometimes affirms (most often only wishes he could affirm) the constructive potential of logos-power, he characteristically reverts to an attitude of despair over the inadequacy and deceptiveness of words.[15] In contrast, Wells believes, or tries to believe, more and more in the power of words to effect utopia, even though he usually despairs of the human ability to realize such linguistic potential.

That Wells begins to lose interest in supernormal embodiments of the "unseen" and to relocate the "unseen" within language as the ineffable "secret" (*FMM*) or the "something" (*TB*) which language does not surrender is hardly surprising when one realizes that an all-consuming interest in universal order underlies both concerns.[16] Literature of the supernatural almost inevitably posits fundamental questions of order: "it begins by assuming that life is rational and morally ordered, then begins to worry about that assumption when something inexplicably threatening creeps in . . . With doubt comes a gradual dismemberment of the narrator's comfortably structured world."[17] Although Poe's and Wells's works usually depend more upon the *reader's* assumptions that "life is rational and morally ordered" than upon any such notion inherent in the fictions themselves,[18] both Poe's and Wells's interest in varieties of the gothic genre derives from their mutually profound concern with the questions of universal order that the genre traditionally evokes. Relocating such basic questions specifically within the context of language, Wells's works finally explore aesthetic issues which Poe's works only anticipate. *Tono-Bungay*, then, may be seen to represent a transitional phase in Wells's career when his interest in language presides over his interest in the fantastic, although he still maintains primarily a Poe-esque notion of the "deceptiveness" of words.

With matters of language as its central concern, *Tono-Bungay* exhibits a narrator whose life is shaped by his own essentially Poe-esque orientation within his environment; vacillating between heroic, supernal aspirations and cynical surrender to the mundane, he is obsessed with order and perversely fascinated with chaos. His narrative, an attempt to impose a tidy chronological structure upon a "series of impressions" and "inconsecutive observations," organizes itself "in no sort of neat scheme" around three Poe-esque "feminine persons" (*Works* 12: 8). In the end he emerges a Tamerlane figure, a martyr to the "ideal," somewhat disillusioned with language, existing simultaneously as a cosmopolitan with a paracultural world view, and as an exile belonging nowhere.

Mapping the "trajectory" of his life, George Ponderevo's narrative describes in Poe-esque terms a conventional nineteenth-century heroic rise-and-fall pattern.[19] Like several of Poe's narrators—for example, those in "William Wilson" and "Usher," and even the speaker in "Tamerlane" who remembers his "boyhood" as "a summer sun"—Ponderevo recalls a blissfully ordered, harmonious youth disrupted during adolescence when he falls in love and falls from grace as Bladesover House. An eighteenth-century anachronistic community socially and geographically sequestered from the tumultuous forces of nineteenth-century industrialism, Bladesover remains throughout George's life a paradigm for the security and orderliness he thinks the universe ought to manifest. Ironically, despite his fondness for order, George at fifteen commits an act of social insubordination resulting in his expulsion from Bladesover into Chatham, a cacophonous microcosm of the world at large, a "place that had the colours and even the smells of a well-packed dustbin" (*Works* 12: 56-57). Ponderevo's life subsequent to his exile consists alternately of "Bladesover" and "Chatham" phases—periods of idealistic "soaring" and of demoralizing falls back into the mundane—significantly punctuated toward the end by his attempt to resolve questions of order and disorder through acts of language.

The events of Ponderevo's life organize themselves not only around "three separate feminine persons" but also within three distinct categories of experience that these women symbolically represent. The first woman is Beatrice, George's first love whom he meets as a boy at Bladesover House. Wells apparently models her closely after Poe's Ligeia as the embodiment of supernal "Beauty":

> I'd never heard a woman before in all my life who could lay bare and develop and touch with imagination all that mass of fine emotion every woman, it may be, hides. She had read of love, she had thought of love, a thousand sweet lyrics had sounded through her brain and left fine fragments in her memory;

> she poured it out, all of it, shamelessly, skilfully, for me. I cannot give any
> sense of that talk, I cannot even tell how much of the delight of it was the
> magic of her voice, the glow of her near presence. (*Works* 12: 432)

As an embodiment of the ideal, Beatrice cannot be rendered earthly, and so
when George finally has a chance to marry her, both agree that their relationship
can never survive the obstacles of the mundane world. They part, leaving
George "alone like a man new fallen from fairyland" (*Works* 12: 433).

Idealized as she is, Beatrice cannot be dragged down onto the ordinary
planes of existence. She admonishes George when he pursues her, telling him
that her role for him has been a "magical" one and refusing to "go down to
become a dirty familiar thing with [him] amidst the grime" (*Works* 12: 511).
Echoing the "conqueror worm" poem Ligeia recites just before her death (which
prefaces Poe's narrator's fall into the mundane realm with Rowena), Beatrice
says to George: "You have had the best and all of me . . . Today my light is out"
(*Works* 12: 513-16; Wells's ellipsis). Like Ligeia, who functions for her lover as
a supernal muse and who cries, "Out—out are the lights—out all!" (*Works* 2:
257), Beatrice announces the extinguishing of her "light" for George, the end of
her role as the embodiment of otherworldly Beauty. Just before he loses sight of
her forever, he misunderstands the last word in her statement that her "light is
out." George wonders, "To this day I cannot determine whether she said or
whether I imagined she said [instead of Ligeia's "out all"] 'chloral'" (*Works* 12:
513-16). Indeed, Beatrice's effect on George (recalling Ligeia's effect on Poe's
narrator), specifically owing to her abilities with language, has been that of
chloral—a substance once used as a hypnotic and an anaesthetic.[20]

The phases of George's life most shaped by the "Beatrice" and "Bladesover"
principles are periods of idealism and prosperity—when he aspires to capture
"Life" in language, when he "soars" in gliders and balloons, and when marketing
Tono-Bungay, a tonic substance much like chloral in that its effects are more
psychological than physical, he rises to the top of the financial world.
Unfortunately, each of George's "soaring" phases precedes a "sinking" phase, a
pattern in his life most clearly illustrated emblematically when his balloon, the
Lord Roberts ß, sinks into the ocean.

The second woman in George's life is Marion, diametrically opposed to
Beatrice, like Rowena to Ligeia, in representing everything quotidian. In
contrast to Beatrice who speaks of love with real "imagination," Marion is
inarticulate and draws her notions of love from banal popular novels. Her ideas
and values are utterly conventional, and contrary to Beatrice, who cannot be
dragged down into the mundane world, Marion, for all George's tugging, cannot
be dragged out of it. The failure of their marriage results largely from Marion's
inability to act as a supernal muse, to inspire George's imagination. During the
"Marion" phases of his life, George conforms socially at the expense of his own
creativity and builds destroyers instead of airplanes and balloons.

The third "feminine person" important in George's life is his Aunt Susan, of
all three women the one whose character most clearly exhibits the sort of
ambiguities with which he is fascinated. Her personality combines Beatrice's
refined sensibility with Marion's practical ability to survive. Playing the dual
role of muse and mother to George's child-like uncle and Tono-Bungay

impressario, Edward Ponderevo, she can admit that "Life's a rum Go, George!" and yet she has been able enthusiastically to "make what [she] could of it" for herself and her husband (*Works* 12: 347). Enigmatic as life itself, Susan's personality becomes recognizable to George in his maturity as suggestive of "something" he senses at "the heart of life" that is both beautiful and elusive.

Just this "something"—"a quality, an element, one may find now in colours, now in forms, now in sounds, now in thoughts" (*Works* 12: 529)—is what George wishes to articulate through narrative. He hopes that proper arrangement of "inconsecutive observations" and close scrutiny of "impressions" may apprise him of life's intimated "secret"; but in his efforts "to render . . . nothing more nor less than Life," he finds language difficult and "the restraints and rules of the art . . . impossible" (*Works* 12: 8). In the final paragraphs of his narrative, which has been an attempt to discover some fundamental principle of order, he grudgingly capitulates to chaos and inarticulateness:

> We tear into the great spaces of the future and the turbines fall to talking in unfamiliar tongues. Out to the open we go, to windy freedom and trackless ways. Light after light goes down . . . This is the note I have tried to emphasize . . . a note of crumbling and confusion, of change and seemingly aimless swelling, of a bubbling up and medley of futile loves and sorrows. (*Works* 12: 528)

Finally unwilling to endorse such a sad "note," George goes on to assert that "through the confusion sounds another note. Through the confusion something drives, something that is at once human achievement and the most inhuman of all existing things. Something comes out of it . . . How can I express the values of a thing at once so essential and so immaterial . . . It is something that calls upon such men as I with an irresistible appeal" (*Works* 12: 528-29). George's repetition of the word "something," even as he insists that all is not finally chaos, reveals the extent to which he finds his own powers with language inadequate to penetrate to "the heart of life."

In George's linguistic pursuit of "something" he discovers in language a paradoxically creative and destructive power much like that of "quap," an element he mines on Mordet Island during one of his "sinking" phases. A visionary financial venture, George's "quap" expedition is a "fairy tale" come true, then transformed into a horror story. Lying about in "heaps," the energy-rich substance constitutes a potential fortune for anyone who can successfully collect it. Unfortunately, "quap" is also a "cancerous," destructive element which disintegrates the hold of his ship, the *Maud Mary*. When late in the novel George refers to his own narrative as a "heap," he deliberately associates the properties of "quap" and those of language, which evinces analogous creative-destructive potential. Language makes the Ponderevo fortune, for the success of Tono-Bungay derives less from its medicinal properties than from an intensely powerful verbal marketing campaign: "£150,000—think of it—for the goodwill in a string of lies and a trade in bottles of mitigated water!" (*Works* 12: 206). Language also effects the decline of the Ponderevo empire when Edward becomes careless about the kind of "lies" he tells, crossing the fine line between lies of "goodwill" and those of forgery: "I done something," he tells George in desperation. "Writin' things down—I done something" (*Works* 12: 475-76).

Like "quap," language contains within itself both creative and destructive energy,[21] specifically the power to create and destroy such illusions as Poe remarks in the *Marginalia*. Tono-Bungay, essentially created by language, perishes through language. Like "chloral," which induces euphoria, and like "quap," which also disorders the mind, language creates illusions and disintegrates those same illusions. One of George's major insights in his narrative suggests that all form eventually degenerates into formlessness.[22] Certainly he includes the forms constructed out of words, for his paragraphs themselves quite often trail off in a series of elliptical dots. He communicates the same notion in the closing scene of *Tono-Bungay* as he discusses the panoramic view of England from his place aboard a ship headed out on the Thames toward the sea:

> England and the Kingdom Britain and the Empire, the old prides and the old devotions, glide abeam, astern, sink down upon the horizon, pass—pass. The river passes—London passes, England passes . . . . [Wells's ellipsis] I fell into thought that was nearly formless, into doubts and dreams that have no words . . . I have come to see myself from the outside, my country from the outside—without illusions. We make and pass . . . We are all things that make and pass, striving upon a hidden mission, out to open sea. (*Works* 12: 530)

All structures, whether social or linguistic, "pass" because at their inception they contain the germ of dissolution. Like Bladesover, which to young George "seem[s] to be in the divine order," all systems, even as they appear most stable, are "already sapped . . . The [are] forces at work that . . . carry all . . . elaborate . . . system[s] . . . to Limbo" (*Works* 12: 11). (Such cosmological notions recall Poe's theory of the expanding and collapsing universe that is expounded in *Eureka*.)

For the alert reader, however, a subdued, highly qualified but nevertheless affirmative attitude underlies Wells's ostensibly pessimistic acquiescence to formlessness. To "make and pass" is to exercise some measure of power, and a "hidden mission" implies purpose and design, albeit with much blind groping. (Later, in *The Undying Fire* and in *The Outline of History* [1920], Wells defines human progress in terms of a "Will feeling about.") George's "making," his act of language, although in his estimation it fails to disclose enough, serves him through its power to *dis-illusion*. Through language George propels himself "to the open . . . to [the] windy freedom and trackless ways" of pure possibility. Although like Tamerlane he is spiritually and physically an exile, he draws nearer the position of Israfel, Poe's heavenly bard free of mundane constraints.

NOTES

1. *Nature* 50 (26 July 1894): 301.

2. David Y. Hughes and Robert M. Philmus, "A Selective Bibliography (With Abstracts) of H. G. Wells's Science Journalism, 1887-1901," in *H. G. Wells and Modern*

Science Fiction, eds. Darko Suvin and Robert M. Philmus (Lewisburg: Bucknell University Press, 1977), p. 194. See also Philmus' comments on the connection between Poe and Wells in "H. G. Wells as Literary Critic for the Saturday Review," *Science-Fiction Studies* 4 (1977):166-93.

3. Critics remarking Wells's debt to Poe include David Ketterer in *New Worlds for Old* (Garden City: Doubleday, 1974), p. 67; Roger Bowen in "Science, Myth, and Fiction in H. G. Wells's *The Island of Dr. Moreau*," *Studies in the Novel* 8 (1976):318-35; and William J. Scheick in *The Splintering Frame: The Later Fiction of H. G. Wells* (Victoria, B. C.: University of Victoria English Literary Studies, 1984), pp. 71-80.

4. H. G. Wells, *The Works of H. G. Wells* (New York: Charles Scribner's Sons, 1924), 10: 333. Henceforth, all references to Wells's works, unless otherwise specified, will be to the Atlantic Edition, cited parenthetically in the text as *Works* with volume and page number [Vols. 1-4, 1924; 5-14, 1925].

5. On this subject, see Darrel Abel, "A Key to the House of Usher," *University of Toronto Quarterly* 18 (1949):176-85; James Gargano, "The Question of Poe's Narrators," *College English* 25 (1963):177-81; and G. R. Thompson, "The Face in the Pool," *Poe Studies* 5 (1972):16-21.

6. H. G. Wells, *The Time Machine/The War of the Worlds*, ed. Frank D. McConnell (New York: Oxford University Press, 1977), p. 13. Henceforth, all references to *The Time Machine* will be to the Critical Edition, cited in the text parenthetically as *TM* with page numbers.

7. Studies of the ways in which Poe cultivates such ambiguities and complex verbal effects include John Carlos Rowe's "Writing and Truth in Poe's *The Narrative of Arthur Gordon Pym*," *Glyph* 2 (1977):102-21; Alan C. Golding's "Reductive and Expansive Language: Semantic Strategies in *Eureka*," *Poe Studies* 11 (1978):1-5; and Ray Mazurek's "Art, Ambiguity, and the Artist in Poe's 'The Man of the Crowd,'" *Poe Studies* 12 (1979):25-28.

8. On Poe's epistemological concerns in *Pym*, see Rowe (note 7 above), Daniel A. Wells, "Engraved Within the Hills: Further Perspectives on the Ending of *Pym*," *Poe Studies* 10 (1977):13-15; and Patrick Quinn, *The French Face of Edgar Poe* (Carbondale: Southern Illinois University Press, 1957), pp. 169-215.

9. For discussions of Poe's management of deceptive appearances in *Pym*, see Joseph J. Moldenhauer, "Imagination and Perversity in *The Narrative of Arthur Gordon Pym*," *Texas Studies in Literature and Language* 13 (1971):267-80; and Rowe (see note 7 above).

10. Edgar Allan Poe, *The Complete Works of Edgar Allan Poe*, ed. James A. Harrison (New York: Fred de Fau, 1902), 3:277-78. Henceforth all references to the prose works (the Virginia Edition) will be cited parenthetically in the texts as *Works* with volume and page numbers.

11. Robert L. Caserio shows how Poe's works equate the formulation of reality with the narrative process in *Plot, Story and the Novel: From Dickens and Poe to the Modern Period* (Princeton: Princeton University Press, 1979).

12. See Arthur H. Quinn's discussion of Poe's cosmic dialogues in *Edgar Allan Poe: A Critical Biography* (New York: Cooper Square Publishers, 1969).

13. Although the breakdown of narrative language is indeed a Gothic convention, Poe is innovative in his employment of this convention. Traditional Gothic horror stories show an inverse relationship between heightened emotion and precise use of language. Poe's works, and later Wells's, employ this convention to investigate fundamental questions about the relationship between language and notions of order.

14. See Bernard Bergonzi, *The Early H. G. Wells* (Manchester, England: Manchester University Press, 1961). Bergonzi argues that Wells's early works reveal a concept of human development that is essentially devolutionary.

15. See Poe's many pessimistic remarks to this effect throughout the *Marginalia*.

16. Instead of "supernatural," I use the word "supernormal" because it describes Wells's science-fictional as well as his Gothic embodiments of the "unseen."

17. *Elegant Nightmares* (Athens: Ohio University Press, 1978), p. 131.

18. Sullivan, *Elegant Nightmares*, discusses reader expectations in Poe's, Wells's, and other writers' Gothic stories.

19. Kenneth B. Newell discusses the rise-and-fall pattern of Wells's *Tono-Bungay* in *Structure in Four Novels by H. G. Wells* (The Hague: Mouton, 1968), pp. 73-83.

20. *Oxford English Dictionary*.

21. Other features of George's use of language are discussed in Lucille Herbert's *"Tono-Bungay: Tradition and Experiment," Modern Language Quarterly* 33 (1972):140-55.

22. The implications of this observation vis-a-vis society in the novel are discussed by David Lodge in *"Tono-Bungay* and the Condition of England" in *Language of Fiction* (New York: Columbia University Press, 1966), pp. 214-42.

Ann Veronica (1909)

Mr. Wells's New Novel

W. H. Chesson

um," as an ejaculation, is consecrated to the use of discreet disapprovers; but, without context, it has the demerit of being unsaleable as "copy." If it were saleable, it is likely that the majority of the Press notices of Mr. Wells's latest novel [*Ann Veronica*] would read like a chorus of bees. For as long as Mrs. Grundy loves art, her chickens (only less numerous than Mother Carey's) will feel pain in saying or writing more than a monosyllable in disparagement of a good work of art, let its morality be what it may. It is impossible that Mr. Wells should write an immoral book, but one man's morality is another man's anarchy, and there are those who will say that his book is subversive of their morality.

For, lo and behold! it is a novel of a young woman who "did," and flourished exceedingly, though her man had been ignominiously a co-respondent and had a wife at the time she eloped with him. Such a novel is bound to offend, because, to countless men and women, the inviolability of marriage is a guarantee of peace. The wedding-ring is to them as potent as Solomon's seal to confine and suppress the hungry passions. It is a bondage which confers on countless people freedom to do their work unworried and unagitated by erotic ambitions. Such people do not want to read the novels of France and Italy, and from their standpoint Mr. Wells will have deteriorated. They will wish that he had stuck to his marvels—to his Martians [in *War of the Worlds*] and Selenites [in *First Men in the Moon*]—and, in my opinion, they would have wished wrong.

For *Ann Veronica* is almost—not quite—a perfect work of realism. The heroine, whose name supplies the title, is the daughter of a solicitor with a scientific hobby and taste for "chromatic" novels. By preventing her from going in Turkish trousers to a fancy-dress ball and by refusing to allow her to attend certain biological classes, he causes her to leave his house and live in lodgings. Her beauty and ignorance speedily embarrass her. A hypocritical and middle-aged stockbroker lays her under monetary obligation, and crudely strives to add her to his list of conquests. Despair makes her go to gaol as a militant suffragette, and, on issuing thence, engage herself to a minor poet of imposing stature. Finally, she breaks her engagement and offers herself frankly, and courageously to a biologist, whose wife has declined to live with him.

The story has no plot—it is not in the least ingenious—and yet it is masterly, for it has all the qualities one would hope to find in an autobiography of a living Ann Veronica, written in the third person. [William Makepeace] Thackeray could not have failed to admire this piece of satire[,] which occurs after Ann Veronica has broken her engagement with the poet:

> She paused again.
> "I—I am sorry—I didn't explain . . . I love someone else."
> They remained looking at each other for three or four seconds. Then Manning flopped back in his chair and dropped his chin like a man shot. There was a long silence between them.
> "My God!" he said at last with tremendous feeling, and then again, "My God!"
> Now that this thing was said her mind was clear and calm. She heard this standard expression of a strong soul wrung with a critical coldness that astonished herself. She realised dimly that there was no personal thing behind this cry that countless myriads of Mannings had "My God!"ed with an equal gusto at situations as flatly apprehended.

In the sketch of Ann Veronica's father, Mr. Wells records with curious felicity the pettiness of human egoism; and no man alive has a keener appreciation of the funniness of a mixture of elementiveness and sentimentality. The sketches of suffragettes are careful and good, and it may be that a prison chaplain, who sits down while conversing with suffragettes in their cells, will wince to find himself anonymously conspicuous in these pages. In writing about love, Mr. Wells is eloquent almost to newness. "I wish," says his heroine, "I could roll my little body up small and squeeze it into your hand and grip your fingers upon it."

Truth to tell, I am fond of her. Till Tuesday morning she will have de-Grundified me[,] and I shall stay at home to avoid adventures trying to the nerves. This is a tiny tribute to Mr. Wells, but it is sincere and well-deserved. For as a bright realistic document, touched with kindly audacity, his book may be cordially recommended to seasoned worldlings.

The History of Mr. Polly
(1910)

A Fictioneer of the Laboratory

H. L. Mencken

 t seems to be pretty generally agreed by the critics, at least in the United States, that H. G. Wells has stepped into the long vacant boots of Charles Dickens, and for that notion, it must be confessed, there is no little excuse.

Wells, in truth, and to change the figure, has rediscovered and staked out for himself the English lower middle class that Dickens knew so intimately and loved with such shameless sentimentality—that hunkerous, uncleanly, tea-swilling *garde du corps* [bodyguard] of all the more disgusting virtues, traditions, superstitions, and epidemic diseases of the Anglican people. The other novelists across the water strike either above it or below it—above it at the magnificent and, as it were, almost supernatural indecency of the aristocracy, or at the moral anarchy of the self-conscious class of social climbers; or below it at the ingenious swinishness of the herd. Thus we have, on the one hand, a copious outpouring of novels of the "Dodo" school (even [George Moore's] *Esther Waters* [1894] and [Henry James's] *What Masie Knew* [1897] belong to it), with their melancholy presentations or perfumed polygamy; and, on the other hand, a steady supply of novels of the Hardy-Phillpotts-Morrison school, with their tedious prying into the amours and political ambitions, the theology and gnosiology of Wesleyan farmhands, seduced milkmaids, Whitechapel paupers and other such vermin. Now and then, of course, a writer may be found who belongs to both schools, or who flits irresolutely from one to the other— George Moore, for example; but it is seldom that any halt is made between the two. In other words, little attention is given in the current English fiction to the average Englishman. You will find plenty of degenerate dukes there, and plenty of Parliament men conducting low intrigues with clergymen's wives, and plenty of felonious parlor maids and derelicts of the Embanckment; but you will seldom find an honest English haberdasher, lawfully married to one wife, and a true believer in hell, monogamy, Beecham's pills, and the British constitution. I know not why, and do not guess, but so it is.

It is to this common and intensely human man, to this private soldier in the ranks of Christian civilization, that Mr. Wells turns in his new novel, *Mr. Polly*. Dickens would have loved Mr. Polly—loved him for his helplessness, his doggish joys, his calflike sorrows, his incurable nationalism—but it quickly appears that Mr. Wells loves him no more than a bacteriologist loves the rabbit whose spine he draws out through the gullet; and so we arrive at the notion that, despite a good deal of likeness, there are many points of difference between Dickens and Wells. They are, in truth, as far apart as the poles, for Dickens was a sentimentalist[,] and Wells is a scientist[;] and between sentiment and science there is even less in common than between kissing a pretty girl and kissing her mamma. Dickens regarded his characters as a young mother regards her baby; Wells looks at his as a porkpacker looks at a hog. Dickens believed that the way to judge a man was to test his willingness to give money to the orphans; Wells believes that it is safer and more accurate to find out the percentage of hydrochloric acid in his gastric juices.

As a matter of fact, the history of Mr. Polly, as Wells presents him to us, is a history of Mr. Polly's stomach. We are told, on the very first page of the book, that the low spirits in which we find him are due to the fact that his wife is an atrocious cook. "He suffered from indigestion . . . nearly every afternoon . . . but as he lacked introspection he projected the associated discomfort upon the world. Every afternoon he discovered afresh that life as a whole, and every aspect of life that presented itself, was 'beastly.'" It is the business of the first half of the book to trace the origin of Mr. Polly's indigestion—in coarse, ill-cooked food; in badly ventilated sleeping quarters; in lack of exercise; in the dull, sedentary life of a haberdasher in a small town, with a sluttish, unimaginative wife and no means of escape from her—and to show its lamentable consequences. Mr. Polly goes constantly from bad to worse, from mere discomfort to pessimism and despair. His day's work becomes intolerably painful; he is eternally irritated; he quarrels with his neighbors; he begins to lose money in his shop. Finally he decides to put an end to his woes by burning down that shop and cutting his throat.

The first of these desperate acts is accomplished with brilliant success, but Mr. Polly loses courage when he comes to the second. Thus he finds himself still alive and still very uncomfortable, but with a hundred pounds of insurance in his wallet instead of a wad of bills payable. What to do? Set up another shop? The thought of it sickens! Take to the woods? Well, why not? It is a short step from the idea to the act. Mr. Polly separates that insurance money into two parts, puts one where his wife will find it—and fares forth into the open country. He is a free man again, an opulent bachelor, the most enviable of creatures.

Thereafter the story describes the salvation of Mr. Polly's stomach, and through it, Mr. Polly's immortal soul. He happens one day, quite by chance, into a quaint sixteenth-century hostelry on a river bank—the Potwell Inn, to wit—and the motherly old soul who owns it sets a plate of honest roast beef before him. Mr. Polly eats and is thrilled.

Eight years afterwards he is still there—still eating the nourishing, digestible victuals of that saintly and accomplished cook, and moving ever upward and onward in the scale of brute creation. He becomes a sound man, a brave man, an efficient man, a happy man. As we part from him, he is sitting on the river bank in the cool of a golden summer evening, tranquilly smoking his pipe and meditating upon the great problems of existence. "Whenever there's signs of a good sunset," says Mr. Polly, "and I'm not too busy, I'll come and sit out here." Enviable man! True philosopher! He has found the secret of life at last!

Mr. Polly is written with all of Mr. Wells's customary facility and humor. The sheer fluency of the writing, in truth, is one of the book's faults. One feels that more careful polishing would have improved it—that it should have remained in the author's desk a year or so before going to the printer. Another fault lies in the fact that Mr. Wells is sometimes just a bit too scientific. Intent upon exploring Mr. Polly as a biological specimen, he seems to forget, now and then, that Mr. Polly is also a human being. In other words, a dash of Dickensian sentimentality would often add something to the flavor of Wells. But I have no hesitation whatsoever in saying that Wells, as he is, entertains me far more agreeably than Dickens. I know very well that the author of *David Copperfield* [1849-50] was a greater artist than the author of *Mr. Polly*, just as I know that the Archbishop of Canterbury is a more virtuous man than my good friend, Fred the Bartender; but all the same, I prefer Wells and Fred to Dickens and the Archbishop. In such matters one must allow a lot to individual taste and prejudice.

The New Machiavelli (1911)

The New Machiavelli

Arnold Bennett

 pretty general realization of the extremely high quality of *The New Machiavelli* has reduced almost to silence the ignoble tittle-tattle that accompanied its serial publication in the *English Review*. It is years since a novel gave rise to so much offensive and ridiculous chatter before being issued as a book. When the chatter began, dozens of people who would no more dream of paying four-and-sixpence for a novel that happened to be literature than they would dream of paying four-and-sixpence for a cigar, sent down to the offices of the *English Review* for complete sets of back numbers[,] at half crown a number, so that they could rummage without a moment's delay among the earlier chapters in search of tit-bits according to their singular appetite. Such was the London which calls itself literary and political! A spectacle to encourage cynicism!

Rumour had a wonderful time. It was stated that not only the libraries but the booksellers also would decline to handle *The New Machiavelli*. The reasons for this prophesied ostracism were perhaps vague, but they were understood to be broad-based upon the unprecedented audacity of the novel. And really in this exciting year, with Sir Percy Bunting in charge of the national sense of decency, and Mr. W. T. Stead still gloating after twenty-years over his success in keeping Sir Charles Dilke out of office—you never can tell what may happen!

However, it is all over now. *The New Machiavelli* has been received with the respect and the enthusiasm which its tremendous qualities deserve. It is a great success. And the reviews have been on the whole generous. It was perhaps not to be expected that certain Radical dailies should swallow the entire violent dose of the book without kicking up a fuss; but, indeed, Mr. [R. A.] Scott-James, in the *Daily News*, ought to know better than to go running about after autobiography in fiction. The human nose was not designed by an all-merciful providence for this purpose. Mr. Scott-James has undoubted gifts as a critic, and his temperament is sympathetic; and the men most capable of appreciating him, and whose appreciation he would probably like to retain, would esteem him even more highly if he could get into his head the simple fact that a novel is a novel.

I have suffered myself from this very provincial mania for chemically testing novels for traces of autobiography. There are some critics of fiction who talk about autobiography in fiction in the tone of a doctor who has found arsenic in the stomach at a post-mortem inquiry. The truth is that whenever a scene in a novel is *really* convincing, a certain type of critical and uncreative mind will infallibly mutter in accents of pain, "Autobiography!" When I was discussing this topic the other day[,] a novelist not inferior to Mr. Wells suddenly exclaimed: "I say! Supposing we *did* write autobiography!" . . . Yes, if we did, what a celestial rumpus there would be!

The carping at *The New Machiavelli* is naught. For myself[,] I anticipated for it a vast deal more carping than it has in fact occasioned. And I am very content to observe a marked increase of generosity in the reception of Mr. Wells's work. To me[,] the welcome accorded to his best books has always seemed to lack spontaneity, to be characterized by a mean reluctance. And yet[,] if there is a novelist writing to-day who by generosity has deserved generosity, that novelist is H. G. Wells. Astounding width of observation; a marvelously true perspective; an extraordinary grasp of the real significance of innumerable phenomena utterly diverse; profound emotional power; dazzling verbal skill: these are the qualities Mr. Wells indubitably has.

But the qualities which consecrate these other qualities are his priceless and total sincerity, and the splendid human generosity which colours that sincerity. What above all else we want in this island of intellectual dishonesty is some one who will tell us the truth "and chance it." H. G. Wells is pre-eminently that man. He might have told us the truth with cynicism; he might have told it meanly; he might have told it tediously—and he would still have been invaluable. But it does just happen that he has combined a disconcerting and entrancing candour with a warmth of generosity towards mankind and an inspiring faith in mankind such as no other living writer, not even the most sentimental, has surpassed.

And yet in the immediate past we have heard journalists pronouncing coldly: "This thing is not so bad." And we have heard journalists asserting in tones of shocked reprehension: "This thing is not free from faults!" Who the deuce said it was free from faults? But where in fiction, ancient or modern, will you find another philosophical picture of a whole epoch and society as brilliant and as honest as *The New Machiavelli* ? Well, I will tell you where you will find it. You will find it in *Tono-Bungay*. H. G. Wells is a bit of sheer luck for England. Some countries don't know their luck. And as I do not believe that England is worse than another, I will say that no country knows its luck. However, as regards this particular bit, there are now some clear signs of a growing perception.

The social and political questions raised in *The New Machiavelli* might be discussed at length with great advantage. But this province is not mine. Nor could the rightness or the wrongness of the hero's views and acts affect the artistic value of the novel. On purely artistic grounds[,] the novel might be criticized in several ways unfavourably. But in my opinion[,] it has only one fault that to any appreciable extent impairs its artistic worth. The politically-creative part, as distinguished from the politically-shattering part, is not convincing. The hero's change of party, and his popular success with the policy of the endowment of motherhood are indeed strangely unconvincing—inconceivable to common sense. Here the author's hand has trembled, and his persuasive power forsaken him. Happily[,] he recaptured it for the final catastrophe, which is absolutely magnificent, a masterpiece of unforced poignant tragedy and unsentimental tenderness.

Marriage (1912)

H. G. Wells and
Mrs. Humphry Ward

John R. Reed

 he was an established international best-seller, the starchy descendant of a famous intellectual family, well-acquainted with people of significance, and, though Tory in her politics, recognized for her successful ventures on behalf of the lower classes. He was a brash young man from the lower middle class who had dropped out of university to enter the rough-and-tumble world of popular journalism and to promote Socialist ideas; and his remarkably original first novel was starting him on a career that would soon skyrocket him to fame and influence. Not a likely match, though the two writers shared almost as many similarities as they did differences, making an examination of their slight but intriguing connection worthwhile.

The year was 1895, and H. G. Wells's *The Time Machine* was stirring imaginations and promoting a new literary ware in England—science fiction. In the same year, Mrs. Humphry Ward's thoroughly conventional *The Story of Bessie Costrell* was appearing in three installments in *The Cornhill Magazine*, for which she was paid a comfortable £560. Mrs. Humphry Ward was already a major presence on the literary scene in England; H. G. Wells was only just achieving recognition, though he would soon go on to assume a position not unlike that Mrs. Ward enjoyed in the years following 1895. Mrs. Ward believed that an aristocracy of sorts should govern England but devoted a good deal of energy to improving physical care and education among the poor and the working classes. Wells was a Socialist who nonetheless endorsed the idea of government by an elite ruling order. Mrs. Ward began as an intellectual novelist concerned with religion, politics, and society, and she ended mainly as a romance novelist of sorts. Wells began as a writer of scientific romances and ended as an intellectual novelist concerned with religious, political, and social issues. In many ways Mrs. Ward was the antithesis of all that Wells looked for in literature, but at the same time she represented some of the very aims that he came to value. Wells's references to her indicate a sensitivity to and understanding of her work that does not constitute praise but is not dismissive either.

From the beginning Wells knew where to place Mrs. Ward. In an article in *The Saturday Review* he complained that the Turgenev "novel of types" did not exist in England and that the great Russian novelist was not read seriously there. "He stands a Lilliputian beneath the towering columns that commemorate the latest triumph of Mrs. Humphry Ward.   Surely abuse had been more honourable." This is not direct attack, but it relegates Mrs. Ward to a literary position incommensurate with the degree of praise accorded her. In the same review Wells credits Mrs. Ward with evincing modern types and modern influences in her fiction. Of Mrs. Ward's *Sir George Tressady* (1896) he similarly wrote that it had "the indisputable stamp of truth," though it possessed "neither very much humor nor very much wit."[1]

Chiefly Wells seems to have objected to the superficial and formulaic character of Mrs. Ward's novels. Mrs. Ward would have agreed with Wells's assertion in "The Contemporary Novel" (1914) that "the novel has inseparable moral consequences." For Wells, however, Mrs. Ward did not properly employ the devices of serious fiction. Wells assumes that, like Arnold Bennett and Samuel Richardson, who admire their created characters, "Mrs Ward considers her Marcella a very fine and estimable young woman." In traditional fiction, however, such model characters are patently fabricated and not credible entities. "And I think it is just, in this," Wells continues, "that the novel is not simply a fictitious record of conduct but also a study and judgment of conduct, and through that of the ideas that lead to conduct, that the real and increasing value—or perhaps to avoid controversy I had better say the real and increasing importance—of the novel and the novelist in modern life comes in."[2] For Wells, the novel is to become an instrument for action; for Ward, according to Wells, it remains a mere representation of a supposed social order.

Wells had raised a similar contrast more explicitly in his earlier essay, "The Novels of Mr. George Gissing" (1897), where he complained that, with the exception of Gissing, contemporary English novels had not measured up to the socially significant continental fiction of Émile Zola, Leo Tolstoy, and Ivan Turgenev. English writers such as "George Eliot and Mrs. Humphry Ward veil a strongly didactic disposition under an appearance of social study rather than give us social studies." By contrast, Gissing is one of a very few modern English writers "who have set themselves to write novels which are neither studies of character essentially, nor essentially series of incidents, but deliberate attempts to present in typical groupings distinct phases of social life."[3]

Wells was himself one of this new breed of writers, and critics acknowledged the difference. Reviewing *The New Machiavelli* in *The Daily News* (19 January 1911), R. A. Scott-James wrote: Wells's "hero is not one of Mrs. Humphry Ward's puppets set up to be great politicians. Remington as a thinker *is* almost a great man; he *is* a profound analyst of society on its human side; he *is* a gifted critic of public institutions."[4] Despite his humble origins, Wells had sufficient experience and powerful enough imagination and intellect to create a believable politician. Mrs. Ward could only establish the type and allow her narrator and characters to *say* that he is a great politician, as with Aldous Raeburn in *Marcella* (1894). Arnold Bennett briefly summed up Ward's strengths and weaknesses as he saw them: "Let me duly respect Mrs. Humphry Ward. She knows her business. She is an expert in narrative. She can dress up even the silliest incidents of sentimental fiction . . . in a costume of plausibility. She is a conscientious worker . . . Mrs. Humphry Ward's novels are praiseworthy as being sincerely and skillfully done, but they are not works of art." Bennett deplores Mrs. Ward's unbelievable heroines and refers to them as "harrowing dolls."[5]

Like Wells, Bennett could not understand how the intellectual press could continue to offer abundant praise for Mrs. Ward's fiction while ignoring superior artists such as Turgenev, or even equally popular ones, such as Maria Corelli. The answer, he concludes, is that other writers do "not please nearly so many respectable and correct persons as does Mrs. Humphry Ward."[6]

Ultimately the case against Mrs. Ward seems to have been that her works were fictional constructions appealing to a respectable, conventional, and conservative audience who did not want or expect fiction to change the social order. These works were not art. In some ways this indictment is particularly sad because, at least in the earlier part of her career, Mrs. Ward labored to master her craft, going so far as to solicit instruction from the Master himself, Henry James, and she surely anticipated that her engaged fiction, by taking up contemporary problems in religion, politics, and social relations might have an immediate positive effect. But by the time H. G. Wells's star was rising, a young generation of writers was already dismissing Mrs. Humphry Ward, although her novels continued to sell well for some time to come. Ezra Pound referred to her as "the Great Mary," confusable with the Virgin Mother; and Rebecca West denounced "her limitless faith in the decency and respectability of reaction."[7] Gordon N. Ray says that West "patronized the still celebrated Mrs. Humphry Ward as a belated example of the psychology of the Victorian clergyman class."[8]

Wells was critical of Mrs. Ward's contribution to English literature, but he was not merely a savage mocker like Rebecca West, or a sly one like Oscar Wilde.[9] As in so many other aspects of his career, Wells took his subject seriously and gave credit for strengths in the writer he criticized. Since Mrs. Ward was to publish a significant assessment of Wells as a novelist in 1918, it is worthwhile to see what he had to say about her in his fiction.

There are few allusions to Mrs. Ward in Wells's scientific romances, as one might suppose, but she does appear in the more overtly didactic *In the Days of the Comet* (1906). In this story, which seems to draw some portion of its inspiration from William Morris's *News From Nowhere* (1891), an aged William Leadford tells of the great redemptive change that comes upon the world when a comet passing close to the Earth alters the chemical composition of the air. The hostile and aggressive human community is suddenly transformed to a brotherhood of mutual concern and assistance. Soon after this change has occurred the English cabinet meets to make plans. The narrator says these men brought up by similar schools and universities constitute a recognizable type:

> These fifteen men who ruled the British Empire were curiously unlike anything I had expected, and I watched them intently whenever my services were not in request. They made a peculiar class at that time, these English politicians and

statesmen, a class that has now completely passed away. In some respects they were unlike the statesmen of any other region of the world, and I do not find that any really adequate account remains of them . . . Perhaps you are a reader of the old books. If so, you will find them rendered with a note of hostile exaggeration by Dickens in "Bleak House," with a mingling of gross flattery and keen ridicule by Disraeli, who ruled among them accidentally by misunderstanding them and pleasing the court; and all their assumptions are set forth, portentously perhaps, but truthfully so far as people of the "permanent official" class saw them, in the novels of Mrs. Humphry Ward. (*Works* 10:239-40)

Mrs. Humphry Ward is here allied with the privileged class itself, but more notably she is included among a group of distinguished writers whose accounts are dependable and whose works survive into the illuminated future. This is far from reckless mockery and reflects, instead, a degree of qualified respect.

Predictably Mrs. Ward shows up more frequently in the novels of class and social concern. In *Kipps* (1905) Chester Coote is an educated young man who undertakes to teach Kipps what it means to be a gentleman. Kipps encounters him when he seeks improvement at the Folkestone Young Men's Association where Coote reads a paper on Self-Help. Coote is described as "a young man of semi-independent means who inherited a share in a house agency, read Mrs. Humphry Ward, and took an interest in social work" (*Works* 8:63). This allusion is innocuous enough, except that Coote and (by extension) Mrs. Ward represent a condescending class attitude associated with the directing of the lower classes by a privileged elite. *Kipps*, of course, describes a modest but determined rebellion against this attitude. Kipps escapes from his engagement to the genteel Helen Walsingham for the humbler but more genuine love of the servant girl, Anne Pornick, in whom he had earlier been interested. Seated before a labyrinthodon on the grounds of the Crystal Palace, Kipps and Anne notice the resemblance between Coote and the prehistoric fossil. Here, as elsewhere in Wells's fiction, the identification with an extinct species suggests the inevitable extinction of the social type as well.

I have suggested that Wells maintained a balanced attitude toward Mrs. Ward, appreciating her influence and the force of her representations, while disapproving of the social and political values she espoused and her inartistic mode of conveying them. As we have seen, R. A. Scott-James considered Remington in *The New Machiavelli* a true rendering of a politician in contrast to Ward's less credible types. Yet in this novel Wells acknowledges the significant presence of Ward on the political and social scene. Writing of his early years, Remington says that his contemporary students at Trinity College were still under the shadow of the great Victorians—figures like William Gladstone, Benjamin Disraeli, Sir William Harcourt, Mr. Evesham, and the Duke of Devonshire. "One heard of cabinet councils and meetings at country houses. Some of us, pursuing such interests, went so far as to read political memoirs and the novels of Disraeli and Mrs. Humphry Ward" (*Works* 14:126). Although Mrs. Ward is thus relegated to a position among the outdated Victorians, she is nonetheless placed in very reputable company and credited with the power of satisfactorily depicting the life of the politically effective classes. Later in the novel, another dimension of her dubious influence is acknowledged in the portrait of Altiora Macvitie, "who came into prominence as one of the more able of the little shoal of young women who were led into politico-philanthropic activities by the influence of the earlier novels of Mrs. Humphry Ward—the Marcella crop" (*Works* 14:221).

Wells had Mrs. Ward very much in mind with *The New Machiavelli*. She was at the height of her influence, though it was already apparent to literary people, if not to the public, that her reputation was fast diminishing. Wells's novel dealt with precisely the same subject matter as many of Mrs. Ward's novels, such as *Marcella* (1894), *Sir George Tressady*, and *The Marriage of William Ashe* (1905). Despite her conservative social views, Mrs. Ward had also dealt with sexual relationships boldly, though not offensively. It is not strange, then, that Wells should have compared his first genuinely political novel with a serious and controversial sexual element to Mrs. Ward's fiction.

The New Machiavelli was regarded as immoral by some readers because it dealt so openly and sympathetically with adultery, but Wells defended his book, claiming that its love passages served the purposes of the story and were not lubricious. "I would sooner cut off my right hand than write deliberately to excite sexual passion," he said. To reinforce his chaste intentions, he also remarked: "There is not a single passage [in *The New Machiavelli*] that offends either against decency or against the established code of morals. Judged by the standards of Mr. Maurice Hewlett, or Mrs. Humphry Ward—in *David Grieve* [1892], for example—the work is coldly chaste."[10]

This is a complicated statement for various reasons, and it is not free from irony. Wells purposely names Mrs. Ward's most risqué novel. In it a young Englishman travels to France with his sister. In Paris, David Grieve falls passionately in love with a young French painter, pursuing her so vigorously that he neglects his dangerously willful sister. When David goes off on a sexual holiday with his lover, Louie takes that opportunity to move in with a talented but feckless sculptor. David's idyll ends and, to make Louie honest, he pays over his inheritance of £600 to persuade Montjoie to marry her, a marriage that soon proves disastrous. Though treated circumspectly by Mrs. Ward, these sexual adventures are far more prominent and "romantically" engaging than anything in *The New Machiavelli*.

Writing much later, Wells admitted that *The New Machiavelli* was written more or less against Mrs. Humphry Ward's brand of fiction:

> The *New Machiavelli* is all the world away from overt eroticism. The theme is simply a fresh variant upon the theme of *Love and Mr. Lewisham* and the *Sea Lady*; it stressed the harsh incompatibility of wide public interests with the high, swift rush of imaginative passion—with considerable sympathy for the passion. The Marcella-like heroine of the *Sea Lady* is repeated, but the mermaid has become a much more credible young woman, and it is to exile in Italy and literary effort, and not to moonshine and death, that the lovers go.[11]

Mrs. Ward was still immediately present to Wells's mind as he began his next novel, *Marriage* (1912). The heroine, Marjorie Pope, is an appealing and impressionable young woman of the upper middle class who evokes in many people a desire to shape and influence her. Among these is Marjorie's aunt, Mrs. Plessington. "She spoke of training her niece to succeed her, and bought all the novels of Mrs. Humphry Ward for her as they appeared, in the hope of quickening in her that flame of politico-social ambition, that insatiable craving for dinner parties with important guests, which is so distinctive of the more influential variety of English womanhood" (*Works* 15:11). There is a wry dismissive tone to this passage, and the narrative voice clearly disapproves of the model provided by Ward's novels. It is thus dismaying that Marjorie succumbs to her aunt's influence. "The world reformed itself in Marjorie's fluent mind, until it was all a scheme of influence and effort and ambition and triumphs. Dinner-parties and receptions, men wearing orders, cabinet ministers more than a little in love asking her advice, beautiful robes, a great blaze of lights; why! she might be, said Aunt Plessington rising to enthusiasm, 'another Marcella'" (*Works* 15:92).

Wells had long since focused on *Marcella* as the basic example of Mrs. Ward's fiction, and I shall return to discuss that novel at greater length. At present, it is enough to note that *Marcella* follows the career of its heroine from Socialism to enlightened Toryism among members of Parliament and the upper class. *Marriage* aims determinedly to guide its heroine away from such a superficial life. After almost suffocating her brilliant husband's intellectual life, Marjorie Trafford follows him into the wilderness and saves his life, an experience that forms the basis of a new and richer partnership. Wells commented on much more than Mrs. Ward's fiction in this novel, but she was by this time clearly a fixed symbol to him of a way of life that he considered increasingly pernicious, not the least because Mrs. Ward herself was becoming strident in her opposition to causes that Wells supported—such as Woman's Suffrage.[12]

Mrs. Ward had, by 1912, ceased to be an important antagonist for Wells. Now she was merely part of a convenient shorthand. We know what to think of Ellen Harman in *The Wife of Sir Isaac Harman* (1914) immediately when we are told that she "sat in the most comfortable garden chair, held a white sunshade overhead, had the last new novel by Mrs. Humphry Ward upon her lap, and was engaged in trying not to wonder where her daughter might be" (*Works* 16:165). Such a person must be saved from herself.

And then came *Boon* (1915), which, though Wells did not fully appreciate the fact at the time, marked his separation from the world of Art. In *Boon* Mrs. Ward is presented as "the last of the British Victorian Great" in a sardonic, telegraphic manner: "Expressed admiration of Mr. Gladstone for her work. Support of the *Spectator*. Profound respect of the American people. Rumour that she is represented as a sea goddess at the base of the Queen Victoria memorial unfounded" (*Works* 13:486). This passage, though part of some complicated and ambiguous fun, is nonetheless more dismissive than it sounds, compactly presenting a popular view that might have been held of Mrs. Ward at the time, except that Wells had indicated early in *Boon* that Mrs. Ward, among other pretenders, had failed to fill the vacated thrones of the departed Victorian Greats. Moreover, support from Gladstone and *The Spectator* would have seemed dubious credentials to advanced thinkers in 1915, and American admiration counted for little. *Boon* deplores American taste. America ignores, for example, her own Stephen Crane. "And she'll let Mary Austin die of neglect, while she worships the 'art' of Mary Ward. It's like turning from the feet of a goddess to a pair of goloshes" (*Works* 13:479).[13]

If, for Wells, Mrs. Ward is a failed Great Victorian, she nonetheless represents the outmoded ideas and methods of the Victorian era. If she is still valued by a broad international readership, it is a readership that cannot appreciate genuine art. For Wells at this point, Mrs. Ward has become a monument of obsolescence, and she effectively disappears from his fiction for a decade or two and then surfaces only in passing. In *The Bulpington of Blup* (1932), however, she makes a curious sort of appearance. The narrator describes the atmosphere in which Bulpington grows up, an atmosphere concerned mainly with the artistic perception of experience. Among literary figures to whom values are attached, Bulpington is aware of "George Moore who was certainly all right and [Thomas] Hardy who perhaps wasn't. George Moore said he wasn't. And Hall Caine and Mrs. Humphry Ward who were simply hell" (23). Wells here mocks the aesthetic pretensions of Bulpington's set, but in placing Caine and Ward among the abominated, he in some sense treats them sympathetically and at the same time criticizes his own earlier denunciations of these novelists.

Wells rarely refers to Mrs. Ward outside his fiction. We have already noted his treatment of her in his 1914 essay, "The Contemporary Novel." When he does comment on her, it is only to class her with other fossils of Old England. A stranger in the future visiting England might be shown over the Houses of Parliament, he muses, "and do his puzzled best to imagine what that strange narrow life was like, assisted by extracts from Hansard, carefully preserved gramophone records of important speeches, enlarged photographs of Mr Gladstone, movie glimpses of Mr Neville Chamberlain in a state of indignation, and the still surviving political novels of Mrs Humphrey [sic] Ward."[14]

Wells was most intrigued by Mrs. Ward near the beginning of his career, after he had made his mark with the scientific romances and when he was turning his attention to what we might call the social novel, a form of "engaged" fiction by which Mrs. Ward had made her reputation. Her *Robert Elsmere* (1888) examined questions of religious faith, aesthetic values, and social action on behalf of the poor. It was Mrs. Ward's first successful novel and became an immediate and overwhelming best-seller. *David Grieve* traced the career of a poor but intelligent rural boy as he made his way in the book selling and publishing trade, substituting a faith in human effort for the dour dissenting faith in which he was raised, while experimenting with profit-sharing in his successful business. *Marcella* described the maturation of a young woman as she progressed toward "sensible" religious, social, and political views. Novels that followed, such as *Sir George Tressady*, *Helbeck of Bannisdale* (1898), and *Eleanor* (1900) contain similar ingredients. All of these novels include, as well, love stories involving numerous complications.

Wells seems to have read a fair number of Ward's novels, but the one that remained his touchstone for Wardsian traits was *Marcella*. He devoted an entire novella to a serious parody of it. In his working manuscript notes for *The Sea*

Lady (1902) Wells names *Marcella*, *Sir George Tressady*, and *Eleanor*, thus revealing his direct purpose in addressing Ward's fiction.[15] Though I have touched on this relationship elsewhere, I think it is worthwhile to explore a little more closely how *Marcella* and *The Sea Lady* are related.[16] Of his own novel, Wells wrote in his autobiography: "Chatteris is a promising young politician, a sort of mixture of Harry Cust and any hero in any novel by Mrs. Humphry Ward, and he is engaged to be married to a heroine, quite deliberately and confessedly lifted, gestures, little speeches and all, from that lady's *Marcella* "[17]

Marcella Boyce, the heroine of Mrs. Ward's novel, has an independent nature, having been educated away from her family. Returning to the family estate, from which her father had been exiled as the result of a scandal, but which he has now inherited, Marcella brings to the Tory neighborhood her Socialist principles acquired among her London friends. Aldous Raeburn, the wise, practical, and high-minded grandson of Lord Maxwell (the chief local landlord), soon falls in love with Marcella, and the relationship progresses despite their incompatible political views. Marcella's efforts on behalf of working people in the neighborhood create tensions, however, which culminate in her support of James Hurd, one of a group of poachers responsible for the death of Lord Maxwell's gamekeeper and assistant. The trial and execution of Hurd leads first to a postponement and then abandonment of Marcella's marriage. Meanwhile, Marcella has become interested in the ideas and character of Harold Wharton, a small landowner and effective public speaker who champions Socialist ideas and seeks reform of game and property laws.

After her break with Raeburn, Marcella returns to London where she becomes a nurse. Raeburn and Wharton are both now in Parliament and are intellectual antagonists. Marcella is gradually drawn into Wharton's circle again but is equally influenced by the idealistic Edward Hallin, whose Socialist views are far more moderate and paternalistic than Wharton's. Marcella cannot help realizing how fine a man Aldous Raeburn is, but she has no hope of a reconciliation and comes close, instead, to accepting Wharton's marriage proposal. But Wharton is soon revealed to have taken a bribe to assist managers in their effort to break a workers' union. Wharton eventually marries a titled lady for money, while Marcella and Raeburn resume their romance with an enlightened marriage in view.

Wells's heroine in *The Sea Lady* is Miss Adeline Glendower, an heiress twenty-one years old, who has "dark hair and grey eyes and serious views" (*Works* 5:315). After the death of her father, she comes out strongly:

> It became evident she had always had a mind, and a very active and capable one, an accumulated fund of energy and much ambition. She had bloomed into a clear and critical socialism, and she had blossomed at public meetings; and now she was engaged to that really very brilliant and promising but rather extravagant and romantic person, Harry Chatteris, the nephew of an earl and the hero of a scandal, and quite a possible Liberal candidate for the Hythe division of Kent. (*Works* 5:316).

Miss Glendower is introduced reading *Sir George Tressady*, "a book of which she was naturally enough at that time inordinately fond" (*Works* 5:318).

Into this arrangement comes the Sea Lady who, Wells pointed out, stands for "the magic of beauty."[18] She has a tendency to "underestimate the nobler tendencies of the human spirit," to "treat Adeline Glendower and many of the deeper things of life with a certain sceptical levity," and to "subordinate reason and right feeling to passion" (*Works* 5:334-35). Mrs. Bunting describes Adeline to the Sea Lady as a good helper for Chatteris. She reads government Blue Books and "knows more about the condition of the poor than anyone I've ever met . . . And you know she can talk to workmen and take an interest in trades unions, and in quite astonishing things. I always think she's just Marcella come to life" (*Works* 5:344).

By this point in Wells's narrative his target has become perfectly clear. He mocks the condescending and patronizing nature of the "Socialism" represented by Ward's *Marcella*. The connection becomes explicit when the narrator's cousin Melville says of the younger Adeline: "'She posed . . . she was 'political,' and she was always reading Mrs. Humphry Ward." Melville regards "this great novelist as an extremely corrupting influence for intelligent girls. She makes them good and serious in the wrong way, he says. Adeline, he asserts, was absolutely built on her. She was always attempting to be the incarnation of *Marcella* " (*Works* 5:378). Adeline has the same "disposition towards arrogant benevolence, that same obtuseness to little shades of feeling that leads people to speak habitually of the 'Lower Classes,' and to think in the vein of that phrase. They certainly had the same virtues, a conscious and conscientious integrity, a hard nobility without one touch of magic, an industrious thoroughness" (*Works* 5:378-79). But Adeline is not Marcella, no matter how much she wishes to be, and Chatteris does not wish to be a Lord Maxwell, as Ward's Aldous Raeburn becomes.

What follows in Wells's tale is an account of how Miss Doris Thallassia Waters, as the Sea Lady is called, wins Chatteris's heart away from the "highly earnest and intellectual" Adeline (*Works* 5:373). Her appeal is in her claim that there are better dreams for people to follow than the dreary illusion to which they now submit. She dismisses Adeline as unreal:

> She's a mass of fancies and vanities. She gets everything out of books. She gets herself out of a book . . . And what does she care for the condition of the poor after all? It is only a point of departure in her dream. In her heart she does not want their dreams to be happier, in her heart she has no passion for them, only her dream is that she should be prominently doing good, asserting herself, controlling their affairs amidst thanks and praise and blessings. (*Works* 5:403)

Chatteris chooses the Sea Lady because she represents the mysterious and the beautiful against the artificiality of Adeline and her Mrs. Humphry Ward world.

The Sea Lady is Wells's early and definitive *statement* on Mrs. Humphry Ward's fiction and its deleterious effects. His definitive *act* may have been making love with Elizabeth von Arnim with her buttocks resting on a copy of the *Times* featuring a moral lecture by Mrs. Ward.[19] But whatever Wells's comments about Mrs. Ward, she had a word or two to say about him as well.

Henry James was a friend of both Ward and Wells, and treated them with similar circumspection. When asked to evaluate other writers' fiction, James would claim that, as a technician, he could read only critically, constructively, and reconstructively. Leon Edel remarks that in saying this, "James was up to his old tricks; this was the way he always dealt with Mrs. Humphry Ward or H.G. Wells." James lectured both authors on the art of fiction, but never really admitted either into the elite circle of true art. Of Ward, James wrote to Edmund Gosse: "She is incorrigibly wise and good, and has a moral nature as Patti has a voice . . . but somehow I don't especially when talking art and letters, *communicate* with her worth a damn." Similarly, when asked whether Mrs. Humphry Ward could be compared with George Eliot, James purred: "George Eliot was a great woman. I have the profoundest respect for the cleverness of Mrs. Humphry Ward."[20]

James gave up on Wells as an artist once he had committed himself to socially responsible fiction. Ironically, it was to Mrs. Ward that he wrote his private eulogy upon Wells as an artist. "Strange to me—in his affair—the co-existence of so much talent with so little art, so much life with (so to speak) so little living! But of him there is much to say, for I really think him more interesting by his faults than he will probably ever manage to be in any other way; and he is a most vivid and violent object-lesson."[21]

Mrs. Ward very likely took her lead on Wells from James. At any rate, her estimate of his talents in *A Writer's Recollections* (1918) sound familiar. She credits Wells and Bennett as the leaders of the New Novel, which she sees as a compound of realist and argumentative fiction. Then she offers a capsule summary of Wells's place in the world of the modern novel: "Mr. Wells seems to me a journalist of very great powers, of unequal education, and much crudity of mind, who has inadvertently strayed into the literature of imagination." She credits him with some successful early story-telling and some effective passages, but dismisses most of his fiction as being essentially Wells's own voice speaking cleverly but devoid of character creation. Who, she asks mordantly, "after a few years more, will ever want to turn the restless, ill-written, undigested pages of *The New Machiavelli* again?" Wells, she adds, has no charm but writes "for a world of enemies or fools, whom he wishes to instruct or show up."[22] He is an able journalist, she concludes, not an artist. It is a damning assessment that echoes, with its own variation, Wells's judgment on Ward's own fiction.

In "The Contemporary Novel" Wells had insisted that the novel has inescapable moral consequences. As early as 1914, he was already well entrenched in the camp of those who regarded the exclusively artistic novel as an insipid illusion. Following this code, Wells went on to write many novels that, with increasing impetus, sped him into the ranks of writers "with a message." It is generally agreed that the later didactic fiction does not measure up to Wells's early successes.

The trajectory of Wells's career resembles Mrs. Ward's. After the highly successful early problem novels, Mrs. Ward's popularity began a steep decline with the publication of *Daphne* (1909), an anti-feminist, anti-divorce novel. At about this same time, Ward was becoming active as a journalist and as a supporter and even spokesperson for conservative government causes. After

1915 or thereabouts, Wells too saw a sporadic decline in appreciation of his fiction, despite an increasing interest in his journalism and social prophesying. His causes were generally directly opposed to those to which Mrs. Ward gave her energies, but the patterns of their careers must otherwise have seemed very similar to contemporary onlookers. Perhaps one of the great ironies in this literary relationship was Mrs. Ward's prediction that "*Mr. Britling Sees It Through* is perhaps more likely to live than any other of his novels,"[23] for it is in this novel that Wells comes closest to Mrs. Ward's own brand of religion, presenting a central character very close to Wells himself, who senses "the Master, the Captain of Mankind, it was God, there present with him" (*Works* 22:539).   Wells developed this inkling of Mr. Britling's at length and in expository form in *God the Invisible King* (1917).

Mrs. Humphry Ward died a couple of years after the end of the first world war; Wells lived on many months past the end of the second world war. By the times of their deaths, both might have been described by a younger generation as fierce and dedicated preachers yearning to educate a benighted people, preachers who somehow wandered into the rarefied world of imaginative literature where they found the atmosphere too thin for their practical imaginations and who, to survive, therefore descended once more to labor in the vineyards on the lower slopes of Olympus.

NOTES

1. Patrick Parrinder and Robert Philmus, eds. *H. G. Wells's Literary Criticism* (Brighton, Sussex: The Harvester Press, and Totowa, New Jersey: Barnes and Noble Books, 1980), pp. 67, 71.

2. H. G. Wells, *The Works of H. G. Wells* (New York: Charles Scribner's Sons, 1925), 9:368-69.   Subsequent page references to this Atlantic Edition appear parenthetically in my discussion.

3. Parrinder and Philmus, p. 146.

4. Patrick Parrinder, ed. *H. G. Wells: The Critical Heritage* (London and Boston: Routledge and Kegan Paul, 1972), p. 184.

5. Arnold Bennett, *Books and Persons: Being Comments on a Past Epoch 1908-1911* (New York: George H. Doran Company, 1917, pp. 49-50. Bennett could not resist a coda to his generally even-tempered evaluation of Ward's heroines in which he devised a terrible destiny for them. "They ought to be caught, with their lawful male protectors, in the siege of a great city by a foreign army. Their lawful male protectors ought, before sallying forth on a forlorn hope, to provide them with a revolver as a last refuge from a brutal and licentious soldiery. And when things come to a crisis, in order to be concluded in our next, the revolvers ought to prove to be unloaded. I admit that this invention of mine is odious, and quite un-English, and such as would never occur to a right-minded subscriber to Mudie's. But it illustrates the mood caused in me by witnessing the antics of those harrowing dolls" (52).

6. Bennett , p. 50

7 William Peterson, *Victorian Heretic: Mrs Humphry Ward's* Robert Elsmere (Leicester: Leicester University Press, 1976), p. 3.

8 Gordon N. Ray, *H. G. Wells & Rebecca West* (New Haven: Yale University Press, 1974), p. 8.

9. John Sutherland mentions Oscar Wilde's claim that reading *Robert Elsmere* "reminded him of the sort of conversation that goes on at a meat tea in the house of a serious Nonconformist family," among many other jibes by other writers of the day: *Mrs Humphry Ward: Eminent Victorian Pre-eminent Edwardian* (Oxford: Clarendon Press, 1990), pp. 2001.

10. *The Bodleian*, 2 (January 1911): 166. I want to thank William J. Scheick for calling this interview to my attention.

11. H. G. Wells, *Experiment in Autobiography* (London: Victor Gollancz Ltd and The Cresset Press Ltd, 1934), 2: 473-4.

12. Sutherland explores this aspect of Mrs. Ward's career in Chapter 25 of *Mrs. Humphry Ward..*

13. David Smith gives a brief description of Wells's acquaintance with Mary Austin, a young American who wrote stories and books about the American West: *H. G. Wells: Desperately Mortal* (New Haven and London: Yale University Press, 1988), pp. 390-91. Wells was generous to Austin, as he was to many young writers, but he appears to have been mistaken in his high estimate of her talent. Austin recalled her friendship with Wells in her memoir, *Earth's Horizon* (1932).

14. H. G. Wells, *The Fate of Homo Sapiens* (London: Secker and Warburg, 1939), p. 211.

15. The manuscript of *The Sea Lady* is in the special Wells collection of the library of the University of Illinois at Urbana.

16. I discuss the relationship of *Marcella* and *The Sea Lady* in "The Literary Piracy of H. G. Wells," *Journal of Modern Literature*, 7 (1980):319-38. This material was subsequently incorporated in *The Natural History of H. G. Wells* (Athens: Ohio University Press, 1982).

17. *Experiment*, p. 468.

18. *Experiment*, p. 469.

19. The action constituted a form of social protest against Ward's opinions as well as having its immediate value. See G. P. Wells, ed., *H. G. Wells in Love: Postscript to an Experiment in Autobiography* (London: Faberand Faber, 1984), p. 89.

20. Leon Edel, *Henry James: The Treacherous Years (1895-1901)* (Philadelphia and New York: J. B. Lippincott Company, 1969), p. 293; Edel, *Henry James: The Master (1901-1916)* (Philadelphia and New York: J. B. Lippincott Company, 1972), pp. 196, 278.

21. For some reason, this letter does not appear in Leon Edel's edition of *Henry James Letters: Volume IV: 1895-1916* (Cambridge: The Belknap Press of Harvard University Press, 1984).

22. Mrs. Humphry Ward, *A Writer's Recollections* (New York and London: Harper and Brothers Publishers, 1918), 1:244-46

23. *Recollections*, 1:245.

The Research Magnificent
(1915)

The Novel of Ideas

Rebecca West

he cretinous butlers who make up the mass of respectable English critics have always disliked Mr. Wells. This is partly because he is alive. Admitting the greatness of the dead means platform tickets and one's name in the *Times*, long dinners passing into a drowse of speeches spiced with the better-known quotations from Horace, and all the treats that make up the literary "bean-feast" known as the centenary. But to hail the greatness of the living is to admit that something planted in the same soil as oneself has grown to a mightier flower. Moreover[,] the butlers very rightly fear that if Mr. Wells goes on as he is doing the household will be broken up[,] and they will be turned out of their pantries; for he has inspired the young to demand clear thinking and intellectual passion from the governing classes, instead of the sexual regularity which was their one virtue and which, he has hinted, is merely part of a general slothfulness and disinclination for adventure. Ostensibly they are not butlers at all. They pretend to be priests of art, and as such they are attempting to object to Mr. Wells['s] latest and most dangerous book, *The Research Magnificent*.

They say it is not beautiful; it is as physically beautiful as a bowl of roses, as a ray of sunshine striking deep through cold green water, as mists full of rainbows on a wet mountain. They say the characters are puppets; if they have never met Benham, the white-faced researcher after aristocracy, it is only because he is still half the world away, standing in the mad Indian moonlight of the jungle, facing the tiger as it draws itself lengthily from the darkness into the frosted silver of the clearing, and lifting a lean hand to it: "I am Man. The Thought of the world." They say it is a dreary stocktaking of dry things of the mind; it is full of a kind of wisdom that gilds the dull appearances of this world . . . But the butlers no more care for this sweetening and illumination of the world than they marvel that a man who three years ago published that base and absurd book, *The Passionate Friends*, should to-day publish this noble and technically perfect novel. "Mr. Wells," they say, "allows himself to fall into disquisitions. Ideas have no place in a novel."

This dogma that ideas have no place in a novel is poisonous nonsense that ought not to be spread in a society where the mind is unnaturally receptive because it is fatigued by the contemplation of horror. An artist who is inspired to creation not by ideas but only by the stimulus of wild external adventure is an interpretative rather than a creative artist. As a dancer must wait for the music, so he must wait for loud events to give tune for the movements of his imagination. As soon as Rudyard Kipling no longer saw from his window little brown men walking light and sinister like carnivores in the molten Indian sunlight, but looked out instead on the pump and three geese on the village green, his mind refused to dance. It is long since Joseph Conrad left the sea, and his imagination no longer gets its rhythm from the storms. But the man in whose brain ideas circle upwards to the truth has the rhythm of their flight and the adventure of their quest perpetually within him. They are visitants that every artist must harbor if he wants to be permanently in communion with the mind of the world.

The history of literature proves abundantly that an idea is not a motive power that ought to be hidden behind an anecdote as an automobile engine is concealed by the bonnet. [Miguel de Cervantes's] *Don Quixote* [1605, 1615] as frankly and exclusively discusses an idea comically as [Feodor Dostoevsky's] *The Brothers Karamazov* [1879-80] discusses one tragically. Indeed[,] the magic force of an idea depends upon its nakedness. [Émile] Zola and [Leo] Tolstoy were both men of the same epoch who sinned similarly against art and the flesh. Both men pinned life down on the board of realism as one pins down a butterfly, and did not see that thereby they deprived it of the movement which was its essence: the description of the race in [Tolstoy's] *Anna Karénina* [1873-76] is as chill a slab of death as the description of the garden in [Zola's] *La Faute de l'Abbé Mouret* [English translation, 1886]. Both men were not clean about love. There is hardly an affair of passion in the works of Zola which should not have been dealt with by the local sanitary authority. And it is an ironic revelation of Tolstoy's fitness to lead men back to simplicity that he had that shame of nakedness and the body that is found usually in the slum-dwellers who are the victims of the most complicated processes of civilization . . . .

It is plain that Mr. Wells writes about ideas because he is in love with the truth and not because he desires a richer kind of beauty. But this only means that, like all great beauty, like the wonder that emerges from the metaphysical speculation of [William Shakespeare's] *Hamlet* [1601] or the magic that is spun by Dostoevsky's moral discussions, the effect of *The Research Magnificent* is accidental. The people who sit in the great room of his story would seem to any other author compelled to failure by their association with Benham, that white-faced prig who will not look up from his papers. Very pleasantly would Mr. Henry James fill a story with the gleaming good breeding and silvery brightness of Benham's little mother, Lady Marayne, and indeed it is not so long since Mr. Wells himself approved the type in Lady Mary Justin.

Amanda his wife, the wild-haired Amanda of infinite delights, was right to give herself to a courtlier knight when Benham left her to pursue a cold idea. Yet when the torch of the intellect is thrust into the room these appearances melt and change. If aristocracy be our aim and if it means fineness and honesty, then this little woman who spends the wealth of the world on the decoration of her mean little body is an offense to the spirit; and Amanda, as hollow as a troll-woman, had behind her adventurousness so little of "that passion to get things together into one aristocratic aim, that restraint of purpose, that imperative to focus," that a man could stay by her only by the destruction of his soul. Benham, the white-faced prig, is a king pale with striving, and the papers in his hands reveal the magic secret of the world.

If we found that a something sits among the stars and does not know that he is God, does not know that the quaint little world he imagined on one idle day a million years ago was forced thereby into existence, and was even now spinning and dripping blood as it spins, how we would cry up the news to those unknowing ears! It is something as strange as this that Benham tells us. There is "an unseen kingship ruling the whole globe, a King Invisible, who is the Lord of Truth and all sane loyalty. There is the link of our order, the new knighthood, the new aristocracy . . . that must at last rule the earth. There is our Prince. He is in me, he is in you; he is latent in all mankind." Here at last is a temple for our homeless faiths, a place of beauty where we can satisfy the human instinct for high endeavors, a place of power where we compromise our ambition, the leadership of the world. And it has been revealed to us by the despised attribute, the intellect, which we are told should be taken from the hot grasp of the artist and left to the cold hands of the professor.

The Undying Fire (1919)

Keeping the Game Going:
The Re-Vision of Poe in Wells's
Later Fiction

Catherine Rainwater

ells's middle and later works expand the intertextual
dialogue with Poe's that Wells establishes in the early years. Corroborating
Harold Bloom's notion of aesthetic influence, the early works suggest Poe's
dominance over Wells's vision, while the middle and later works perhaps
demonstrate *re-vision* far more than emulation of his American predecessor's
art.[1] Indeed, one important difference between Poe's fiction and Wells's early
works sheds interesting light on the later development of Wells's thought about
Poe: the early works are not grounded within a coherent, articulated
cosmological system such as almost invariably informs Poe's art. Indeed, Poe's
fiction and some of his poetry cannot be adequately interpreted without
reference to this cosmology, most literally stated in his treatise, *Eureka* (1848).

Although Darwinian evolutionary theory underlies Wells's thought from the
beginning of his career, his early novels posit no particular cosmological system.
Eventually, though, Wells formulates his own system, different from Poe's yet
everywhere suggesting itself as a revision of Poe's. Such novels as *When the
Sleeper Wakes* (1899), *The Undying Fire* (1919), *Men Like Gods* (1923), *Mr.
Blettsworthy on Rampole Island* (1928), *The Croquet Player* (1936), and *All
Aboard for Ararat* (1940) suggest Wells's major transformation of the Poe
material, now conjoined with Freudian and Darwinian ideas, and altered by
Well's revisionary cast of mind that continually modified even his own ideas.[2]

Within the Neo-Platonic universe of Poe's creation, characters aspire toward
an ideal realm, which they "remember" as the place of the soul's origin; for Poe,
the human being shares no part in the creation of this unearthly realm. As the
narrator of Poe's "Ms. Found in a Bottle" declares, fearless of even "the most
hideous aspect of death": "It is evident that we are hurrying onwards to some
exciting knowledge—some never to be imparted secret, whose attainment is
destruction."[3] For Wells's characters, however, vague intimations of

"something" to be known or attained (recall Ponderevo in *Tono-Bungay*) lead to their vision of an earthly utopia, yet to be constructed through human will and language. Wells sees language and will as the means for *transforming* the mundane *into* the ideal, not, like Poe, for *transcending* the mundane *toward* the pre-existing ideal. Thus, increasingly in Wells's later works, language plays a liberating, redemptive role within human history, whereas for Poe, language itself is finally transcended in a supernal realm outside of history. Although for Poe, language is transcendentally instrumental, "the old familiar language of the world" (*Works* 4:2) is inadequate to express the vast, cosmic notions of his celestial beings in "The Conversation of Eiros and Charmion" (1839) and "The Power of Words" (1845).

Wells offers a similar argument in *Men Like Gods*, where his utopians communicate through mental telepathy, a highly evolved, perfected form of human language. In this and later works, language in the service of human will is the primary instrument of evolution if the will is constructive, or of devolution if the will is destructive. While both Poe and Wells entertain the same basic notions of what language can do, Wells over the years becomes more preoccupied with what language *ought* to do. His later Poe-influenced works appear to struggle desperately against the deceptive and uncontrollable potentialities of semiosis, whereas Poe's writings more often delight in the same. Apparently, only after Wells better understands his own relationship with Poe's cosmology, as well as his and Poe's resulting divergent attitudes toward language and will, does he begin to incorporate elements of Poe's cosmological system into his own later works. With this understanding come some of Wells's most innovative uses of Poe material.

Like Poe's cosmic dialogues, Wells's *The Undying Fire* opens in a celestial setting where heavenly beings converse on the principles of divine design. Wells's universe is sustained through a dialectic of power between God, representing order, stability and unity, and Satan, the "celestial raconteur," who introduces disorder, instability and uniqueness into the system. In a celestial "chess game," these two beings compete for control of human beings—the progeny of Job of Uz with whom Satan has a long-standing wager. He once predicted that "Job would lose faith in God and curse him."[4]

Job Huss, or "Mr. 'Uss," as his housekeeper calls him, is the human locus of the battle between God and Satan (who says Job represents "us"—humanity). A devoted teacher, Huss spends his life educating boys in the arts, sciences, and languages. Believing in divine order, he attempts to structure these boys' educational experiences in a manner humanly reflecting such order. However, as a middle-aged man, Mr. Huss has a crisis of faith. Satan precipitates this crisis which tests and revises Job's ideas about divine order. Afflicted by a series of tragedies and by what he believes to be cancer, Job nevertheless resists the temptation to despair, to "curse God and die." During his dark night of the soul he maintains belief in an "undying fire" in the hearts of humanity, but he significantly changes his notions about human responsibility and progress. Shocking his academic associates, Mr. Huss spends the hours before surgery explaining his new point of view, which includes many of Poe's notions transformed into Wellsian terms.

Huss believes that proper education can offset the potentially disastrous results of human self-interested action. Educating the individual to act responsibly for the common good includes instruction in languages and history, which can both be redemptive if properly understood within the context of a collective consciousness. Actions undertaken without collective consciousness, although they may appear worthwhile, are actually the masks of "Satanic" individualism. Huss cites the technological advances which produced the U-boat as examples of human progress at odds with the common good: "the marvel of these submarines is that they also torture and kill their own crews. They are miracles of short-sighted ingenuity for the common unprofitable reasonless destruction of Germans and their enemies. They are almost quintessential examples of the elaborate futility and horror into which partial ideas about life, combative and competitive ideas of life, thrust mankind" (*Works* 11:124).

Later, expounding upon the horror of death inside a U-boat, Huss declares: "the water does not come rushing in to drown them speedily . . . the water creeps in steadily and stealthily as the U-boat goes deeper and deeper. It is a process of slow and crushing submergence that has the cruel deliberation of some story by Edgar Allan Poe" (*Works* 11:133). Wells's reference to Poe here is not merely whimsical; Poe's works probably inspired Wells's symbol of the U-boat—a modern technological expression of the subterranean forces at work within the human psyche, collective and individual. These forces act destructively upon civilization. However, no Poe-like transcendence through such destruction occurs within Wells's world, but instead only "futility," "extinction" and waste.

Huss recovers from the operation (he does not have cancer, only a benign tumor—another variety of "subterranean" phenomena), but while unconscious he has a vision of an expanding and contracting universe resembling Poe's in *Eureka* and alternating between "Godly" periods of radiance and "Satanic" periods of darkness: "Was it [the darkness] a veil before the light, or did it not rather nest in the very heart of the light and spread itself out before the face of the light and spread itself and recede and again expand in a perpetual diastole and systole?" (*Works* 11:154). However, Mr. Huss does not awaken with faith in a post-apocalyptic life, but with faith in God as the "undying fire" in the heart. Wells's cosmological drama takes place on earth; and "God" and "Satan" are perhaps only human metaphors for features of the unfolding process.

Wells's revision of Poe's cosmological principles emphasizes the positive features of human development implied by the "undying fire" in the heart; this "fire" corresponds to the "expanding" phase of Poe's Eurekan universe and represents for Wells the quest for order, unity, and the collective good that is counterbalanced by "contracting," disorderly, "Satanic" phases. The "fire" is the godly impulse in human nature. Besides reinventing Poe's Eurekan cosmos, *The Undying Fire* also places Wells and Poe in a God-and-Satan relationship with regard to the composition of Wells's text itself. The first chapter of *The Undying Fire*, "The Prologue in Heaven," juxtaposes the Author of the universe, God, with the spoiler, Satan, who disrupts this universe. Their adversarial relationship suggests that between Wells, the author of the text which expresses utopian order, and Poe, another "raconteur" whose works deny such earthly utopian order, a similar struggle exists. Extrapolating from Bloom's theory of influence, one might infer that Poe's influential works stimulate in Wells a type of anxiety that erupts intertextually as a resistant force against the later writer's desired optimism.

Consider, for example, the roles of God and Satan in the "chess game" they play—within, incidentally, a Poe-like arabesque setting: "The vast pillars [of heaven] vanish into unfathomable darknesses, and the complicated curves and whorls of the decorations seem to have been traced by the flight of elemental particles" (*Works* 11: 3). In the game,

> The Ruler of the Universe creates the board, the pieces, and the rules; he makes all the moves; he may make as many moves as he likes whenever he likes; his antagonist, however, is permitted to introduce a slight inexplicable inaccuracy into each move, which necessitates further moves in correction. The Creator determines and conceals the aim of the game, and it is never clear whether the purpose of the adversary is to defeat or assist him in his unfathomable project. Apparently the adversary cannot win, but also he cannot lose so long as he can keep the game going. But he is concerned, it would seem, in preventing the development of any reasoned scheme in the game. (*Works* 11:5)

Read metapoetically as a commentary upon the intertextual "game" going on between writer and precursor, this passage describes Wells, the godly Author, who struggles for order and control in a text meant to contribute to the creation of an actual utopia; he is vexed by Poe, the "Satanic" predecessor-raconteur whose influence "spoil[s] the symmetry of [Wells's] universe," mires it in "history," and constantly reminds Wells of the "crawling monsters of the early sea," the "hairy beetle-browed and blood-stained" creatures who are the ancestors of humanity (*Works* 11:6, 7, 10). In other words, Poe attributes a dark and irrational psychology to humanity that Wells cannot quite dismiss and that works against the "reasoned scheme" of his collective utopia.

Wells's references to the U-boat, as well as to Job's tumor (like the U-boat, a subterranean destructive agent, similar to "quap" in *Tono-Bungay*), might also be read as intertextual markers of Poe's texts, submerged and exerting a subterranean, troublesome force within Wells's texts. Indeed, to see Poe's fiction as the "U-boat" or destructive subtext of Wells's fiction is to understand how Poe's Manichaean vision, attractive to Wells in his more deterministic early years, threatens always to break through and assert itself in Wells's vision.[5] Unable to believe in an afterlife as Poe apparently did, Wells instead affirms the possibility of human communal perfection, an ideal which Poe's metaphysics certainly contradicts. Wells's utopian argument is troubled by a "Satanic" or Poe-esque undercurrent which seems intent on introducing "a slight inexplicable inaccuracy into each [of Wells's] move[s]." Not surprising, then, is the dream-sequence chapter, "The Operation," which is rife with Poe-like passages and which breaks through the surface of the otherwise quite rational, objective narration to vex the system the text propounds.

Casting doubt on Job's utopian scheme is a dream in which he confronts Satan, who accuses him of speaking ignorantly and without authority: "*Who is this that darkeneth counsel by words without knowledge?*" (*Works* 11:153). Job begs God for true knowledge, but God does not verify Huss's millennial vision.

God leaves open the possibility of humankind's self-destruction. "'Leaving nothing?'" Job asks. "'Nothing,'" answers God. "'Nothing,' he echoed, and the word spread like a dark and darkening mask across the face of all things" (*Works* 11:160). Portending disaster, Huss's dream ends in a Poe-esque collapse of the universe:

> [I]t seemed to him that the whole universe began to move inward upon itself, faster and faster, until at last with an incredible haste it rushed together. He resisted this collapse in vain, and with a sense of overwhelmed effort. The white light of God and the whirling colours of the universe, the spaces between the stars—it was as if an unseen fist gripped them together. They rushed to one point as water in a clepsydra rushes to its hole. The whole universe became small, became a little thing, diminished to the size of a coin, of a spot, of a pinpoint, of one intense black mathematical point, and—vanished. (*Works* 11:160-61)

Although Wells's novel concludes optimistically—Huss's life improves—a subconscious recollection of the dream always troubles Job, just as a subtextual echo of Poe's metaphysics "troubles" the surface of Wells's narrative.

Besides works such as *The Undying Fire* that treat philosophical questions from a broad, even "celestial," perspective, Wells (like Poe) devised narratives that explore the point of view of the individual psyche within the cosmological process. Poe's stories about the dissolution of a single human mind usually conform to the cosmological myth set forth in *Eureka*. Wells likewise develops works such as *Mr. Blettsworthy on Rampole Island* that consider the fate of the solitary individual whose life unfolds within the larger process of collective destiny. *Blettsworthy* extends Wells's dialogue with the Poe material, but unlike Wells's early works that trace the dissolution of an individual mind within no particular cosmological scheme, this later novel insists that individual salvation lies within the human community—Wells's secular utopian equivalent to Poe's supernal realm.

Numerous echoes of *Pym* point to Poe's presence in Wells's thoughts as he wrote *Blettsworthy*, but a proposed advertisement written by Wells himself for the novel affords tangible evidence. In this ad, he refers to the novel's "fantastic events," which he considers as impossible to summarize as "a romance by Edgar Allan Poe."[6] Indeed, *Blettsworthy* is a Poe-esque romance, a study of the dialectic between imagination and actuality, dreaming and waking states, structure and chaos, flesh and spirit, appearances and reality. Like so many of Poe's writings, the work is also a study of human language and of individual personality.

Wells's Arnold Blettsworthy is like many of Poe's narrators who represent warring aspects of psyche struggling for dominance. He inherits his English father's love of method and mathematical precision as well as his Portuguese-Syrian mother's mystical nature and love of language. Aware of his dual sensibility, he admits: "I . . . subordinate reality to a gracious and ample use of language . . . am divided against myself . . . I add to . . . practical complexity, a liability to introspective enquiry."[7] When his mother dies (literally and figuratively in that his own "mystical" nature immediately atrophies), his father sends him to live with an uncle and aunt at Harrow Hoeward. Here Blettsworthy becomes extremely rational in contrast to his childhood years when he seemed to be "surrounded by shadowy and yet destructive powers and driven by impulses that could be as disastrous as they were uncontrollable" (17). However, after this Harrow Hoeward interlude, he reverts to a chaotic state of being, the serene "mask" disguising the "tornado" of existence falling away as he wonders whether "Arnold Blettsworthy" is "no better than the name and shell of a conflicting mass of selves" (55). Reminiscent of Poe's William Wilson, in whom vice and virtue allegorically battle, Wells's Blettsworthy embodies a war between flesh and spirit. In his early adulthood he discovers the "vile cellars" in his own foundation (54). The "breakdown" of his "will and memory" occurs in tandem with a bout of amnesia caused by an accident. A doctor prescribes a relaxing ocean voyage that, ironically, affords Blettsworthy no period of convalescence. Aboard the *Golden Lion*, a Poe-inspired symbolic equivalent of Blettsworthy himself, his sense of "dividedness" of self increases as the crew mutinies and the ship breaks up in a storm.

Quite early in the voyage and despite popular myths about the sea as "open space," Blettsworthy complains of the claustrophobic shipboard environment: "Water. An immeasurable quantity and extent of water about you and below, and wet and windy air above; these are the enormous and invisible walls of your . . . incarceration" (67). Seasick and feverish, he finds his world insubstantial and his rational hold on reality tenuous: "Was all this place no more than a collection of animated masks that looked like a friendly community? . . . Was I, too, anything more than a mask? I had yet to find humanity not only in the world about me but within" (92-93). In the process, Blettsworthy removes "mask" after "mask" to disclose "reality"—without and within—as Rampole Island, Wells's metaphor for self and civilization *dis-illusioned*.

The first "mask" to fall away is Blettsworthy's rational sense of self. Just as Poe in "Ms. Found in a Bottle" equates his narrator's self with the ghost ship he occupies, Wells in *Blettsworthy* links his protagonist with the *Golden Lion*. Blettsworthy's rational faculties falter as the ship's engines fall increasingly "out of tune." Finally, the engines fail, leaving the floating ship "at the mercy" of overwhelming waves "until it was like night under the smother" (106). As the *Golden Lion* founders for days on end, Blettsworthy watches the "wavewashed deck vanishing ever and again beneath swirling foam-marbled water" (107). Once he sees or thinks he sees a large shark on board (108). A series of such passages suggests overwhelming subterranean forces and anticipates the later scene of mutiny and murder recalling that in *Pym*. Pym, Blettsworthy, and the ships that represent them are at the mercy of upwelling, "uncontrollable" powers.

Mirroring his mental confusion, Blettsworthy's initially "explicit" narrative gradually becomes "vague and circumstantial" (57). He admits awakening one morning uncertain of whether he actually heard or dreamed he heard a gunshot. Knocked unconscious during a violent storm, he awakens once again to discover the ship aslant, significantly "down by the head" (110), not merely literally, but also figuratively. Already on the verge of rebellion before the storm, the men turn against the ship's "head," the "mad" captain. During the mutiny, the captain locks Blettsworthy in a closet.

The focus of Blettsworthy's rage, the old man is also a symbolic equivalent of the "madness" into which Blettsworthy lapses (and perhaps also of Poe, the precursor/father whose works underscore the threat—the irrational—to a Wellsian utopia). At the end of the novel, moreover, when Blettsworthy recovers his sanity, he learns of the captain's engagement in "submarine warfare," for Wells a symbolic expression of the collective madness of World War I.

Blettsworthy escapes the closet to find himself and the ship abandoned. He ends up playing the role of sacred lunatic among the "savages" on Rampole Island, modeled perhaps after Poe's Tsalal in *Pym*. He first beholds Rampole Island as a high rocky shore resembling a "clearish blue purple glass" with substantial rosy-pink patches and alabaster-like opaque white veins: "Light was taken into this mineral and reflected from within it as precious stones take in and reflect light . . . A jutting mass of rock in the shape of a woman . . . the Great Goddess" presides over the village itself, which sits in a "narrow gorge" (138). Like Pym's stay on Tsalal, Blettsworthy's stay here offers nothing in accord with the reality he has known. A Poe-esque, claustrophobic enclosure, the village (like the entire island) does not "fit in" with Blettsworthy's "scheme of known things" (145). Thus as he enters the gorge, he speculates that this experience might be death.

However, quite a surprise awaits Blettsworthy. There is no actual Rampole Island. He is in fact rescued from the hulk of the *Golden Lion*, placed in a hospital, and then in the custody of his nurse, Rowena (also the name of the second wife of the narrator in Poe's "Ligeia"—the fair-haired woman aligned with rational existence). Blettsworthy "awakens" in a Brooklyn apartment as a psychiatric patient who has "dreamed" Rampole Island. His concept of reality, shaken sufficiently within the dream, crumbles even further when he realizes how imagination may prevail over exterior phenomena. Indeed, Blettsworthy's experiences, both "real" and imaginary, extensively revise his notions of truth. He decides that Rampole Island is the true reality, and that civilization is merely a "mask" over the "ignoble stresses" of existence (239). Later, as a soldier in World War I, he grows even more convinced of the insanity of so-called civilized human beings.

Blettsworthy's experience forms the basis of his necessary *dis-illusionment*. On Rampole Island he sees only devolution; consequently, he upholds a pessimistic view of human development based on the behavior of the island's huge, destructive animals called the "megatheria." During a stay in the hospital as a wounded soldier, however, he reconsiders. The "aggressive Stoicism" of Lyulph Graves, a reformed old enemy, to some extent stirs Blettsworthy's faith in the possible redemption of the human race through clear language and collective will. Graves insists upon the "soul" and "will" that distinguish humankind from the megatheria. Although Graves's optimism never wholly frees Blettsworthy from his obsession with Rampole Island as reality, the fact that Graves has become an honest man wishing to rectify past injustices gives Blettsworthy moderate hope that, as Graves proclaims, "Rampole Island will pass away."

Typical of Wells's later works, in *Blettsworthy* language and will interrelate. Early in the novel, Blettsworthy becomes depressed at the vacuity of many human conversations. The fact that no communication necessarily occurs when people exchange words disturbs Blettsworthy profoundly. Later, aboard the wrecked *Golden Lion* Blettsworthy's distress is compounded when (reminiscent of Poe's "Ms. Found in a Bottle") he tosses bottled messages into the sea, and they merely float back to him. "I did not like that," he declares (125). Always bothered when his audience seems absent and his messages unreceived, Blettsworthy believes the mark of an ideal society is clear, simple, direct communication through language. (Such language might be as orderly and functional as the Euclidean geometry which so fascinates his rational self.) Only "savages," he contends, are "encumbered with symbolism, metaphor, metonymy, and elaborate falsifications" (147). However, since he considers Rampole Island to be reality, and since, divided against himself, he often "subordinate[s] reality to a gracious and ample use of language," such clarity must necessarily remain a dream of the future. In the present world, the baroque and arabesque capacities of language that Poe's works emphasize exert counterpressure against a willed, rational discourse; this fact, coupled with Wells's post-structuralist premonitions of "absence" in language, trap Wells within a difficult, if not "impossible dialectic" between Rampole Island and the land of *Men Like Gods* (where "language" is perfected in telepathy), just as Blettsworthy is trapped between his maternal, poetic heritage and his paternal, mathematical heritage.

In the meantime, Wells criticizes modern, particularly Freudian, psychology, which underestimates the positive role of the nonrational and the power of the individual's will within the collective process. For example, Blettsworthy's therapist, Dr. Minchett, sees his ideas about Rampole Island as an expression of pure pathology. He does not consider any of Blettsworthy's pessimistic notions to be valid insights into contemporary civilization. Blettsworthy, on the other hand, believes that all people must acknowledge the existence of Rampole Island if the world is to be improved. In Wells's view as in Poe's, however narcissistic the individual psyche may appear, it is nevertheless contained within a Manichaean cosmological process. But from the psychoanalytic point of view as expressed through Dr. Minchett, the breakdown of the individual mind bears no collective significance. Thus Minchett rejects Blettsworthy's idea that he discovered on Rampole Island any truth or "reality" beneath the illusions of civilization; for Minchett believes conventionally in those very illusions as reality, and his job is to convince his patients to believe the same. He insists that Rampole Island is merely a dark mental dwelling space for irrational fears and threatening evils. Through Minchett, Wells satirizes the psychoanalyst as simply another sort of dogmatist automatically rejecting notions not sanctioned by his system. As such, Minchett is no wiser than "Chit," Minchett's counterpart soothsayer in Blettsworthy's dream. Indeed, Chit speaks with a greater degree of Wellsian authority.

Chit, unlike Minchett, respects the role of dreamers, visionaries and "sacred lunatics," who may revitalize society with the unorthodox ideas they proclaim. Modern psychology, however, grants no validity to individual insights derived through madness. When Blettsworthy regains psychological equilibrium sufficient to function in society, he rejects Minchett's counsel. The "truths" his madness produced inform his philosophy of human progress as evolutionary or devolutionary depending upon the disposition of a collective will.

This novel suggests that between 1919, with *The Undying Fire*, and 1928, Wells managed to account for the evolutionary role of nonrationality within the overall reasoned "scheme" which he hoped would prevail in the future. Considering Wells's revised attitude toward nonrationality, one begins to appreciate some of the larger differences between *The Undying Fire* and *Blettsworthy*, which is finally even more transformative of Poe material than the earlier novel. In *The Undying Fire*, Job Huss cannot recall his dream, and his vision of the future is threatened by this virtual amnesia. He cannot recall God's warning and thus cannot use the dream to inform his philosophy and guide his actions. Blettsworthy, however, as a recovered amnesiac, consciously recalls his dream and develops a wiser, more mature optimism than Job Huss's. Such modified optimism prevails in a very late work, *All Aboard for Ararat*, in which Wells's vision of the universe as a constantly revisionary process is cast in Eurekan terms, allowing for irrational phases.

Blettsworthy transforms Wells's Poe-inspired subtext in still another way. If, at a textual level, *The Undying Fire* encodes a "battle" between writer and precursor, *Blettsworthy* moves this "battle" into a less combative phase. Not only has Wells philosophically solved the problem of the opposition between rationality and nonrationality, he has also narratively displayed this synthesis. In *Blettsworthy*, for example, Wells employs narrative strategies quite akin to those of Poe, as I have shown. The narrator is a "divided" self who goes through a series of increasingly irrational, fragmentary experiences culminating in a "storm," both physical and psychological. Each of the narrated chapters begins or ends with an apology for the gap in the information between chapters. Such gaps—caused by amnesia, fever, and illness—remind us of those in Poe's texts in which a narrator explains that no rational way exists to account for a series of bizarre, discontinuous events. In a story by Poe, no explanation of where the soul or psyche has journeyed can ever be forthcoming, because Poe's works locate such places completely outside the phenomenal realm. For Poe, the "gaps" must stand, and precisely these gaps deprive the reader of external, phenomenal standards for interpretation.[8] A reader is thus forced to "explain" events with regard to the narrator's relative insanity or unreliability. Psychological "truth" emerges from the stories, but not phenomenal "truth."

By contrast, Wells's *Blettsworthy* postulates no otherworldly realm which the soul visits but cannot describe. The narrator's inner life or psychological experiences take place within a mental reality granted phenomenal status by the author; that is, if "Rampole Island is reality," then human society is underlaid with a primitive psycho-history accessible to consciousness, just as physical reality is underlaid with fossils accessible to human investigation (a notion contradicting the Freudian theory of the unconscious, and literally stated in archaeological tropes in *The Croquet Player*). Such evolved consciousness is a prologue to the imaginative, willed transformation of the world. Through Blettsworthy's narrative Wells implies that one never (as in Poe) escapes the world but always acts within and upon it—for better or worse. Blettsworthy dreams that he actually visits Rampole Island, but on awakening he recognizes the architecture of the apartment as spatially corresponding to the Rampole Island environment.

Blettsworthy has not escaped or transcended phenomenal reality but, like Job Huss, has perhaps "seen round a metaphysical corner" (*Works*, 11: 169) and remembers his vision. Neither has he escaped "metonymy," one of the devices of language he disdains as "savage" and imprecise. In fact, Wells's text metonymically evokes Poe's texts through a complex matrix of indirect allusions, just as Poe's texts often metonymically evoke his own metapoetical cosmology. Indeed, Wells's intertextual metonymy leads to a truly collective artistic vision. Responding to and revising Poe material, Wells's art points toward a collective textuality which shapes and is shaped by every individual artist. Wells's works anticipate the postmodern view of all language as metonymy and, consequently, of every literary work as an intertextual event.

NOTES

1. See Harold Bloom, *The Anxiety of Influence: A Theory of Poetry* (New York: Oxford University Press, 1973); and "The Breaking of Form," in *Deconstruction and Criticism*, eds. Harold Bloom, et al. (New York: Continuum, 1979), pp. 217-53.

2. On Wells's revisionary practices, see William J. Scheick, *The Splintering Frame: The Later Fiction of H. G. Wells* (Victoria, B.C.: University of Victoria English Literary Studies, 1984).

3. Edward H. Davidson describes Poe's "destructive transcendence" in *Poe: A Critical Study* (Cambridge: Harvard University Press, 1957). See especially his discussion of *Pym* (176-77).

4. H. G. Wells, *The Works of H. G. Wells* (New York: Scribner's, 1924), 11: 8. Subsequent references to Wells's works, unless otherwise specified, will be to this Atlantic Edition, cited as *Works* in parentheses with volume and page numbers. [Vols. 1-4, 1924; 5-14, 1925; 15-22, 1926; 23-28, 1927.]

5. Bernard Bergonzi's *The Early Works of H. G. Wells* (Manchester: Manchester University Press, 1961) argues that Wells's early works represent human development as basically devolutionary.

6. Permission to quote this passage has been granted by the Harry Ransom Humanities Research Center, The University of Texas at Austin.

7. H. G. Wells, *Mr. Blettsworthy on Rampole Island* (London: Ernest Benn, 1928), p. 11. Subsequent references to this novel are cited parenthetically in the text.

8. See Joseph J. Moldenhauer, "Murder as a Fine Art: Basic Connections Between Poe's Aesthetics, Psychology, and Moral Vision," *Publications of the Modern Language Association* 83 (1968):284-97.

The Outline of History (1920)

Ellen Glasgow's Outline of History in *The Shadowy Third and Other Stories*

Catherine Rainwater

> I was conscious of an inner struggle,
> as if opposing angels warred somewhere in the
> depths of my being.
>
> "The Shadowy Third"

 n several letters in her autobiography, *The Woman Within* (1954), Ellen Glasgow mentions reading the works of Poe and Wells.[1] In contemplating these two authors' works, she joined what has now become a wide network of writers whose art bears complex intertextual connections centering around a mutual literary debt to Poe and, frequently, also to one another.[2] Glasgow admits to feeling a "curious . . . kinship with Poe,"[3] and although she calls Wells's novels "dull" (*WW* 203), she owned at least five of them along with an early edition of *The Outline of History* (1920). Apparently, she found the *Outline* intriguing enough to consult in more than one of its many versions.[4] Glasgow's well-known fascination with Darwin might partly account for her interest in Wells's ideas about history, for *Outline* is firmly rooted in Darwinian evolutionary theory. This same interest in Darwinian concepts and their social and philosophical applications might also partially explain her homage to Poe in several short stories published between 1916 and 1923 and collected as *The Shadowy Third and Other Stories* (1923). Although Poe is a pre-Darwinian writer, his works anticipate important, if not biologically based, questions about human evolution and devolution, and about the existence of primitive, irrational depths beneath the surface of civilized society.

Glasgow wrote these Gothic stories suggesting Poe's and Wells's influence during the years immediately surrounding the end of the first World War—a time when Wells claims that "everyone" was in some way or another "outlining" history in response to global conditions.[5] The tales attest to her efforts to account for the shape of things past and things to come, efforts more typically registered throughout her career in numerous realistic novels. Although Glasgow suffered extreme emotional ups and downs throughout her life, several critics and Glasgow herself have observed that the years between 1910 and 1925 marked a critical period of hesitation, reassessment, and redirection of her artistic energies.[6] She wrote short stories at this time, argues Richard K. Meeker, because she had temporarily lost a sense of a "comprehensive view of life . . . Her writings . . . contain increasing references to a world gone mad, uncivilized barbarians, and ugly deviations from human decency . . . It became increasingly hard for her to write on a large scale, to trace the causes and effects that had so fascinated her" in her earlier works.[7]

Indeed, Glasgow's preface to *Barren Ground* (1925) reports a period of "tragedy" and "defeat" from which she claims to have emerged during the composition of this novel. Dismissing most of her previous work as "thin" and "two-dimensional," Glasgow declares that with *Barren Ground* she has arrived at a "turning point" in her life, and that she can now write as she had always intended to write—"of the South, not sentimentally, as a conquered province, but dispassionately, as a part of the larger world"; and "of human nature" rather than "Southern characteristics." She is sure that "different and better work is ahead."[8] Glasgow's sense of the "large scale" and her "comprehensive view of life" had returned along with renewed confidence in "trac[ing] . . . causes and effects" in history.

Despite this renewed confidence, Glasgow never develops any systematic outline of history (indeed, she seems finally to agree with Wells that progress is the tentative result of "Will feeling about"[9]); however, her ghost stories that address history reveal the characteristically dialectical pattern of her thought as she struggled to attain a sense of a universal pattern grounded upon some reliable authority.[10] Between 1916 and 1923, when most of the pieces in *The Shadowy Third and Other Stories* were written and published, the ideas of Poe and Wells (in *The Outline of History*, at least) apparently served Glasgow as thesis and antithesis in the dialectical development of her own view of historical progress. All of the stories imply Glasgow's internalization of a Poe-esque vision coalescent with her own sense of a mad "world . . . [of] uncivilized barbarians, and ugly deviations from human decency," while the1923 stories suggest the substantial role that Wells's *Outline* might have played in her development of a "comprehensive view" of it all. Indeed, Poe and Wells might be seen as "opposing angels" that "warred somewhere in the depths of [her] being"[11] for control of Glasgow's sense of historical design.

The stories in *The Shadowy Third* intertextually connect with Poe's in several ways: at least two—"Dare's Gift" (1917) and "Jordan's End" (1923)—allude overtly to Poe through their use of proper names, and three others strongly suggest Poe's presence in Glasgow's imagination as she wrote. Nearly all exhibit Poe-esque narrative management and, thereby, imply a Poe-inspired worldview with important implications for Glasgow's theory of history. Finally, Glasgow's stories reveal her sympathy with the Southern antebellum ethos of Poe's work, however displaced his regional concerns might be into ostensibly ahistorical contexts.[12] Glasgow seems, on the one hand, to internalize Poe's fearful vision of a dystopian, devolutionary world and, on the other hand, to resist this vision by adopting a typically Wellsian, tentative faith in a better possible future. In fact, we might borrow the trope of a contracting-expanding universe from Poe's *Eureka* (1848) to identify the bipolar phases of Glasgow's thought that are inscribed in the stories comprising *The Shadowy Third*. It is interesting to note that Wells himself went through similar alternating periods of dystopian fears and utopian hopes, and that he transforms this same trope from *Eureka* into his own theory of "systolic" and "diastolic" phases of human development.[13] In her Poe-esque devolutionary, or contractile phase, Glasgow imagines history as a claustrophobic "web" of "destiny," while in her Wellsian, expansive frame of mind, she envisions history as a "spiral" of slow progress.[14]

Though a few other critics have, mostly in passing, remarked Glasgow's literary debt to Poe, none have adequately assessed what Glasgow apparently learned from her predecessor about the subtleties of narrative management and about the worldview that he implies through the dubious claims and judgments of his prototypically unreliable narrators.[15] Glasgow's "The Shadowy Third" (1916) is a case in point. Like most of the stories in the collection, it features a first-person narrator whose credibility dwindles in a decidedly Poe-esque fashion as the details of her narrative unfold. Young and infatuated with Roland Maradick, the charming physician who hires her to tend his ailing wife, Glasgow's narrator has a marked "imagination" and admits that she would "have made a better novelist than a nurse" (5). In the Poe tradition of such deluded, vengeful narrators as appear in "The Tell-Tale Heart" (1843) and "A Cask of Amontillado" (1846), Margaret Randolph might in fact be guilty of murdering a man whose sins against her (and others) perhaps exist only in her mind.

Though some evidence in the story suggests that Maradick himself might be a murderer, the Poe-esque unreliability of the narrator precludes the reader's final judgment of him. Subtle hints of the narrator's suppressed animosity toward the physician appear early in the tale: "I am not the first nurse to grow love-sick about a doctor who never gave her a thought" (7); and "my worship [of him] . . . was a small thing, heaven knows, to flatter his vanity . . . but to some men no tribute is too insignificant to give pleasure" (14). From the outset, the narrator has mixed motives for believing Mrs. Maradick's story of her husband's evil designs; perhaps the wife's charges are based on fact, or perhaps the narrator decides to believe the story that "nobody [else] believes" (20) because of Dr. Maradick's indifference to her "worship."

Additional clues to the narrator's less than objective state of mind include her self-proclaimed psychic "sensitivity" that she boasts of, then denies in an appeal to the reader's credulity: she claims to see beyond the "web of material fact . . . [to] the spiritual form . . . [Unlike other people's], my vision was not blinded by the clay through which I looked" (35). Yet she contradictorily declares, "I am writing down the things I actually saw, and I repeat that I have never had the slightest twist in the direction of the miraculous" (31). Such direct solicitation of the reader's confidence in a self-incriminating narrator's inconsistent account of events is a favorite technique of Poe, who uses it over and over again in such stories as "The Fall of the House of Usher" (1839), "Ligeia" (1838), and "The Tell-Tale Heart."

Frequently insisting upon her own veracity, the narrator also reveals, "I was conscious of an inner struggle, as if opposing angels warred somewhere in the depths of my being. When at last I made my decision [to defy Dr. Maradick's orders], I was acting less from reason, I knew, than in obedience to the pressure of some secret current of thought" (27). This "secret current of thought" overrides common sense and logic. Recalling the narrator in "The Fall of the House of Usher," who unquestioningly accepts Roderick's bizarre explanation for secretly burying his twin in the vault, Margaret avoids asking important questions at crucial moments. She seeks no answers to confirm or deny suspicions about what seems to go on in the house, but instead she grows more confident of her "secret" knowledge. Like the narcissistic Mrs. Maradick (who stagnates within the enclosed psychological space of her self, symbolized by her haunted house), the narrator perversely refuses to look beyond her self-validated, intuitive knowledge to the outside world for corroboration of her suspicions.

Indeed, like Poe's "A Cask of Amontillado," Glasgow's story ends with what might be interpreted as a smug confession, a "signature" to an artful act of murder committed by a narcissistic, self-deluded narrator. Margaret tells us that one night as the doctor descended the stairs,

> I distinctly saw—I will swear to this on my deathbed—a child's skipping rope lying loosely coiled, as if it had been dropped from a careless little hand, in the bend of the staircase. With a spring I had reached the electric button, flooding the hall with light; but as I did so, while my arm was still outstretched behind me, I heard the [doctor's] humming voice change to a cry of surprise or terror, and the figure on the staircase tripped heavily and stumbled with groping hands into emptiness . . . Something—it may have been, as the world believes, a misstep in the dimness, or it may have been, as I am ready to bear witness, an invisible judgment—something had killed him at the very moment when he most wanted to live. (43)

This ending leads to at least two possible conclusions, one supernatural and the other natural: (1) the ghost of Maradick's allegedly murdered stepdaughter has left the rope on the stair; or (2) the narrator herself has done it, ostensibly to avenge the murders of the girl and her mother but also to punish the object of her unrequited love, who is soon to marry another woman. Obviously, "the world believes" Dr. Maradick's fall was an accident, while the narrator insists that "an invisible judgment" struck him down. That such judgment might be her own is implied in the "invisible warning" that she receives earlier—"a current of thought . . . beat from the air around into my brain. Though it cost me my career as a nurse and my reputation for sanity, I knew that I must obey that invisible warning" of Dr. Maradick's evil plot against his wife (33).

The narrator's behavior seems even more strange when Mrs. Maradick finally dies; despite her firm belief in the doctor's guilt, the narrator does not leave his house. She stays on to work for him and, eventually, she decides for no apparent reason that he must be completely innocent, after all. Just when he stands "clear and splendid" in her "verdict of him" (37), she learns that he plans to marry a woman who once rejected him because he was poor. Suddenly, all the rumors of Maradick's plot to inherit his dead wife's fortune seem plausible again. Either jealousy or some ultimate revelation of Maradick's true evil sparks the narrator's return to her previous state of mind. She sees the ghost of the little girl again and, eventually, Maradick ends up dead at the foot of the stairs— whether by accident or by design, the reader can never know for sure.

Like most of Poe's own stories, Glasgow's "The Shadowy Third" reveals little if any *overt* concern with history. However, also like many of Poe's works, Glasgow's story supports an allegorical reading of its implications for a view of history. Several critics have observed that Poe's dystopian tales reveal not only his anxiety over national conditions presaging the Civil War, but also his discomfort as an artist and a citizen in a country without a clear sense of national identity rooted in a distinct heritage. "The Fall of the House of Usher," in particular, can be read as a commentary upon the death of a Southern agrarian aristocracy that is out of step with the progressive, urban, industrialized North.

A significant historical context is implied in "The Shadowy Third" in Glasgow's identification of her narrator (Margaret) and Mrs. Maradick with the South, and of Roland Maradick and the setting of the story with the North. The story takes place in New York, but the narrator recently comes from Virginia, and Mrs. Maradick's mother was from South Carolina. The narrator and Maradick's wife are romantic and otherworldly, and both are trapped in the "web" of a dead past. The ailing Mrs. Maradick refuses to leave the house where she was born and where she claims to see the ghost of her dead daughter. Even her fortune constitutes a constraining past; she inherited it from her dead first husband, whose will imposed limits on her disposal of it. The narrator is similarly unable to free herself from the past and appears compelled—like a Poe narrator—to return to it in telling her story.[16] Maradick, on the other hand, is Northern and the controller of both women's "destiny" (6) in the same way that the nation—reconstructed according to terms of the victorious North—controls the destiny as well as the "wealth" of the former Confederacy. As soon as his wife dies, he sells her house to developers who plan to raze it and build modern apartments. The character of Maradick also seems to suggest allegorically the overall evolutionary pattern of human history. In one passage, the narrator describes his "coat of dark fur" (6), a particularly interesting observation given Glasgow's consistent preoccupation with Darwinian evolution. Maradick, wearing the dark coat of an animal, embodies not only the urban industrial future (the "barbarian" aspect of modernity that Glasgow dreaded), but also the bestial evolutionary past.   Indeed, the narrator's attraction to him is fundamentally an "animal" attraction to his "shining dark" eyes, the "dusky glow in his face," and the sound of his voice.[17]

This passage resonates with another passage in a later story, "The Difference" (1923), in which the evolutionary past is evoked through a Poe-esque image of the "skeleton of the savage" that lies "beneath the civilization of the ages" (229). Poe's description of Usher's house evokes the archetypal image of a death's head and suggests the nonrational dimensions of mind that rationality masks; the image of the skull-beneath-the-veneer-of-civilization is one that Glasgow doubtless also encountered in her reading of Darwin's *Descent of Man* (1871) as well as in the Darwinian vernacular wisdom of her era.[18]

Both "The Shadowy Third" and "The Difference" imply that Glasgow's interest in Poe coalesced with her Darwinian notions of human history.

"Dare's Gift" (1917) is another story with an intertextual relationship to Poe's fiction; furthermore, it is overtly concerned with history, particularly of the South. Richard Meeker has outlined some of the more obviously Poe-esque traits of plot and setting in "Dare's Gift." For example, "Roderick" is the name of the original owner of the ancestral estate. The "house was of great age " (49), and upon close scrutiny, it reveals "architectural absurdities—wanton excrescences . . . The rooms appeared cramped and poorly lighted" (61). The windows appear to be "staring" (63), and a reddish glow surrounds Dare's Gift, recalling the "red litten" windows of Usher's house. Furthermore, a Poe-esque "vegetable sentience" prevails in the house over the rationality and individual will of its inhabitants.

The less obvious features of Glasgow's debt to Poe in this story have gone unremarked, however. Her tale of a haunted mansion implies a claustrophobic view of human history as an unbreakable mold delimiting thought and action. Glasgow's post-Civil-War South is enslaved to a past ideal, according to Dr. Lakeby:

> In every age one ideal enthralls the imagination of mankind; it is in the air; it subjugates the will; it enchants the emotions. Well, in the South fifty years ago this ideal was patriotism; and the passion of patriotism, which bloomed like some red flower, the flower of carnage, over the land, had grown in Lucy Dare's soul into an exotic blossom. (91-92)

Lucy's house, called Dare's Gift, is literally steeped in the history of Virginia. From its first owner's purported betrayal of Nathaniel Bacon (in Bacon's Rebellion), to Lucy Dare's betrayal to the Confederates of her Yankee sweetheart, to Mildred Beckwith's betrayal of her husband (the first narrator) to his legal adversaries, the house exerts a sinister power over its inhabitants, who grow "feverish" and "excited" by their sometimes perverse notions of patriotism the longer they remain on the estate.

Like Roderick Usher, who cannot escape the fate that has befallen his ancestral house, the various descendants of Sir Roderick, such as Lucy Dare and other owners of Dare's Gift, are trapped within an historical pattern that compulsively repeats itself, partially owing to their lack of perspective on the past which the house embodies. Poe's Roderick Usher apparently cannot leave his terrible house; so he summons his analytical friend (from the past) to help him.[19] Instead of helping Roderick, however, the narrator succumbs to the deranging influences of the estate. Like Poe's story, Glasgow's underscores the circularly repetitive and irrational power of the past embodied in a house.

This circularly repetitive historical pattern in "Dare's Gift" is emphasized by Glasgow's narrative structure. She uses a Chinese-box arrangement of stories within stories to suggest that storytelling itself might be one of the ways in which human beings attempt to extricate themselves from historically repetitive patterns. However, Glasgow's narrator resembles Poe's in "The Fall of the House of Usher," who ends up mired in Roderick's history and in need of an audience to listen to his admittedly fantastic tale, presumably to help him, in turn, get some kind of perspective. Glasgow's outermost narrator and latest owner of Dare's Gift, Harold Beckwith, includes old Dr. Lakeby's story within his own in an effort to reach back, through Lakeby's memory, to get a "clear perspective" (47) on his situation. However, nestled inside of Lakeby's narration lies the implacable silence of Lucy Dare, an "ethereal" and "unearthly" (82, 83), Poe-esque woman who no longer remembers her past at Dare's Gift and who, in any case, was "never much of a talker" (103). Ultimately, Beckwith is left with no "clear perspective," but only Lakeby's observation that

> [w]e nibble at the edges of the mystery, and the great Reality—the Incomprehensible—is still untouched, undiscovered. It unfolds hour by hour, day by day, creating, enslaving, killing us, while we painfully gnaw off--what? A crumb or two, a grain from that vastness which envelops us, which remains impenetrable—. (79)[20]

Both 'The Shadowy Third" and "Dare's Gift" end on a note of stagnation, an acceptance of a suffocating, dystopian world of insanity or hollow capitulation to the past. The narrator of "The Shadowy Third" needs to tell her story ten years later, perhaps to find the ever-elusive "perspective." Beckwith and Lakeby in "Dare's Gift," who attempt to tell their story, circle about Lucy's silence and the impenetrable mystery of the house. Like the narrator of "The Shadowy Third," the narrator of "Dare's Gift" opens with a frustrated remark concerning past events that he has yet to comprehend in full: a "year has passed, and I am beginning to ask myself if the thing actually happened" (47). As compulsively as any of Poe's narrators, he engages in a sort of narrative exorcism, as if reciting the past could relieve him of the burden it constitutes.[21]

In "The Shadowy Third" and "Dare's Gift," Glasgow implies that the past is a trap in which we may be caught without comprehension or means of escape. Though she innately resembles both Poe and Wells in her battle with alternating idealism and pessimis,[22] the early stories in Glasgow's collection suggest her particular sensitivity to Poe's dystopian fears (a frame of mind in which, likewise, Wells sometimes found himself.)[23] The stories dated 1923, however, suggest a guardedly optimistic expansion of her thought within the Wellsian frame of reference reflected in *The Outline of History*. These later stories suggest that limited transcendence of ostensibly closed personal spheres—the self, the South—is possible; Glasgow was perhaps affected by Wells's hope for a world synthesis based on tentative notions of will and progress. Indeed, in two of her 1923 stories, the "webs" and "circles" of the early works are replaced with the Wellsian trope of the "spiral" (an image that depicts the overarching pattern of historical evolution that Wells describes in the *Outline*) to represent this idea of tentative progress.[24]

Instead of frustrated efforts to gain an elusive "perspective," Glasgow's 1923 stories conclude with open-ended questions. These questions imply that the present need not be hopelessly constrained by the past, an idea that Glasgow's story called "The Past" (1920) states overtly and that her reading of Wells's *Outline* would certainly have reinforced. (In "The Past," the narrator describes the protagonist's "victory" as a result of "chang[ing] her thought of the past" [146].) As early as 1908, Wells had developed his well-known notion that history is essentially the record of life struggling towards consciousness and of "Will feeling about."[25] In the edition of the *Outline* that Glasgow owned, Wells writes: "[T]he history of our race for the last few thousand years is no more than a history of the development and succession of states of mind and acts arising out of them . . . [T]he world is full of physical evils, but there is this mental awakening to set against them" ([1920] 2:572). He goes on to say that the current era "rises to a crisis in the immense *interrogation* of today [emphasis mine] . . . History is and must always be no more than an account of beginnings . . . Life begins perpetually" (2:579, 594-595).

Wells's evolutionary view of human consciousness and history also stresses the gradual refinement of "free intelligence" as opposed to the atavistic mentality of the primitive past (1:262). This intelligence affords human will the power to modify the apparent designs of destiny. Eventually, according to Wells, all forms of self-serving individualism (greed, nationalism, etc.) will pass away because they are socially maladaptive; Wells's ultimate world synthesis is a secular Nirvana: "The teaching of history, as we are unfolding it in this book, is strictly in accordance with this teaching of Buddha . . . The study of biological progress . . . reveals . . . the merger of the narrow globe of the individual experience in a wider being . . . To forget oneself in greater interests is to escape from a prison" (1:423).

Glasgow's attraction to these and other ideas of Wells registers emphatically in her 1923 stories. "Whispering Leaves" and "Jordan's End," in particular, conclude with tentative hope for the future; literally, they end with a Wellsian brand of "interrogation" suggested by the narrators' questions. In "Whispering Leaves," Pelham and the narrator escape the prison of the past as represented by another Poe-esque, haunted family estate. The story ends with two questions inviting the reader to ponder the nature of the "reality" of the past: "Was [the experience with the ghost] a dream, after all? Was the only reality the fact that I held the child safe and unharmed in my arms?" (197). In "Jordan's End," a female protagonist anticipates and even hastens her freedom from the Jordans, her husband's congenitally insane family. This story seems designed deliberately to force the reader to ponder the same questions that the narrator must ask himself for the next thirty years: Did Judith "kill" her husband, and if she did, was it a morally defensible act? Glasgow's third story of 1923, "The Difference," is not literally a ghost story, but it may (like her ghost stories) be read as the record of a character's escape from the tyrannical influence of history. The main character exercises her will and ultimately frees herself of romantic illusions about her husband. Consequently, she is to some extent liberated from the constraining mold of traditional Southern womanhood.[26] The narrator remarks the "stagnant waters of [the husband's] mind and observes the wife's gaze pass "from his face" to the freedom implied by the "window beyond" (261).

Like most of the other stories in Glasgow's collection, "Whispering Leaves" suggests Poe's influence in its setting (on a remotely located and haunted ancestral mansion which the narrator approaches with some apprehension in the opening of the story) and in its use of the haunted house to represent claustrophobic, enclosed psychological space. However, this story breaks with the Poe tradition in several ways supporting my claim that Glasgow's later stories are marked by Wellsian optimism. First, the ancestral estate is deteriorated and haunted, but it is neither depressing nor frightening to the young female narrator. Indeed, she loves the enchanting songs of birds that she constantly hears, and the old black woman's ghost (Mammy Rhody) appears never to alarm her. Unlike Poe's narrators and unlike the unmoored narrators of "The Shadowy Third" and "Dare's Gift," the narrator of "Whispering Leaves" is reliable. Though she later wonders whether some part of her experience was "a dream" (197), she never gives the reader any reason to question her sanity or judgment, for she maintains a clear-minded skepticism toward her ghostly "hallucinations." A hardy pragmatist, she concludes her story by saying that whether or not the ghost was a dream, what matters is the "reality" of the empirical evidence of her experience (Pelham's miraculous escape from the fire).

"Whispering Leaves," like the other stories, contains an allegory of history. The house is "primitive" (170, 171), and its inhabitants never use lamps, only candles (181). Old Cousin Pelham remains locked within his primitive world in a state of "abnormal egoism" (176). Mammy, the ghost, represents a Wellsian idea of the past. The ghost bears a "secret" or a "message" (166, 172, 188, 197) for the narrator, just as the past bears its messages for the future; but the past, like Mammy's ghost, must pass away once its messages are imparted. Mammy Rhody, the "past," delivers the "future," little Pelham, into the safekeeping of the "present," the narrator. Pelham thus escapes his destiny as suggested by dilapidated family estate. Moreover, the house burns down in a kind of phoenix-rising-from-flames image at the end of the story and liberates Pell, "an unearthly flower of light," from the literal and figurative "darkness" of his origins (185).

In this story, Glasgow employs a "spiral" image associated with time, memory, and the partial transcendence of history. The narrator remarks her clear memory of the events of fifteen years ago: "I have not forgotten so much as the spiral pattern the Virginia creeper made on the pinkish white of the wall" (167). Moreover, the house has a spiral staircase, and at the end of the story, the ghostly face of Mammy Rhody disperses in "spirals of smoke" (197) as she and the boy, Pelham, are freed from Whispering Leaves. Though the word, "spiral," does not occur in Wells's *Outline*, the pattern of historical progress that he describes is, indeed, a spiral one. Like Wells, Glasgow employs this image in connection not only with the gradual evolution of humanity, but also with collective and individual memory. Glasgow doubtless would have observed in the *Outline* several of Wells's implicit and explicit references to the role of memory in tracing the "great lines upon which our affairs are moving" (2:580). Memory aids in the revision of ideas which, in turn, affect the design of a future that Wells hopes will be marked by selfless thought and action—the opposite of the "egoism" that he and Glasgow so abhor.

In "Whispering Leaves," the "abnormal egoism" of the old proprietor of the estate is implied in the type of flowers he favors—narcissus. By contrast (in what is probably a veiled allusion to Walt Whitman), the narrator tells us she prefers lilacs because they seem to hold "the secret of spring," or of new beginnings (169). Reinforcing the narrator's fondness for such new beginnings, the ending of the story marks a new beginning for everyone. The house has burned, Mammy Rhody's ghost is free, and little Pelham Blanton escapes not only the fire but also his circumscribed life at Whispering Leaves. Apparently, he and the narrator leave Virginia, and perhaps even the South altogether.

In "Jordan's End," another Poe-inspired house with a "sinister influence" (272) represents the tyranny of the past. Like the Ushers, the Jordan family is hereditarily mentally ill, perhaps as a consequence of inbreeding. Recalling Poe's narrator in "Usher," Glasgow's narrator obeys a summons to journey through a depressing landscape to the house of *Alan* Jordan (perhaps named for Poe and certainly a "Roderick Usher" type of character). A chthonic, ancient man called "Father Peterkin" joins the narrator along the road, and explains that the Jordans have "'run to seed'" (269) following the Civil War. Their dilapidated ancestral home reflects this history. As in "The Fall of the House of Usher," house and owner are one.

In contrast to the Jordans, Judith, Alan's wife, is a Poe-esque, "unearthly" beauty. The narrator describes her as "very tall, and so thin that her flesh seemed faintly luminous, as if an inward light pierced the transparent substance. It was the beauty, not of earth, but of . . . spirit" (273). Judith's exercise of what Wells might call "free intelligence" as opposed to blind obedience to traditional morality eventually frees her from the apparent prison into which she has married. She revises her future through an act of mercy killing that alters destiny, both the Jordans' and her own.

Like the house in "Whispering Leaves," the Jordan house has a spiral staircase (275). In a small room at the foot of it sit three old women—wives and widows of other deranged Jordan males. Dressed in black and silently knitting, these old women are an emblem of Fate (278-79). The narrator is appalled that one of the old women knits "an infant's sacque," an image suggesting the inevitable birth of more doomed Jordan descendants in the future, at least until Judith intervenes (282). In another room at the top of the spiral stairs sits Alan. Here in the upstairs room is the scene of Judith's mercy killing that liberates Alan into death and Judith into a future different from that which the old women foretell. Though Judith must ascend and descend these spiral stairs a few more times before the chains of history are completely broken (she has a son), she has changed the future through a carefully considered act that both she and Alan approved.

Because he must live with the knowledge of Judith's action, the narrator becomes the true focus of this story. He knows at the time of Alan's death that Judith administered an overdose of medication, but he chooses to ignore the empty bottle on the nightstand. He also knows that Judith plans one day to help her son, Benjamin, escape his fate in the same way, if necessary. Thirty years later, this narrator has abandoned medicine "for literature" (278); unlike the compulsive narrators of "The Shadowy Third" and "Dare's Gift," who narrate the past without "perspective" or comprehension, he tells his story as a complex, ethical "interrogation" of Judith's actions and of his complicity in them. In the end, he is left pondering, and inviting the reader to consider, the very questions that he refused to ask Judith. "I knew that the questions on my lips would never be uttered . . . The thing I feared most, standing there alone with her, was that some accident might solve the [apparent] mystery [of Alan's death] before I could escape" (290).

Together, Judith and the narrator have willed change, but the narrator worries over how and by what means they have intervened in destiny. As a physician-turned-storyteller, he believes he has found a better "outlet" for his "imagination" (278), perhaps in the instructive use of literature to pose questions about the future. The story poses profound ethical questions about the human design of the "new beginnings" that Glasgow contemplates throughout her works and that Wells extols in *The Outline of History* and in many of his novels. Though Glasgow does not necessarily disapprove of euthanasia, her treatment of the subject in *The Shadowy Third* reveals that she shares with Wells an obvious concern with the choices that humanity makes in designing the future. Indeed, she is careful to draw important distinctions between mercy-killing, committed in "A Point in Morals" (1899) and "Jordan's End" for, arguably, ethical reasons, and murder, committed in "The Shadowy Third" for perverse and self-serving ends.

Glasgow's autobiography suggests that she was interested enough in Wells's ideas in the *Outline* to peruse at least one of its post-1920 editions. In *The Woman Within* a quotation from the 1940 edition shows Glasgow returning to a passage in the *Outline* that must certainly have interested her when she read it during the twenties in a slightly different form. The passage concerns Buddhism, a subject that particularly appealed to Glasgow during the years when she wrote her short stories and that continued to interest her throughout her life. Wells's 1920 edition remarks that his evolutionary theory of "history . . . is strictly in accordance with [the] teaching of Buddha," and the 1940 edition powerfully reinforces this notion (1:423). Glasgow quotes the *Outline* of 1940, where Wells "has recently reminded us" that the

> fundamental teaching of Gautama, as it is now being made plain to us by the study of original sources, is clear and simple and in the closest harmony with modern ideas. It is beyond all dispute the achievement of one of the most penetrating intelligences the world has ever known . . . For Nirvana does not mean, as many people wrongly believe, extinction, but the extinction of the futile personal aims that necessarily make life base or pitiful or dreadful. Now here, surely, we have the completest analysis of the soul's peace. Every religion that is worth the name, every philosophy, warns us to lose ourselves in something greater than ourselves. 'Whosoever would save his life, shall lose it.' There is exactly the same lesson. (*WW* 174)[27]

In subsequent pages of her autobiography, Glasgow concurs with Wells on the need for historical transcendence of "personality" and individualism. Like Wells, she sees how "human nature" has, so far, impeded evolutionary progress toward an ideal state of being as exemplified by Buddha, Christ, and St. Francis of Assisi. Throughout history, she complains, such "radiance" has been "blotted out by . . . human nature" (175).

Glasgow's characters in her short stories do not transcend human nature, but the stories that suggest Glasgow's Wellsian frame of mind in the 1920's emphasize the possibility of a better future at the end of the expanding "spiral" of human evolution, whereas her earlier, Poe-inspired stories depict people ensnared in the "webs" of their own circumscribed personal interests and histories. Following the example of both Poe and Wells in their different ways, Glasgow apparently looked forward to the loss of the burden of self, including that portion of the burden comprised of delimiting history.

NOTES

1. See *The Woman Within* (New York: Hill and Wang, 1954), pp. 174 and 203; and *Letters of Ellen Glasgow*, ed. Blair Rouse (New York: Harcourt, Brace and Company, 1958), pp. 27, 35, and 352. Glasgow read and marked passages in Wells's *Outline of History*, which she owned. Carrington C. Tutwiler's *A Catalogue of the Library of Ellen Glasgow* (Charlottesville: Bibliographical Society of the University of Virginia, 1969) records her copy as a two-volume, 1921 Macmillan edition. However, the *National Union Catalog* shows no two-volume edition published by Macmillan in 1921. Perhaps Glasgow's copy was, instead, the 1920 edition. Unfortunately, the Alderman Library at the University of Virginia has not preserved the extensive library that Tutwiler (Glasgow's nephew) gave to them, so it is impossible to check the date on her copy. In any case, the parts of *Outline* that I refer to in this article as interesting to Glasgow appear in some form in the 1920 edition as well as in the 1930 and 1940 editions. Thus, it stands to reason that whether her own copy was a 1920 or 1921 version of the much revised *Outline*, it would have contained the ideas and passages to which I refer here.

2. Twentieth-century writers influenced by Poe are many. They include Wells, G. K. Chesterton, Vladimir Nabokov, Jorge Luis Borges, Paul Bowles, Charlotte Perkins Gilman, Richard Wright, and Theodore Dreiser, to name only a few. Moreover, these writers frequently also read and intertextually refer to one another. Chesterton, Nabokov, and Borges, for example, refer to Wells *and* Poe in their writings. For a thorough discussion of the Poe tradition, see my *Twentieth-Century Writers in the Poe Tradition: Wells, Nabokov, and Borges* (DAI 1982); my two essays on Poe and Wells reprinted in this volume; and my essay entitled, "'Sinister Overtones,' 'Terrible Phrases': Poe's Influence on Some Works of Paul Bowles," *Essays in Literature*, 11 (1984):253-266.

3. Rouse, p. 352.

4. She owned and marked passages in her own edition (see note 1 above), and she quotes directly from p. 395 of the 1940 Macmillan edition of *Outline* in *The Woman Within* (see p. 174).

5. H. G. Wells, *The Outline of History* (New York: Macmillan 1940), p. 2.

6. During this time, several family members died, her romantic relationship with Henry Anderson began and ended, and in 1918, she apparently attempted suicide, though the seriousness of the attempt is unclear. Her feelings about her work and her literary competitors (Cather, Wharton) were also a source of stress. On Ellen Glasgow's life, see E. Stanley Godbold, Jr., *Ellen Glasgow and the Woman Within* (Baton Rouge: Louisiana State University Press, 1972) and J. R. Raper, *Without Shelter: The Early Career of Ellen Glasgow* (Baton Rouge: Louisiana State University Press, 1971).

7. "Introduction," *The Collected Stories of Ellen Glasgow*, ed. Richard K. Meeker (Baton Rouge: Louisiana State University Press, 1963), p. 6. See also Rouse, p. 194, on Glasgow' ideas about the decline of American society.

8. Ellen Glasgow, *Barren Ground* (San Diego: Harcourt Brace Jovanovich, 1985), pp. vii-viii.

9. Wells uses this phrase or its equivalent in *Tono-Bungay* (1908), *The Undying Fire* (1919) and the various revised editions of *The Outline of History* .

10. Glasgow shares Wells's sense of human experience as a search characterized by trial and error.   On Glasgow's dialectical thought in this "search," see my "Consciousness, Gender and Animal Signs in Ellen Glasgow's *Barren Ground* and *Vein of Iron*," in *Ellen Glasgow: New Perspectives* ed. Dorothy Scura, special issue of *Tennessee Studies in Literature,* forthcoming; and "Narration as Pragmatism in Ellen Glasgow's *Barren Ground*," *American Literature,* 63 (1991):664-682. See also Raper's *Without Shelter*, pp. 2, 10-11; and "Invisible Things: The Short Stories of Ellen Glasgow," *Southern Literary Journal* , 9 (1977):66-90.

11. "The Shadowy Third," *The Shadowy Third and Other Stories* (Garden City: Doubleday, Page and Company, 1923), p. 27. Henceforth all references to stories in this volume are noted with page numbers in parentheses.

12. On Poe's historical consciousness, see Lewis P. Simpson, *The Brazen Face of History: Studies in the Literary Consciousness in America* (Baton Rouge: Louisiana State University Press, 1980), especially pp. 101-102; Louis D. Rubin, *The Edge of the Swamp: A Study of Literature and Society of the Old South* (Baton Rouge: Louisiana State University, 1989), esp. pp. 146-147; and Donald E. Pease, *Visionary Compacts: American Renaissance Writings in Cultural Context* (Madison: University of Wisconsin Press, 1987).   Despite some serious mistakes in factual and bibliographical data concerning Poe, Pease makes some insightful observations about Poe's historical awareness.

13. See my "Encounters with the "White Sphinx":
The Re-Vision of Poe in Wells's Later Fiction," reprinted in this volume.

14. Though Poe also uses a version of the spiral image—the vortex or whirlpool— he emphasizes contractile spiral motion to suggest transcendence of history through material destruction, whereas Wells uses an expanding spiral to suggest secular historical development.

15. Classical discussions of Poe's narrators include Darrel Abel's "A Key to the House of Usher," *University of Toronto Quarterly,* 18 (1949):176-85; James Gargano's "The Question of Poe's Narrators," *College English,* 25 (1963):177-81; and G. R. Thompson's "The Face in the Pool," *Poe Studies,* 5 (1972):16-21.

16. Wells develops a similarly compulsive set of narrators in *The Croquet Player* (1937), who must keep repeating what they see as a terrifying story. On *The Croquet Player* and narration, see William J. Scheick, The *Splintering Frame: The Later Fiction of H. G. Wells* (Victoria, B. C.: University of Victoria English Literary Studies, 1984). It is also interesting to note that the stories in *The Shadowy Third* and several of Glasgow's novels, such as *Barren Ground,* suggest that she shares with Wells (in *Outline*) the notion that the act of writing is connected with the gradual emergence and liberation of humanity into fuller consciousness.

17. Glasgow had not yet worked out her equation of animals and men that I explore in my "Consciousness, Gender and Animal Signs."

18. Both Wells and Glasgow use this skull image, with its source not only in Poe, but also in Darwin's *The Descent of Man, and Selection in Relation to Sex* (New York: A. L. Burt, 1871); especially pp. 191-192. This image occurs throughout Wells's *The Croquet Player* as well as *Mr. Blettsworthy on Rampole Island* (1928).

19. Many studies of Poe have by now remarked Poe's equation of the narrator with reason, Roderick with irrationality, etc. Many have also observed how the narrator's propensity for rational analysis in the opening of the story diminishes as he succumbs to Roderick's madness. Donald Pease notes in particular how Roderick's summons to the narrator involves a plea not only for rational analysis, but also for an audience to listen to his story and help him get free of the past.

20. Perhaps by an odd coincidence, this speech by Glasgow's character greatly resembles speeches by Wells's characters in such works as *Tono-Bungay* and *The Undying Fire*. See, for example, Ponderevo's concluding remarks in *Tono-Bungay*, cited in my article on Wells's early works included in this volume.

21. See Scheick on "exorcising the ghost story" in *The Splintering Frame*.

22. Indeed, this extreme vacillation between periods of idealism and pessimism seems to be the common characteristic of Poe, Wells, and Glasgow that accounts for the latter two's interest in Poe and for Glasgow's interest in Wells. On Glasgow's battle with idealism and pessimism, see my "Narration as Pragmatism."

23. On Wells's dystopian frame of mind, see Bernard Bergonzi, *The Early H. G. Wells* (Manchester, England: Manchester University Press, 1961). Bergonzi argues that Wells's early works reveal a concept of human development that is essentially devolutionary. See also my two other essays on Wells reprinted in this volume.

24. Poe's, Wells's, and Glasgow's sources of this spiral image are many, including Plato and the Romantics, and (for Wells and Glasgow) the Transcendentalists. Both Poe and Wells would also have served as a source for Glasgow's use of the image.

25. See note 9 above.

26. For feminist readings of the stories in *The Shadowy Third and Other Stories*, see "Visions of Female Community in Ellen Glasgow's Ghost Stories," *Haunting the House of Fiction: Feminist Perspectives on Ghost Stories by American Women*, eds. Lynette Carpenter and Wendy Kolmar (Knoxville: University of Tennessee Press, 1991), 117-141.

27. See Wells's *Outline* (New York: Macmillan,1920), pp. 422-423; see also the 1940 Macmillan edition, pp. 395-396.

The World of
William Clissold (1926)

Mr. Wells's New Novel

E. B. Osborn

ovels with prefaces that explain or excuse resemble the drawings of small children which bear such inscriptions as "This is a Cow." Just as the cow in a picture thus described is seldom obviously cow-like, so there is apt to be something lacking in a story that requires a Preface, even if—as almost always happens—it is an attack on the "insolent" or "indolent" reviewers.

In the Preface to the first volume (there are to be three in all), which is published to-day, of *The World of William Clissold*, by H. G. Wells, quite a number of distracting explanations, not to say excuses, are suddenly released. It reminds us of a story of a French entertainer with a troupe of nineteen kangaroos, who found to his disgust that there was a heavy duty on performing animals entering Bulgaria, where he hoped to have a profitable tour. However, his kangaroos were nicely graduated in size, and in order to bilk the Customs officials he caused the smallest beast to enter the pouch of the second smallest, which entered that of the third smallest, and so on until only the largest kangaroo of all remained visible to pay duty on.

The weather was hot, however, and the Customs people painfully slow—so that the poor, congested animal could not hold in her complex contents, and suddenly exploded, the whole landscape being filled with a flight of released kangaroos, to the terror and amazement of all the beholders. This insolent, indolent reviewer is both terrified and amazed at the multiplicity of questions, both great and small, suddenly let lose in Mr. H. G. Wells's Preface, and the ingenious author must try to forgive him [the reviewer] for dealing with only two or three of the larger ones.

Two of these questions "concern the treatment of opinion in works of fiction and what is called 'putting people into books.'" To take the second first, Mr. Wells claims that William Clissold, like all his [Wells's] other characters in this and previous novels, is a fictitious person. As to William Clissold, he says, "His views run very close at times—but not always—to the views his author has in his own person expressed; nevertheless, is it too much to ask that they should be treated here as his own?" To be brutally outspoken, it is far too much to ask. Of all living authors[,] Mr. Wells is the most of an egoist, and his varied and vivid self is the stuff, a sort of psychological plasticene, out of which his characters have been moulded from the first. He admits that there was never a character created by an imaginative author from the inside which did not contain the quite unavoidable element of self-projection. "Even Hamlet is believed to be a self-projection of Shakespeare."

But we are very sure that Mr. Wells has never yet realised the extent to which his characters, and the affairs—especially the love affairs—wherein they are involved, are autobiographical. He has lost nothing by the habit of pulling his emotions, and other people's emotions, up by the roots in order to make succulent salads for popular consumption. He is so profoundly interested in himself that the interest is contagious, and the general reader has been intrigued by all the Wellsian variants, from Kipps to Ann Veronica's lover, and so on.

For these and still other reasons, we cannot grant Mr. Wells's request, and we are compelled, on the contrary, to say that William Clissold is more like Mr. Wells than he is like himself. It is in vain that he introduces living personages into his book in order to throw us off the personal and peculiar scent, as of the attar of egoism. Dr. [Carl Gustav] Jung turns up and talks in a London flat. The {George Bernard} Shaw of the Eighties "blows" (Mr. Wells's word) into a Kensington evening, Mr. [John Maynard] Keynes lunches with Clissold, and Dean Inge is met at dinner. But—a fatal omission!—Mr. H. G. Wells never appears to make his bow to the pretty ladies, and "argue high and argue low, and also argue round about him." If, say, Noel Coward had been faced with this problem of camouflage[,] he would never have perpetrated such a deadly sin of omission.

There are symptoms of a story in the book, so far as it has gone, but it is not in the least interesting. The sad truth is that the arteries of Mr. Wells *qua* story-teller have become sociologised. The fate of Clissold's father—a financier, who suggests both Whittaker Wright and Horatio Bottomley in his career and lamentable ending—does not worry us in the least. Clementina, the light of love who flutters over the surface of Clissold's personality, is not substantial enough even to be a nuisance. There are clever bits of characterisation and descriptions, such as that of a Provençal *mas*, which are like glimpses of a novel that is a true drama in its dramatic setting. Mr. Wells has not lost his genius for making a picture in a phrase. But the book is really an orgy of opinions—what might perhaps be called an example of the novel of ideas, though the Shavian "discussion" is in some respects a better term.

"Is it not quite as much 'life' to meet and deal with a new idea as to meet and deal with a new lover?" The answer is in the negative; except for old men, thought can never have the poignant appeal of emotion. But the novel of ideas should attract thoughtful persons, provided the ideas are new. But the arguments and opinions here set forth are for the most part familiar to all the readers of the Wellsian treatises concerning all things in the Universe and a few others. For example, the old attacks on the orthodox conception of Deity are renewed in dissertations on the "two Mr. G.'s" (the other one is [Herbert]

Gladstone), and the scholar historian, who sifts the dust of circumstance scientifically, thus performing an indispensable service to all save a Gibbon of the tree-tops, is pulverised in the old, futile fashion.

In the discussion of Karl Marx and the new Socialism, however, Mr. Wells's opinions, as uttered through the Clissold gramophone, show a change of orientation. Evidently he is moving slowly but surely towards the Right, and if his present rate of progress is maintained, he will in almost five years become an unofficial member of the Conservative Party. He still calls himself a revolutionary, but the mildest Menshevik would refuse to accept him as such.

Meanwhile (1927)

Mr. H. G. Wells's Pamphlet Novel

Richard Jennings

he pamphlet novel . . . still commends itself to Mr. Wells. There is an interesting letter of his, somewhere in the correspondence of Henry James, in which he declares that he aspires to be a journalist, rather than a romance-writer. What a pity! For we already have a good many working journalists, expressing opinions, scattering views; we have only one living writer who can give us such books as *Kip[p]s*, *The Time Machine*, or *The Island of Dr. Moreau*. But, since Mr. Wells prefers, in these days, to be journalist and pamphleteer, we must submit. We bow our heads. It is his freedom of choice.

I had hopes for this new book [*Meanwhile: The Picture of a Lady*] when I read the sub-title, adapted from an early novel by that same Henry James. *The Picture of a Lady*!

What Lady?

She is the young, and at first very happily married, Mrs. Rylands[,] who lives in Italy, in one of those delightful villas that invite the immorality of indifference—make one forget all but the passing hour and the present beauty: if only one's visitors would permit such delicious oblivion. But young Mrs. Rylands is visited by two tiresome people.

One of them, Miss Puppy Clarges, disturbs the prevalent peace by having an "affair" with Mrs. Rylands's rich husband, Philip. And that is a grief, naturally, to the "lady." The other tiresome visitor is a long, ungainly Mr. Sempack, who comes to the villa in very much the talkative disposition as marked Mr. William Clissold—comes to talk about world-affairs, particularly, about progress.

Mr. Sempack regards progress as inevitable[,] and he lets everybody know about it. For him the scientific outlook, the efficiently organising intellect *must* in time get control, and suppress the wild violences and crude impulses of our life. I need say no more. I need not linger over the creed of Mr. Sempack, which is familiar, surely, to all students of the later optimistic Wells, who is so far removed on this point from the early pessimist of *The Time Machine*, as from the sceptic of *Tono-Bungay*.

Mr. Sempack believes. And, briefly, his argument seems to be that if you do *not* believe in the cleansing capacity of scientific and rational adaptations, what the deuce *are* you to believe in? Which, of course, is no argument at all. Why, having renounced belief in other obvious untruths, should you take to belief in another very doubtful truth?—for example, in the applied science which is just as likely to bring ruin as salvation upon humanity? This Mr. Sempack is a donkey.

But I will say one thing for him. He is human enough to allow himself to be kissed by a person called Lady Catherine in Mrs. Rylands's garden in Italy. Other things happen in that garden. A victim of Fascism hides there, for one thing, and Mrs. Rylands's attention is directed towards Fascism. But mainly one may say that what happens in Italy isn't nearly so important as what is happening contemporaneously in England.

Young Mr. Rylands (much ashamed of his naughtiness with Miss puppy Clarges) penitently leaves for London, and, influenced by Mr. Sempack's copiousness of utterance, proceeds to write a series of very long letters to his wife, who is about to make him a father. Philip Rylands writes, in fact, a frankly abusive History of the General Strike, for which he blames the Government—spelling it "Goverment" all the time. Philip undergoes a great awakening . . . .

Philip is, for a moment, Philip, a rather vague nobody much. But he has to be Mr. Wells's mouthpiece. Miraculously, and in an epistolary form, he grows more and more like Mr. Wells. He at any rate is no portrait, but a peg. His mental clothes don't fit him.

And the lady? Poor Mrs. Rylands! She is equally vague—a recipient, instead of a talker. Her mind is a sort of ready postbox for others' communications. We look all over the book for her true portrait.

H. G. Wells's and Henry James's Two Ladies

Janet Gabler-Hover

I cannot detect any mother fixation, any Oedipus complex or any of that stuff in my make up.
H. G. Wells[1]

Wells's promiscuity may be due to a mother-fixation.
Ingvald Raknem[2]

n his 1934 *Experiment in Autobiography*, H. G. Wells had this to say, among other things, about Henry James. "I bothered him," Wells remarks, "and he bothered me."[3] Most James and Wells critics follow Wells's lead in assuming that the quarrel between Wells and James was a result of their conflicting aesthetic theory.[4] Wells thought that art should be subordinated to its social message, while James responded that art "*makes* life." Wells had earlier written James, "To you literature like painting is an end, to me literature like architecture is a means, it has a use."[5]

Critics concur that Wells's commitment to social change caused him to espouse the discursive mode of the "Shandian novel" as opposed to "any more rigid form imposed on that accuracy."[6] An exhaustively complete and formal presentation of character, argued Wells, would close off the possibilities of depicting "impermanent realities" since "in a changing world there cannot be portraits without backgrounds, and the source of the shifting reflected light upon the face has to be shown."[7] Wells rejected James's conception of the "novel of completely consistent characterization arranged beautifully in a story and painted deep and round and solid" (*Experiment* 414) for a "splinter[ed] frame"; the exhortation of social ideas in fiction would undoubtedly include narrative meditations, shifts, and meanderings that would likely destabilize the formal coherence of the text and would put the development of social ideas before the development of characterization.[8] Wells not coincidentally calls his discussion of this in the autobiography a "*Digression* about novels" (410) [italics mine].

With Wells's commitment to social change in mind, one can easily see how Wells and James disagreed not only on the form and purpose of fiction, but also about its implicit ideological values. The formal structure implicit in history, stasis, and a world of social wealth line up on James's end, while future change and the destabilization of social classes and past privilege line up on the other. But there is a deeper level at work, I would argue, fueling their intensely felt antipathy. In commenting on his and James's conflicting theories of the novel, Wells, rather puzzled, admits, "I had a queer feeling that we were both incompatibly right" (*Experiment* 414).

One could plausibly argue that a psychological synonym for "queer" in this context is "uncanny." Two rightnesses—James's and Wells's two ways of looking at the world and of structuring their fiction according to this light—become uncanny when one way of looking at the world is found to be intensely threatening to someone else's. In consequence, one either denies or represses the threatening other, who is consequently experienced as uncanny. Another way to gloss Wells's use of "queer" is to address its sexual implications. At one point in his autobiography, Wells comments ruefully that James wanted his younger novelist acolytes to call him Cher Maitre (411). This patronizing endearment and Wells's resistance to it gain resonance in the context of *fin de siecle* sexual mores. Elaine Showalter notes that "queer" meant homosexual in English slang by 1900.[9] And *fin de siecle* sexual politics included "the late nineteenth-century upper-middle-class eroticization of working-class men as the ideal homosexual objects."[10] Of working-class origin, Wells conceived of James to represent the aristocratic elite; but Wells obviously wanted his readers to know that he never called James "Dear Master."

James may have either consciously or unconsciously made veiled sexual references to Wells in his correspondence about Wells's fiction, as we shall see. Less problematic is the fact that Wells and James shared some surprisingly similar family dynamics and some consequent attitudes about their sexuality that they chose to defend against in their lives and in their fiction in uncomfortably opposite ways. Undoubtedly, social concerns can be highly personal and constitutive of one's way of being in the world. But if we follow Wells's lead and assume that his quarrel with James's fiction was primarily ideological, I believe that we miss the more primary underlying basis for the uneasy linkage between Wells and James as well as for the antipathy they eventually expressed for each other's work. There is a level of psychological disturbance in exchanges between Wells and James; many of these exchanges are sexually evocative and highly charged with potential ambiguity.

Such disturbance is evident also in Wells's infamous indictment of James's fiction in a chapter of *Boon* (1913). But there is a more rarely acknowledged fictional treatment of Henry James that comes later in Wells's career with *Meanwhile: The Picture of a Lady* (1927). It has been recently observed that Wells probably meant his *Meanwhile* to respond to James's *Portrait of a Lady*,[11] and in fact a contemporary reviewer for *The Daily Mirror* assumed that Wells got the sub-title for *Meanwhile* from James's *Portrait*.[12]

Although I do not claim in this essay to study the work of either Wells or

James in a phenomenological sense that would account for their entire canon, I want to suggest that a fictional instance where one author consciously revises another provides a special case for the most emphatic dramatization of the differences between the two. These differences in *Portrait* and *Meanwhile* are most apparent on the level of narrative strategy: James and Wells "emplot"[13] or strategize their narratives defensively to mitigate against sexual anxiety. Consequently, James's and Wells's plots take exactly opposite turns. In *Meanwhile*, Wells's fictionalization of his social-utopian ideas includes an "exposure" of his own sexual promiscuity. How that exposure functions to ease Wells's anxiety I will attempt to explain later in this essay. As a counterpart to Wells's, James's fictionalization of sexuality in *Portrait* is more discrete and covert, also more rejecting. The one instance of sexual explicitness in the novel—Isabel's famous kiss with Caspar Goodwood—implies that sexuality is threatening and overwhelming. Other than that instance, sexuality in the novel seems "hidden" by the narrative presentation. It is worth noting, given this difference in Wells's and James's narrative strategy, that these very terms of exposure and retention figure insinuatingly and derisively in the criticisms that James and Wells level against each other in their correspondence (which will include *Boon* and Wells's autobiography since most of Wells's letters to James are not extant). This correspondence, once analyzed, provides a context for the discussion of the novels.

1

James and Wells corresponded with each other, publicly and privately, ostensibly *about* each other's fiction. But Wells and James also addressed each other's personal lives. Under the guise of good will and admiration on James's part and with a more candid critical tone on Wells's part, a kind of guerrilla warfare emerged. It should not be surprising that their discussion of each other's fiction was also so personal. Both authors sensed intuitively that their personalities were embedded in their fiction and that fiction writing was life survival.

The struggle that James underwent to individuate from his overwhelming family is generally known through Leon Edel's biography and other sources. Becoming a writer of fiction was his way of doing it.[14] Less generally known, except to his scholars, is Wells's desperate struggle to disentangle himself from his own family's paralyzing economic dynamics. Wells did this first by acquiring an education against enormous odds, and then he became a writer of fiction, which was lucrative for him, indeed.

The family dynamics of Wells and James share the presence in the life of each of a dominating and repressive mother. Both Henry and H. G. had to prove to doubting mothers that their fiction would secure them a living. James's mother managed the family through the fluctuating interest of her husband's annuity. Henry had a kind of credit balance with her early in his career when payments for his work went into his father's account. He felt the "maternal pressure" of proving his solvency to his mother.[15]

Wells's mother Sarah did not have the luxury of an income-sustaining husband. Her charming but dissolute husband excelled only in playing cricket. Not only did Wells loathe his mother's aristocratic pretensions for herself—she eventually ensconced herself as an ineffectual housekeeper at Lady Fetherstonhaugh's in Up Park—but he resented the narrow ambitions his mother forced upon his own life, although he conceded that "nearly every boy in the British lower and lower middle classes . . . were 'put to a trade' and bound" (*Experiment* 102). Wells gained his freedom at last when he left his apprenticeship as a draper early one morning and walked seventeen miles to Up Park to convince his mother he must pursue the financially assisted education that he had solicited for himself (*Experiment* 123). Anthony West reminisces that Sarah remained even at the end of her life "more convinced than ever that [his] father [was] riding for a fall."[16]

Freudian interpretation has encouraged critics to judge the effect on both Wells and James of their repressive mothers. There is a general critical argument since Edel that, according to the usual Freudian reading, Henry James became homosexual because "paternal ineffectuality and maternal oversolicitude" resulted in his "failure to bond with [his] father." James thus remained joined to the mother and desired "what she desire[d]: men."[17] It has been argued as well that H. G. Wells became promiscuous as a result of his relationship to his mother. Ingvald Raknem points out without her full endorsement that Wilfrid Lay made this suggestion in 1917, based on a claim that Wells's promiscuity indicated an "unconscious longing . . . to return to [his] mother."[18] I believe that it is potentially damaging to assume the Freudian thesis that James's homosexuality was linked to a dysfunctional relationship with his mother, for if we concede this, we implicitly suggest that homosexuality is a pathological behavior.[19] Whether, on the other hand, Wells unconsciously sought out a mother figure in his fiction, and whether he attempted to compensate for the type of mother that he had, will be one focus later in this discussion.

One can say that James and Wells shared a similar reticence about intimacy in relationships that can be tied at least in part to an overbearing parent.[20] It is also worth noting that both James and Wells had good reason during the *fin de siecle* to fear that the sexual habits of homosexuality or promiscuity could cause a scandal that might disrupt their highly public careers. A "culture of oppression" surrounded homosexuals in England during the nineteenth century.[21] James was certainly aware of this persecution. Wells, too, not only had many of his books censured because of his candid treatment of sexual promiscuity, but he was also aware that his own promiscuity could threaten his career. Amber Reeves's father, for example, made Wells's affair with his daughter "a scandal" from which Wells finally retreated into his marriage with Jane.[22]

While James kept sexuality covert in both his life and fiction, Wells elected to expose the sexual lifestyle he lived and wrote about. Wells's open exposure of his sexuality in his fiction apparently discomforted James immensely; this discomfort surfaces somewhat ambiguously in the letters that James wrote to Wells about his fiction. It would not be surprising if Wells *were* mortally offended by those letters, as his son Anthony suggests.[23] In James's patronizing offers to re-write Wells's books,[24] in his implicitly derisive descriptions of Wells's fiction in sexual terminology that I will discuss, and in his later more blatant criticism, James could have reminded Wells of Wells's critical and repressive mother.

If Wells knew of James's homosexuality, which his correspondence suggests to me that he may have, this might even more have been the case. Sarah Wells not only predicted throughout her life that her son's career might end in waste; she also "raise[d] the issue of sexual identification in the context of [her son's] childhood," according to Anthony West.[25]   Sarah had lost "her one sweet and tractable child, her Fanny, her little 'Possy.'"   "It is my conviction," wrote Wells, "that deep down in my mother's heart something was broken when my sister died two years and more before I was born" (*Experiment* 44). According to West, Sarah Wells caused gender confusion in her son early in his life by making him feel that he was betraying her by not being a girl. West recalls a photograph of his father at four dressed in a frock. He hastens to add that such feminization in dress was common at that time for boys under the age of five.[26]

The photograph, included in Wells's *Autobiography* (facing 22), is a powerful piece of iconography, nevertheless. The elder brother stands with his arm poised on H. G.'s shoulder, and H. G. sits on an ornate thronelike chair, looking very demure and very much like a girl in his frock.   If James "patronized [Wells] relentlessly"[27] and requested to be called the Master, positioning Wells in the role of an obedient girl; further, if James wrote in his correspondence to Wells in terms that even suggestively posited Wells as a sexual object, Wells might have perceived himself as gender marginalized by James's criticism, an impression exacerbated if James implicated Wells in his correspondence in a fantasized homosexual relation where James seemed to function as the male.

Wells and James apparently met in 1898. James shared with Wells the kind of correspondence about their fiction that James shared with other young writers, such as Joseph Conrad.   When Wells and his family moved to Spade House, Sandgate across from James's residence at Rye, Wells and James began to meet frequently, and the correspondence accelerated. James welcomed Wells as a "confrere," according to Leon Edel and Gordon Ray, while Wells felt an "underlying *malaise* which James's euphemisms and extensive propriety of manner had inspired in him."[28]   But those euphemisms and linguistic circumlocutions—the courtly salutations where James "beseeches" Wells to forgive him his tardy response, or spends several lengthy sentences baroquely discussing the honor that Wells has done him[29]—serve to confuse or obscure, even render an *apologia* for, James's epistolary likening of the reading of Wells's fiction to a sexual experience.

In one letter, for example, James likens reading Wells's *Anticipations* to sexual ravishment: "The right hour came, and I gave myself up—utterly, admirably, up—to the charm; but the charm, on its side, left me so spent, as it were, with saturation, that I had scarce pulled myself round before the complications of Xmas set in." James discloses that reading Wells kept him from the duty of his New Year's correspondence; yet his description of the aftermath of reading implies the kind of guilt, rather, that might accompany a sexual act of self-gratification: "And then I was ashamed—and I'm ashamed still. That is the penalty of vice—one's shame disqualifies one for the company of virtue. Yet, all this time, I've taken the greatest pleasure in my still throbbing and responding sense of the book."[30]

If Wells perceived, consciously or unconsciously, that there was *this* sort of sexual nuance in James's correspondence, even on the level of play, it would not have pleased him. Wells was a disciple of Havelock Ellis,[31] whose psychology confirmed that only heterosexual love was "natural."[32] Wells himself referred George Bernard Shaw's problems, and those of his lover, Odette Keun, to similar sexual acts: "Essentially they [Shaw and Keun] are masturbators. With me she led a normal sexual life; but occasionally ⟨ . . . the old system of habits asserted itself . . . Her face and complexion changed for the worse. Then it was she was most self-assertive, most vindictive and treacherous."[33]

James was not only writing about Wells's books; he also made the point that Wells's books *were* Wells—that Wells was exposed in them—so that if James described himself as having the sexual experience of reading Wells's books, he was "having" the author as well. The "great source of interest" in a Wells novel, James wrote Wells, "was simply H. G. W. himself. You, really, come beautifully out of your adventure, come out of it immensely augmented and extended."[34]

There are similar terms in a 1904 letter to Wells. James calls a book of Wells "a record of romantic adventure of which You are the Hero."[35] Then he recounts that a book of Wells's tales "hurr[ied] [him] prematurely to [his] couch." At this point James uses his later famous image of the orange to describe the experience of "eating" Wells. It is a description suggestive, perhaps, of oral intercourse: "They [the tales] were each to me as a substantial coloured subject or bonbon . . . which I just allowed to *melt*, lollipop-wise, upon my imaginative tongue. Some of the colours seemed to me perhaps prettier than the others, as some oranges are the larger and some the smaller, in any dozen. But I (excuse me!) sucked *all* the oranges."

Other safely tucked away sexual allusions in James's epistolary rhetoric can be found. Wells reduces James "to mere gelatinous grovel." He converts James "to quivering pulp"; Wells "let[s] fly the shaft that has finished [James] in the fashion to which [he] now so distressfully testifi[ies]."[36] One cannot be certain how much of this Wells perceived. At one point he responds kindly to James's criticism: "You put your sense of the turbid confusion, the strain and the violence of my book so beautifully that almost they seem merits." Additionally, there is a responsiveness to James's intensity: "I wish you were over here. I rarely go to the Reform without a strange wild hope of seeing you."[37]

But the relationship was to deteriorate when James eventually found that his discomfort for Wells's way of being in his fiction and in the world overrode the pleasure that the experience of Wells's fiction gave him. At some point it must have become clear to James that he was sacrificing his own aesthetic principles for the sake of finding this pleasure in Wells:

> I have read you, as I always read you, and as I read no no-one else, with a complete abdication of all those 'principles of criticism,' canons of form,

references to the idea of method or the sacred laws of composition . . . which I totter . . . by the fond yet feeble theory of, as I advance under your spell, with the most cynical inconsistency.

This was *James's* self-abandonment for the pleasure of experiencing Wells: "I live with you and in you (almost cannibal-like) *on* you, H. G. W., to the sacrifice of your Marjories and your Traffords."[38] Wells's fiction, that *was* Wells for James, and it often exposed Wells's sexual lifestyle, his sexual promiscuity. Apart from ethical objections that James undoubtedly had to sexual licentiousness, what probably equally troubled as well as enticed James was the spectre of Wells's sexual exposure.

When James wrote his 1914 summary criticism for the *Times Literary Supplement*, "The Younger Generation," on Wells and other young writers (Arnold Bennett, Joseph Conrad, among others), Wells determined that "Henry James broke the unspoken truce that had been present" between them.[39] Perhaps Wells had perceived a bartered interchange where he would take quite literally the praise James lavished upon him in James's personal letters, while overlooking their verbal gyrations to the effect that it was against James's better judgment to do so. Unfortunately, it was inevitable that James would turn against Wells. James "had given himself up" to the economy of indiscriminate sexual spending in Wells's fiction, but this experience would inevitably give way to James's higher sense that life/art/sexuality must have a constraining form to provide it with meaning. Predictably, the images of lavish expenditure that overwhelm James's rhetoric in his personal letters give way in "The Younger Generation" to images of waste. Metaphorically this waste is described as the leakage of fluid.

James, one recalls, sucked all the oranges of Wells's delectable tales to saturation. In James's critical essay, what is squeezed is the orange of fictional material, which is indiscriminately squeezed to saturation: "They [Wells *et al.*] squeeze out to the utmost the plump and more or less juicy orange of a particular acquainted state and let this affirmation of energy, however directed or undirected, constitute for them the 'treatment' of the theme."[40]

Wells in particular is singled out for not treating his theme with proper discretion. As most James scholars and all scholars of Wells are aware, James quarrels with a scene in Wells's *Marriage*. He laments how the plot (that renders a young aviator and the young woman he accidentally meets sexually intimate) is not causally assisted by enough character motivation to explain why the maiden is so precipitously wooed. Wells and his critics judge this criticism to be a prime example of the contrasting values placed by James and Wells on character development as opposed to the novel of ideas (*Experiment* 410-414). But this is an overly anaesthetized and superficial interpretation of James's intention.

Not coincidentally, James picks away at a scene that results in a kiss. That kiss, which is not convincingly prompted by a reasoned motivation, is called by James a "miscarriage of 'effect'" (191), a miscarriage because the "seed" of the relationship, James laments, had been "already sown." James seems to imply that sexual acts informed by no causal motivation are indiscriminate sowing. Likewise, the author of the *Marriage* episode and of the novel *Marriage* in general, a novel which "is literally Mr. Wells's own mind" (189), is also indiscriminately spilling the "reservoir" (190) of his own creative—I would suggest, implicitly seminal—fluid:

> We ask ourselves again and again why so fondly neglected a state of *leakage* comes not to be fatal to *any* [italics James] provision of quantity, or even to stores more specially selected for the ordeal than Mr. Wells's always strike us as being. [Some other author's store of fluid, possibly James's, is implicitly finer?] Is not the witnessed pang of *waste*, in fact, great just in proportion as we are touched by our author's fine offhandedness as to the value of the stores, about which he can for the time make us believe what he will? [my emphasis]

James derides Wells for the sexual impotence of indiscriminate spillage: "We wince," James writes, "at a certain quite peculiarly gratuitous sacrifice to the casual in 'Marriage' very much as if seeing some fine and indispensable little part of a mechanism slip through profane fingers and lose itself" (190).

For James, the sexual experience is "saved"—from wasteful spillage, from indiscriminate promiscuity—by a judging mind that selects its sexual occasions cautiously, gives them reasons for happening, and invests them with a permanence and thus a meaning. In his essay on the artist Gabriele D'Annunzio James denounces love depicted having "neither duration, nor propagation, nor common kindness, nor common consistency, with other relations, common congruity with the rest of life." D'Annunzio's vulgarity is "not . . . the space he allots to love-affairs, but the weakness of his sense of 'values' in depicting them."[41] Apt at this point is Geoffrey Dellamora's interesting observation that in Victorian culture nature, procreation, heterosexual sex, and a constructive economy were culturally linked on one hand, while art, the "waste of semen in masturbation or in love between males," and a wasteful economy were linked on the other.[42] James's awareness of these associations may help to explain his avoidance of "exposure," and why he rejects "the terrible *fluidity* of self-revelation"[43] that he finds in fictional autobiography. Only if "the observant and recording and interpreting mind . . . has intervened and played its part," can "the exhibition of 'Love' *as* 'Love'—functional Love . . . keep . . . somehow interesting and productive (though I don't mean *re*productive!)."[44] Implied here is James's awareness of the cultural shibboleth that homosexual love and art possibly, meant the unreproductive spilling of seed. James saves himself in his fiction from the painful exposure of his own homosexuality through the strategy of narrative indirection;[45] he also "saves" un*re*productive art and sexuality by making them productive through the retention and framing of sexual experience within the context of meaningful human intercourse, or exchange.

"Squeezing out," "waste," "leakage," "expose:" James's words refer to an indiscretionary spillage of bodily resources. Wells strikes back, in his parody of James in *Boon* and his comments about James in *Experiment in Autobiography*, with derogatory images of unhealthy bodily retention. Although Wells's arguments do definitely have a content protesting "the elaborate, copious emptiness of the whole Henry James exploit"[46] with its demand for unity, resistance to change, and reliance on "etiquette, precedences, associations, claims" (*Boon* 453), even with these aesthetic arguments one cannot help but be reminded of their personal resonance as well. What Wells implies about James's sterility of ideas, he notes also in fact about his mother's: "I do not think my mother ever had a new idea . . . her ideas faded out, that was all" (*Experiment* 154). With Wells, as with James, it is virtually impossible not to read their sexual selves imprinted experientially onto their theoretical disagreements.

Wells attacks James's fiction, implicitly James, for sexual impotence—unproductivity—and he invokes the impression of bodily retention through his conceit about James's bladder. James, Wells writes in his autobiography, is "like some victim of enchantment placed in the centre of an immense bladder" (451). James's bladder urges have been suppressed for so long the bladder is "disten[ded] and only "a difficult parturition" will finally result in "the loud, sonorous bursting of a long blown bladder" (*Boon* 459). James is evidently self-repressed. Wells, on the other hand, thinks of himself as having fought the "ugly, threatening, and humiliating gestures" from the world that "screwed [himself] up for self-repression and a fight, and [I] fought and subdued [myself] until [I] was free" (*Experiment* 156).

Wells implies the further irony that James and his prose are bloated with the retention of actually *nothing*. James is as big as an "elephant" (*Boon* 453); he is a "hippopotamus." James is as "edentate as a pseudopodium," (*Experiment* 413), that is, he lacks teeth and is unsubtly constructed like an amoeba who has to move and ingest food through a temporary cytoplasmic protrusion! Besides the obvious taunt about James's weight, what is the argumentative point of these conceits? The intention seems clear. James is a simple, static organism with sedentary bodily functions, an organism which keeps expanding beyond its capacity when there is really nothing—no bodily fluids—to expand. Correspondingly, his characters are "eviscerated" (*Boon* 455)—they have no bowells. They also seem to have no functional sexual organs; they "never make lusty love" (*Boon* 455). Nor do they have "thought or possibility of children" (*Boon* 461).

Wells implies the unproductive nature of James's fiction and life. "I," he declares in *H. G. Wells in Love*, "am ineradicably heterosexual" (113). James, Wells observes, was "an unspotted bachelor" with "no [fictional] penetration" (*Experiment* 451; *Boon* 453). The well-known bachelor taxonomy in Victorian fiction was "marginalized" and "housebroken by the severing of [its] connections with a discourse of genital sexuality"; as such, the bachelor was "one possible path of response to the strangulation of homosexual panic." By the post-Victorian era, "that renunciatory high ground of male sexlessness [had] been strewn with psychic landmines."[47] Wells certainly must have been aware of the politics of this type. Perhaps he meant its nuances to attach to James, and to James's "impotent" fiction. He could avenge himself against James's oblique attack on the sexual indiscretion in his fiction and life; he would defend in some sense his own means of adaptational survival.

Speaking, one last time, of oranges in *Boon*, Wells names a character Mr. Orage, a "gifted editor of the *New Age* " (where the actual Alfred Richard Orage would pseudonymously savage Wells's book).[48] The fictional Orage is not admitted to the literary "conference upon the Mind of the Race." He finds instead "a point of vantage in a small pine-tree overlooking the seaward corner of the premises" (442; 443). This character is shown for the last time in the narrative presumably about to fling "a large and very formidable lump of unpleasantness" (447) over the wall. This incident recalls the occasion that amused Wells so much when Henry was horrified with his brother William's "scandalous" behavior in peeping over the wall at Rye House for a look at G. K. Chesterton (*Experiment* 453-454). I cannot help wondering if Wells intended to twit James by calling up this incident with the fictional Mr. Orage. Wells's amusement at James's fear of exposure is equally invested in Henry's bachelorhood and in the intimate yet troubled relationship James had with his brother. Could there be a subtle blackmail behind Wells's mockery of James's sexuality, his habits, his fear of exposure? At the least, James and Wells reveal in their criticism how central their economy of sexuality is to their narrative strategies and how opposite these strategies of exposure/concealment and expenditure/retention actually are.

2

Before a final discussion of how these oppositions are "emplotted" in James's *Portrait* and in Wells's *Meanwhile*, I would like to discuss the more or less literal ways that Wells's *Meanwhile* invokes and revises the earlier work. H. G. Wells seems to have intended several things by writing *Meanwhile*. First, the book serves as a tribute to Wells's dying wife Jane in his fictional portrait of the brave wife Cynthia. He also wrote the book as one of his social manifestos against fascism.[49] Finally, the book is a response against Henry James's aestheticism, especially as it implicitly manifests itself in James's own portrait of a lady.

Meanwhile is set in a wealthy palazzo in the Italian countryside. Cynthia Rylands, who has become a member of the aristocracy through her marriage to her adored Philip, is feeling the vague sense of ennui that might beset an intelligent and idealistic young wife who has been experiencing a succession of house parties where nothing of importance seems to be acted out or said. In the midst of her musings about this situation, and after the arrival of the utopian philosopher Mr. Sempack, who has brought new promise of meaningful conversation into her house, Cynthia inadvertently gains an impression that seems to shake the basis of her entire world. She sees her husband Philip in a sexual dalliance with one of the new, racier type of young women, Puppy Clarges. Considering Puppy's loose morals, "strident and hard," Cynthia had thought of her dismissively: "Who could love that body of pot-hooks and hangers?"[50]

Cynthia's anguish is overridden by the wisdom of the "Utopographer" Sempack, who informs Cynthia that she has the fate of her husband and herself in her hands. Philip was meant for better things than the listlessness of life in the country. He was meant to go to England, to become involved in political and social action and, more specifically, to struggle with the problem of the national coal strike. Since Philip is constitutionally stronger to face action than she is—she is also in the weakened state of being pregnant—Sempack argues that Cynthia must sacrifice her lesser grievance as inconsequential and irrelevant to the real case in point.

Philip's infidelity is merely a symptom of wasted energy. Furthermore, Philip's sexuality should never be a central concern. As Sempack counsels, "It is a matter of bracing yourself up to the new idea that this sort of thing is likely to happen again in your lives." Cynthia must go "beyond jealousy" to support her husband in the true focus of their lives; she should help Philip to "understand and serve." Only then can he realize his potential for great social action in the world (79).

Cynthia is indisputably a paean to Wells's wife Jane, about whom Wells wrote that her "humour and charity and the fundamental human love between us, were to be tried out [by Wells's consistent infidelity] very severely in the years that lay ahead. Suffice it here to say that they stood the test" (*Experiment* 392).[51] Wells saw the dividend of this struggle in his own ability to pursue his fiction and the struggle for "worldly freedom" (390).

Cynthia is also crafted with an eye to James's Isabel. Cynthia Rylands and Isabel Archer are linked analogous names. "Archer" suggests the goddess Artemus with her ambiguous dual function of bringing fertility to mankind while remaining a cruel virgin huntress who kills any man who sees her naked. Wells obliquely refers to his revision of *Portrait* with his use of "Cynthia," an epithet for Artemus/Diana, although Wells's Cynthia retains only the fertility associations of the original.

One may imagine from Wells's revision what he thought about Isabel. Wells's book begins in Italy; he skips the succession of suitors Cynthia might have had and shows Cynthia already married, while James's *Portrait* takes Isabel to Italy where she will meet and marry Gilbert Osmond much later in the novel. Isabel is definitively unmarried for the first half of the novel. Further, while Isabel is concerned with her own egotistical needs, and she views marriage as a constraint to her freedom in *Meanwhile*, Cynthia thinks of her husband: how can Philip "find a way of release to be the man, the leader, the masterful figure in human affairs she surely believes he might be"? (45). Granted, Isabel marries Osmond from "the sense that life was vacant without some private duty that might gather one's energies to a point," (297) but, unlike Cynthia with her conception of duty to her husband, Isabel is concerned with the intensified direction of her own energies, not her husband's.

Wells's Philip is more like James's Lord Warburton, who also has vague notions about how society can be reformed. Wells would likely disdain Isabel's selection of Osmond (and James's pursuit of this line of interest) for its aestheticism and resistance to social issues. There is a character, Mr. Plantagenet-Buchan, in *Meanwhile*, who seems meant as a portrait of Henry James. As such, the pretentiously named Plantagenet-Buchan is Wells's all-out critique of James's aestheticism, which Wells pits against the larger social awareness and consciousness of his own stand-in, Sempack. Plantagent-Buchan is a "most highly cultivated and Europeanised American" for whom it is "forbidden to . . . be naive" (23-25). About him, Cynthia wonders, "'Do you think a man like Mr. Plantagenet-Buchan ever makes love to women—I mean, really makes love—actually?'" (105). That James really does not make love—actually—seems to have been the rumored consensus about James's ambiguously intimate relationship with the novelist Constance Fenimore Woolson. James used Woolson "compulsive[ly]" in "intense, but peculiarly furtive, intimacies" with her to shore up his own compulsion toward heterosexuality.[52] How interesting that in *Meanwhile* it is "dear accommodating Miss Fenimore" who, for the convenience of Plantagenet-Buchan, is separated from her pretty room in the tower (12).

But it is James's aestheticism that gets the most damaging treatment in Plantagenet-Buchan. Mr. Sempack's moral philosophy, which advocates futuristic vision as opposed to frittering one's life away on the "meanwhile," causes the Jamesian character to brood about his own sense of values: "He liked to think of his existence as a very perfect and polished and finished thing indeed," the narrator reveals. He looks in a mirror, his interest, like James's, fixed on "varying the point of view," here,

> comparing himself with Mr. Sempack. He was struggling with the perplexing possibilities that there might be a profounder subtlety than he had hitherto suspected in the barest statement of fact and opinion, and a sort of style in a physical appearance that looked as though it had been shot out on a dump from a cart [an obvious allusion to Wells's own heterogenous style].
>
> His discontent deepened. 'Little humbug!' he said to the elegance in the mirror . . . He touched brutality. 'Little *ass*!' he said. (37)

In his sense that "the general substance of things was beauty," Plantagenet-Buchan reminds Cynthia

> of those people, now happily becoming old-fashioned, who will not look at a lovely landscape except through a rolled-up newspaper or some such frame . . . So while in practice he was for sealing up himself and his sensations in a museum case as it were with beauty, she was for lying open to the four winds of heaven, sure that beauty would come and remain . . . And so while art for him was quintessence, for her it was only a guide. (124)

In *Meanwhile*, Wells argues that an aesthetic vision of life must be replaced by a social one. He argues, also, through his characters Sempack and Cynthia, that male animal passions are not only inevitable but irrelevant to a woman's truer frame of reference with her husband. Wells argues that a woman obsessed with her husband's betrayal as a result of his animal passions, past or present, is being negligently self-indulgent when there are so many larger social issues in the world with which to be concerned. A real lady, Wells suggests, is like his character Cynthia (and his wife Jane): Cynthia dismisses her husband's infidelity and helps him to realize a democratization of his own family's exploitative interests in the coal industry. While in *Portrait* Isabel's child dies after six months, in *Meanwhile* Cynthia gives birth to a son. Hence, Cynthia's bearing/forebearing nature allows for reproductivity and social affirmation—a +2, of sorts—whereby Wells's *Meanwhile* replicates his criticism that James's fiction withholds sexuality (including parturition) and turns away from its social mission. It has the negativity of 0.

In *Meanwhile*, Wells has it both ways: he attacks James's inflated (retentive) prose by implying that, as in *Portrait*, it produces nothing; and he refutes James's accusation that his own promiscuous style is wasteful. Indeed, his promiscuous style (which switches midway through the text from narrative report to combined report and epistle) and his plot featuring promiscuity (which exposes sexual indiscretion) both result in creative and socially acceptable reproduction on the microcosmic (familial) and macrocosmic (societal) levels.

3

Several James scholars recently concur—albeit unknowingly—with Wells's assessment that *Portrait* is about "nothing." James knew, William Veeder suggests, that in his society business was equated with "men-life-presence" and pleasure with "women-death-absence." Henry, or any man involved with art, was thus invariably feminized; Isabel was thus a surrogate for Henry James. Since for Isabel/James "the only way to deal with the fear of being killed is to kill it—which means to kill the self," "Isabel fights her fear of death by embracing Osmond, her 'ultimate nada.'"[53]

For Deborah Esch, the nothingness in *Portrait* refers to the lack of memory, to Isabel's coveting of "the liberty to forget."[54] Isabel thus predictably forgets the lesson about her husband that she learned in her midnight vigil, and this forgetfulness, says Esch, prevents her from learning how to translate the past "into a future that would be something other than the repetition of a past error."[55] And for Millicent Bell, the midnight vigil itself demonstrates Isabel's lack of memory, for it reveals "a history curiously bare of recollected incident, a history of attitudes and inner responses."[56]

However, it does not seem that forgetfulness and nothingness drive the central impulse of *Portrait*, while forgetfulness *is* the central plot impulse of Wells's *Meanwhile*. To illustrate this point, one needs to distinguish between the diegetic, or story, level of a text (which is the level on which characters commit actions) and the higher-level movements of the plot that may even run counter to the characters' actions and conclusions in a story. In both *Portrait* and *Meanwhile*, extra-heterodiegetic narrators tell the story; that is, narrators both outside and above the level on which the story take places are the agents of its telling. In *Portrait*, for example, Isabel's temporal knowledge is clearly surpassed by that of the narrator. The narrator knows about the occurrence of events when Isabel has not been temporally present; he relates, for example, Madame Merle's meetings with Gilbert Osmond when they plot Isabel's marriage. He also moves through time at will with prescience or with an accelerative force beyond Isabel's time-bound vision.

A further level of story emplotment exceeds even that of a extra-heterodiegetic narrator, I would argue, although the extra-heterodiegetic narrator is the one who, amongst all possible narrators, is most capable of omniscience and authority.[57] I conceive this level as that of the implicit author; she is existential and poetic in her spatial configuration of time. This implicit author—James or Wells in this essay—constructs a paradigmatic plot to correspond with his own ethical vision, his psychological needs, thus, his very way of being in the world. The extra-heterodiegetic narrator, on the other hand, must lay out this plot in linear time. And a character, such as Isabel, is even further limited; she can only follow linear time and reconfigure in her head, such as she does in her midnight vigil, an awareness of the past and of how the past fits into the present. She can also only anticipate, and then with uncertainty, what may follow in the future.

With these levels of story telling in mind, I want to argue that, true to the description of the psycho-sexual defenses that James and Wells intuitively perceived in each other's fiction, James's plot in *Portrait* is indeed configured by a special kind of retention. However, this is not the retention of "nothing." It is a memory of sexual incident. Wells's plot in *Meanwhile*, on the other hand, throws away, or discards, the sexual incident that it claims to expose.

In James's *Portrait*, the retention, or remembrance, of sexual incidence seems the central lesson in the tale. Esch and others point out that Isabel is not particularly eager to remember, especially if the knowledge gained from the accretion of information will clip her wings or disillusion her. Yet, typically, ethics in a James novel hinges on memory. James "emphasizes the interconnection, the hanging together, the continuity, for bliss or for bale, of the moral life. Something done can never be undone. All our doings, along with what their results cause to be done in their turn, form one indestructible web."[58] Hence, Osmond and Merle's adulterous liaison, which is committed prior to the novel, forms the background of James's *Portrait*.[59] And, although the adultery between Gilbert Osmond and Madame Merle takes place preceding the novel's events—hence, according to one critic, Isabel has "*no specific* outrage to charge Osmond with—he was neither an adulterer or a wife-beater"[60]—the effects of the liaison unquestionably poison any "truth" in Isabel's marriage. And she will be forced, through finally having to "see" this liaison, to realize that her thoughts and actions have indeed been constrained and that she is different, estranged, from her husband, in some unalterable ways that she must finally acknowledge.

The implicit author of *Portrait* emplots the novel towards this end of Isabel's knowing. Using a strategy such as prolepsis, the extra-heterodiegetic narrator confines Isabel inevitably within her eventual knowledge of her sorrowful fate. Here, for example, is the narrator considering Isabel's thoughts about potential marriage to Osmond: "Her imagination, as I say, hung back: there was a last vague space it couldn't cross—a dusky, uncertain tract which looked ambiguous and even slightly treacherous, like a moorland seen in the winter twilight. But she was to cross it yet" (4:22). This passage remembers forward to Isabel's disastrous marriage; it ominously foreshadows—and centrally focuses—the web of events that consist of Merle and Osmond's intimacy, Isabel's subsequent sense of betrayal, and her ultimate realization of how estranged she is from her husband.

The storyline is strategically emplotted, as well, toward the goal of Isabel's "remembering" her husband's infidelity (while the narrator here "remembers forward"; one might say these events are configured in opposition to her own resisting desire to forget. Isabel is given impressions that ultimately coerce this awareness from her. Immediately after Isabel decides that "there had been no plot, no snare" between Osmond and Merle to arrange her marriage, the narrator reports that Isabel "had received an impression": she sees Osmond and Merle poised in colloquial familiarity in the drawing room. Toward her enhanced awareness, "the thing made an image, lasting only a moment . . . Their relative positions, their absorbed mutual gaze, struck her as something detected" (4:160; 4:164; 4:165). This impression leads to Isabel's midnight vigil. It is this memory that will continue to haunt her: "She stopped again in the middle of the room and stood there gazing at a remembered vision—that of her husband and Madame Merle unconsciously and familiarly associated" (4:205); "Sometimes, at night, she had strange visions; she seemed to see her husband and her friend—his friend—in dim, indistinguishable visions" (4:278).

The Countess Gemini finally informs Isabel of all the facts of the sexual perfidy; the implicit author arranges this *deus ex machina* so that Isabel will finally know all (4: 365). We may ask why the implicit author of *Portrait* is so intent on exposure and remembrance of the sexual facts surrounding this disastrous marriage. One recent psychological reading argues convincingly that Gilbert Osmond is a surrogate for Henry James's brother William. Henry felt like "the woman scorned" when William wed in 1878. In response, Henry wrote a fantasized version of William's failure in marriage in *Portrait*, wreaking psychic revenge thereby.[61]

What is gained by Isabel in the novel, however, and thus presumably by the implicit author as well, is the lingering ineradicable sense of difference or estrangement that one person inevitably feels in the presence of the other in an intimate relationship, unless the identity of one partner is annihilated by the ego of the other. Isabel Archer and Gilbert Osmond feel existential nausea in the presence of this difference, which is always in some primal Freudian sense the experience of sexual difference as well. They cannot recuperate any meaning; their marriage is unreproductive. But the residual of this sad tale is the sense of ineradicable difference. There is an authenticity and an honesty about the acceptance of this that promises the possibility of psychological exploration and growth.

Seemingly more confrontational about sexual issues, *Meanwhile* is emplotted to forget the sexuality that it exposes. The subsequent myth that emerges is compensatory and recuperative of the great sense of betrayal and loss that accompanied the death of Wells's wife Jane. Anthony West talks about this loss in a way evocative of what Jane symbolized for her husband:

> Jane died, and Easton Glebe became an empty shell. This was a departure from the agreed game plan that my father had altogether failed to foresee. In his script Jane was always to be dependably there in the home he had made for her; and wherever he had been and whatever he might have been doing, she was to receive him with understanding, forgiveness, tolerance, and pride on his return. And there it shockingly was. She had broken out of the role, and he was left with no one to confess to and to be absolved by when his latest break-out was over.[62]

Wells obviously fantasized Jane in the role of the nurturing mother that he had never had. Wells even splits off a part of his wife Amy Catherine and names her Jane, to accord with this fantasy life:

> To most of our friends and acquaintances she was Jane and nothing else. . . .

> Jane was a person of much greater practical ability than Catherine. She was the tangible Catherine and made decisions freely, while Catherine herself stayed in the background amiably aloof. Jane ordered a house well and was an able 'shopper;' she helped people in difficulties and stood no nonsense from the plumber. Her medicine cupboard at home was prepared for all occasions. She had gone through a Red Cross course.

The passage continues quite a while in a similar vein.[63]   Jane was unquestionably Wells's Angel in the House.

Jane is also necessarily desexualized by Wells (*Wells in Love* 82); Wells can respond without sexual guilt in desiring the mother. This is not the castrating mother; it is a recuperative one who will view her "child's" sexual escapades with tolerance: "She had always regarded my sexual imaginativeness as a sort of constitutional disease; she stood by me patiently, unobtrusively waiting for the fever to subside.[64]

The ultimate regressive desire of the male, argues Julia Kristeva, is "the maternal paradise in which every demand is immediately gratified."[65] And yet, there is the paradox that the preoedipal mother, in her inaccessibility, "represents both home and not home," and her "body is the site of both presence and absence, plenitude and loss."[66] There are two eerie photographs in Anthony West's biography that Wells took of his mother as she was laid out for burial. They are haunting particularly for the masklike inexpressiveness of the face, for their representation of the distant mother who is finally in her death fully inaccessible (preceding p. 119).

In *Meanwhile*, Wells attempts to recuperate from this loss, which has been triggered again by the loss of his wife. While the implicit author in *Portrait* invokes a *deus ex machina* to cause Isabel to remember her husband's sexual infidelity, the implicit author in *Meanwhile* invokes a surrogate Wells in the guise of the utopographer Sempack, who counsels Cynthia to simply forget it. The "real" Cynthia Rylands, Sempack explains to her, will understand that "*there is nothing to forgive* " (78; my emphasis). The emplotment in *Meanwhile* erases the very infidelity it supposedly exposes.

The plot of the novel must forget sexuality, since the ultimate fantasy in the novel is to merge with the mother, and "mother" in Western thinking is asexual while woman as eroticized object is Eve.[67] In *Meanwhile*, the plot displaces an estranged and potentially threatening (m)other sexual side of Philip/Wells to a social agenda and to a social self that is fully conscious. This is similar to Wells's own strategic use of Jung to split his Lover-Shadow, an *"other* consciousness" which is "sexual in origin," from his *persona*, "the rapid envelopment and penetration of my egotism by socialistic and politically creative ideas."[68] The split between the unconscious and conscious in the novel is accommodated on the diegetic level by a shift from dialogue before the sexual indiscretion to mostly epistolary written discourse in the latter part of the novel after the discretion has been canceled.

There is an unusual narrative retroversion in the first half of the novel that helps to explain how for Wells oral discourse may have a relation to the unconscious. Cynthia is listening to Sempack discuss with the others his utopian philosophy about the future and its interaction with the concept of "meanwhile." Cynthia's perception of the conversation is delivered in a narrative report liberally mixed with free indirect thought. The free indirect form of narration can present the illusion that we as readers are actually situated inside the mind of the character. As Cynthia starts losing the drift of the conversation because she is falling asleep, the reader is equally mystified.

The morning after, Cynthia reconstructs the discussion again, but this time she miraculously knows how to fill in the gaps in conversation that she missed the night before when she was falling asleep. Cynthia reasons that she can now fill in the gaps because "in any talk much of what was said was like the wire stage of a clay model and better forgotten as soon as it was covered over" (38). Since the information was not accessible to her the night before, it seems that she must be recovering her material from the unconscious state related to falling asleep. She also seems to perceive her own role in this reconstruction to be creative, since she selects only the material from the unconscious that she wants to remember.

What strikes Cynthia about written discourse, as opposed to speech, is its indelibility. She worries about the letters she will get from Philip because "things said can be forgotten. Or you recall the manner and edit and rearrange the not too happy words. Things written hammer at the eye and repeat themselves inexorably" (136). In Philip's letters, which take up a large section of the novel's second half, Philip remembers better and better in written form; great value is placed on the fact that ideas begin to proceed in a more orderly fashion. Thus while Cynthia can safely negotiate the unconscious, male narrative such as Philip's is only safe in the rational realm of the conscious, where nothing that resides in the unconscious, such as the sexual self, can leak through. Hence, Philip's conscious mastery over written discourse marks his successful transition to his social persona.

By contrast, Cynthia retains throughout the novel a special relationship with the unconscious, it seems, because of her pregnancy. Julia Kristeva suggests that "an 'enceinte' woman loses communal meaning, which suddenly appears to her as worthless, absurd, or at best, comic—a surface agitation severed from its impossible foundations." There is a "regressive extinction of symbolic capabilities"—that is, of language employed referentially—and, instead, a celebration of poetic language disruptive of the symbolic, social level.[69] Along with Cynthia's increasingly poetic sense of the beautiful as she progresses in her pregnancy, it is interesting to note as well in the light of Kristeva's description that Cynthia twice "forgets" normal word sequence. On the night of discussion, she hails Sempack, "You scatter pollen like a freeze scats ideese" (23) [You scatter ideas like a fir tree scatters pollen]. Cynthia's word sense lapses again at the end of the novel when she has delivered her baby. "'Dju finka vim ?'" [Do you hear him?] she nonsensically asks her husband (223).

As I have mentioned, her state of "enceinte" also disposes her to "an ever deepening and intensifying realisation of the beauty in things." Predictably, this perception of beauty in the material world is for Cynthia "inseparably mingled with the conception of discovering God" (124). While Isabel at the end of *Portrait* fears drowning in the "rushing torrent" provoked by Goodwood's kiss (4:435), and, thus, one might suppose, by the whole realm of sexual possibility,

Cynthia meets the "narrow gorge and inevitable rapids" of her "crisis of maternity" with the knowledge that "for the present she was with God. So near, so palpably near was He to her that her whole being swam in His. He would be with her in the darkness; He would be with her amidst the strangeness and pain" (219). In Wells's myth, Philip experiences that "divinity—for it was divinity" as it is embodied in Cynthia (221). Cynthia is "'Wife of my heart and Mother of my Soul'" (222).

This divinity is depicted as both erotic in its potential—Cynthia is described as luxuriating in her indolence—and yet safely inaccessible to sexual intercourse, or so it would seem in the novel. Feminine sexuality is strangely neutralized in *Meanwhile*. After delivery, Cynthia reminds Philip "grotesquely of a toy dog" (222). The narrator observes early on that "Cynthia's ruffled hair made her look like a very jolly but rather fragile boy" (38). Even Philip's amour *Puppy* Clarges is de-feminized. She is "strident and hard," "angular and aggressive" (49, 50).

Undeniably, there is much to admire in Wells's and his character Philip's devotion to social responsibility. Nevertheless, it is distressing to note how women are marginalized in this defensive strategy aimed at transcending the complicated split Wells saw in himself between his social, ethical self and his sexuality. It seems fair to say that neither the James revealed in *Portrait* nor the Wells revealed in *Meanwhile* is comfortable with sexual intimacy. Their narrative strategies cope with this discomfort by exposing and dwelling on sexual dis-ease in the instance of James, and by narratively forgetting or canceling out sexuality on the part of Wells. But the discomfort with sexual intimacy still remains. This discomfort seems to be the link between Wells and James, and their opposite narrative strategies for addressing this discomfort seems to be the source of their antipathy.

NOTES

1. H. G. Wells, *Experiment in Autobiography* (New York: Macmillan, 1934), p. 51.

2. Ingvald Raknem, *H. G. Wells and His Critics* (Oslo/Bergen: Universitetsforlaget, 1964), p. 334.

3. Wells, *Experiment*, 410.

4. Vivien Jones, *James the Critic* (New York: St. Martins, 1985), p. 146; and Robert Bloom, *Anatomies of Egotism: A Reading of the Last Novels of H. G. Wells* (Lincoln: University of Nebraska Press, 1977), pp. 28-29; and Leon Edel and Gordon N. Ray, *Henry James and H. G. Wells: A Record of their Friendship, their Debate on the Art of Fiction, and their Quarrel* (Urbana: University of Illinois Press, 1958), p. 11.

5. In Edel and Ray, to Wells, July 10, 1915, and to James July 8, 1915, pp. 267 and 264 respectively. Subsequent letters mentioned in the notes are from this edition of letters, unless otherwise noted.

6. Jones, 154.

7. *Experiment in Autobiography*, p. 424. Subsequent references to this edition are noted parenthetically.

8. See William J. Scheick, *Fictional Structure and Ethics* (Athens: University of Georgia Press, 1990, pp. 40-46, 75-91 for a discussion of how Wells privileges structure

over characterization for ethical reasons.

9. *Sexual Anarchy: Gender and Culture at the Fin de Siecle* (New York: Penguin, 1991), p. 112.

10. Showalter, p. 111.

11. William J. Scheick, *The Splintering Frame: The Later Fiction of H. G. Wells*, (Victoria, B. C.: University of Victoria Press, 1985) p. 51.

12. Richard Jennings, "Mr. H. G. Wells' Pamphlet Novel," *The Daily Mirror*, July 28, 1987, p. 4. (As noted by Scheick in *Splintering Frame*.)

13. I am taking the liberty of using Paul Ricouer's noun "emplotment" in verbal form. Ricouer says, "I see in the plots we invent the privileged means by which we reconfigure our confused . . . temporal experience. *Time and Narrative*, Trans. Kathleen McLaughlin and David Pellauer, Vol. 1 of 3 vols., (Chicago: University of Chicago Press, 1984-1988, p. xi. I use "emplot" in a liberal adaptation of Ricouer, then, to refer to plotting in narrative time of a spatial configuration.

14. See, for example, Leon Edel, *Henry James: A Life*, (New York: Harper & Row, 1985), p. 19.

15. Edel, pp. 153-154.

16. *H. G. Wells: Aspects of a Life*, (New York: Random House, 1984), pp. 18-19.

17. William Veeder, "The Feminine Orphan and the Emergent Master: Self-Realization in Henry James," *Henry James Review* 12 (1991):26.

18. Raknem, pp. 330-331.

19. See the discussion of homosexuality as Freudian pathology, for example, in Alan P. Bell, Martin S. Weinberg, and Sue Kiefer Hammersmith, *Sexual Preference: The Development in Men and Woman*, (Bloomington: Indiana University Press, 1981).

20. Wells's son Anthony wrote that his father could not meet any emotional demands made on him by women, *Aspects*, pp. 88-89.

21. Richard Dellamora, *Masculine Desire: The Sexual Politics of Victorian Aestheticism*, (Chapel Hill: University of North Carolina Press, 1990), p. 11.

22. H. G. Wells, *H. G. Wells in Love: Postscript to an Experiment in Autobiography*, (Boston: Little, Brown, and Company, 1984), p. 79.

23. *Aspects*, pp. 41-42.

24. See letters in Edel and Ray, pp. 81-82, 172-173.

25. *Aspects*, p. 180.

26. *Ibid.*, pp. 180, 181.

27. *Ibid.*, p. 41.

28. Pp. 17, 23.

29. January 20, 1902, p. 74; and January 24, 1904, p. 93.

30. January 20, 1902, p. 75.

31. Raknem, p. 323.

32. Eve Kosofsky Sedgwick, *Between Men: English Literature and Male Homosexual Desire*, (New York: Columbia University Press, 1985), pp. 194-195.

33. *Wells in Love*, p. 122.

34. January 20, 1902, p. 75.

35. January 24, 1904, p. 94.

36. November 20, 1899, p. 61.

37. April 25, 1911, p. 130.

38. October 18, 1912, pp. 166-167.

39. David Smith, *H. G. Wells: Desperately Mortal: A Biography*, (New Haven: Yale University Press, 1986), p. 170.

40. Henry James, "The Younger Generation," in Leon Edel and Gordon Ray, pp. 182-83.

41. "Gabriele D'Annunzio," *Literary Criticism: French Writers, Other European*

Writers, The Prefaces to the New York Edition, ed. Leon Edel, (New York: Library of America, 1984), p. 937.

42. Dellamora, p. 111.

43. "Preface to *The Ambassadors*," *The Art of the Novel: Critical Prefaces*, ed. R. P. Blackmur, (New York: Scribner's, 1962), p. 128. I am indebted to Edel and Ray for connecting this passage to James's discussion of autobiography, p. 128.

44. To Wells, March 3, 1911, p. 129.

45. Ann Kosofsky Sedgwick, "The Beast in the Closet: James and the Writing of Homosexual Panic," *Sex, Politics, and Science in the Nineteenth-Century Novel*, (Baltimore: Johns Hopkins University Press, 1986), discusses James's narrativizing of homophobia, pp. 162-182.

46. H. G. Wells, *Boon*, vol. 13, *The Works of H. G. Wells*, (New York: Charles Scribners Sons: London: Unwin, 1924-1927), p. 456. Subsequent references to this edition are noted parenthetically.

47. Sedgwick, "Beast," pp. 156, 159, 162.

48. *New Age*, 13 (October 16, 1913): 730.

49. Smith, 286.

50. H. G. Wells, *Meanwhile: The Picture of a Lady*, (London: Ernest Benn Limited, 1962), pp. 49, 50. Subsequent references to this edition are noted parenthetically.

51. See also Patricia Stubbs, *Women and Fiction: Feminism and the Novel 1880-1920*, (New York: Harper & Row, 1989), p. 190.

52. Sedgwick, "Beast," pp. 166, 163.

53. Veeder, pp. 24, 53.

54. Henry James, *The Portrait of a Lady*, Vols. 3 and 4 in *The Novels and Tales of Henry James*, (New York: Scribner's, 1907-9), 3: 322. Subsequent references to this edition are noted parenthetically.

55. "'Understanding Allegories': Reading The Portrait of a Lady," Henry James's The Portrait of a Lady, ed. Harold Bloom, (New York: Chelsea House, 1987, p. 153.

56. *Meaning in Henry James*, (Cambridge: Harvard University Press, 1991), p. 120.

57. See Shlomith Rimmon-Kenan, *Narrative Fiction: Contemporary Poetics*, (London: Methuen, 1983), p. 95 for her discussion of how extra-heterodiegetic narrators are usually invested with authority.

58. J. Hillis Miller, *The Ethics of Reading*, (New York: Columbia University Press, 1987), p. 103.

59. Miller, p. 106.

60. Bell, p. 89.

61. Veeder, pp. 26, 35.

62. *Aspects*, p. 113.

63. *Wells in Love*, p. 25.

64. *Ibid.*, p. 82.

65. Julia Kristeva, *In the Beginning Was Love: Psychoanal-ysis and Faith*, trans. & ed., Arthur Goldhammer, (New York: Columbia University Press, 1987), p. 41.

66. Madelon Sprengnether, "(M)other Eve: Some Revisions of the Fall in Fiction by Contemporary Women Writers," in *Feminism and Psychoanalysis*, ed. Richard Feldstein and Judith Roof, (Ithaca: Cornell University Press, 1989), p. 304.

67. *Ibid.*, p. 305.

68. *Wells in Love*, p. 56.

69. Julia Kristeva, *Desire in Language: A Semiotic Approach to Literature and Art*, ed. Leon S. Roudiez, trans. Thomas Gora et. al, (New York: Columbia University Press, 1987), p. 240.

Brynhild (1937) and *Apropos of Dolores* (1938)

Schopenhauer, Spengler, and Wells

William J. Scheick

eactions, early and late, to both *Brynhild* (1937) and *Apropos of Dolores* (1938) have been far from flattering. These novels have been shunted aside as insignificant undertakings presumably impoverished by Wells's preference for proselytizing ideas in lieu of caring about artistic expression. By way of reconsideration, I find both works to be remarkable aesthetic experiments and, as such, neglected documentation of the maturation of Wells's artistry. They strike me as rich texts, especially when read through the filter of Schopenhauerian and Spenglerian thought. These books, it seems to me, represent two of Wells's most sophisticated applications of his technique of the splintering frame.

1

Readers of *Brynhild* might first be struck by its spare, old-fashioned story of both the breakdown of a marriage and a consequent brief affair involving a wife, who struggles for a degree of self-awareness and identity. This is all that happens in *Brynhild*. The novel commences in the middle of a night with Rowland Palace, an author egotistically worrying about his public image, and with Brynhild Palace, his wife of nine years, trying to comfort him. The story actually concerns Brynhild's deepening consciousness, in counterpoint to her husband's increasing lust for popularity. While at a weekend party at a lush estate, Brynhild meets Alfred Bunter, an imaginative poet, a fugitive from the law who has a brief affair with her. By the end of the novel Bunter is gone, and Brynhild is pregnant with his child, a fact she never tells the poet.

As this summary suggests, the plot of *Brynhild* conforms to Wells's belief that art should depict life in all its mundaneness. Wells also argued that beneath the surface of life's particulars startling discoveries await, and so he designed the commonplace plot of *Brynhild* to reveal, through the technique of the splintering frame, a pattern of larger reality embedded within commonplace phenomena. As its subtitle *The Show of Things* intimates, the novel focuses on modes of our perception of reality, a concern expressed through the characters, imagery, and structure of the work.

The interrelation of these three features of the book is suggested by two clues. The first appears early when the narrative voice refers to "Schopenhauer's realization of the importance of Show (*Vorstellung*)."[1]   Modified Schopenhauerian notions provide a philosophical basis for the artistic effects of *Brynhild*. The standard English translation of Schopenhauer's *Die Welt als Wille und Vorstellung* appeared in 1883, seeing numerous editions through the turn of the century. Wells claimed familiarity with this translation, apparently read the extensive section on Schopenhauer in Will Durant's *The Story of Philosophy* (1927), and in a revised edition of *The Outline of History* referred to the "profound and penetrating speculations" of Schopenhuer.[2] However, there is at present no way to determine how much of the German philosopher's work Wells read, how much he learned about it from secondary sources, or how much of what he encountered he understood accurately. Such concerns urge a cautionary note without undermining a sensitivity to the influence of Schopenhauer on *Brynhild*, which exhibits enough similarities to the thought of the German philosopher to warrant comparison. Indeed, as the subtitle of the novel and the specific reference to *Vorstellung* suggest, deep philosophical issues at least related to those of Schopenhauer lie beneath the surface of the novel's apparently mundane plot.

Modified Schopenhauerian thought provides a philosophical basis for the structure of *Brynhild*. But Wells's experiment with structure in this novel required a concrete illustration of Schopenhauer's abstract remarks about art in *The World as Will and Idea*, and he appears to have found what he needed in Ettie A. Rout's *Maori Symbolism* (1926), to which he refers, as a second clue, in the penultimate paragraph of *Brynhild* :

> In New Zealand, as Mrs. Ettie (Rout) Hornibrook showed so ably and interestingly in her *Maori Symbolism*, the decorations on a beam or a pillar may be expanded by an understanding imagination into the most complete and interesting of patterns, and so it is with this book. It is a novel in the Maori style, a presentation of imaginative indications. (302).

By adapting the manner of Maori archetypes or sacred symbols, Wells attempted to give *Brynhild* a structure appropriate to the qualified Schopenhauerian ideas also informing its imagery and characterization.

2

Only four dominant characters emerge in Wells's novel: Rowland and Brynhild Palace, representing the upper levels of society; and Immanuel Cloote and Alfred Bunter, representing the lower levels of society. Save for Brynhild, they are types, and it is quite true, as one critic has observed, that Cloote is Rowland's alter ego and Bunter is Brynhild's secret.[3] But this relationship signifies much more. Cloote and Rowland belong, as it were, to one species of the human race, whereas Bunter and Brynhild belong to another. The fundamental difference between these two species lies in the nature of their will.

The concept of Will is central to the meaning of *Brynhild*, and it is easy to mistake a particular character's view of Will for Wells's. For instance, Brynhild speculates on the possibility that "the will of a woman is different from a man's" (185; italics deleted), that while the male will is initiating and aggressive, the female will is resistant and responsive. In fact, however, Brynhild's subsequent experiences enlarge these ideas, and we, as readers, should perceive that difference in wills is not sexually determined. On the contrary, divergence in the exercise of Will seems more indicative of two distinct kinds of human beings, who are found in both sexes as well as at all levels of society, a conclusion Wells reiterated in *Apropos of Dolores*, his next novel.

Rowland Palace possesses an aggressive will, expressed in an egocentric desire (satirized in the narrative) to manipulate others. Immanuel Cloote, Palace's public relations man, shares in this endeavor as a "secret agent" (99). Together they strive to manage Rowland's image in terms of the "show," presentation, *Vorstellung* of life. In contrast, Brynhild and Bunter possess essentially passive wills. Unlike her husband, who smugly seeks to fortify "the façade he presented to the world," Brynhild inquires "into all the neglected possibilities that might be pining and fretting behind the façade she had hitherto unquestioningly supposed to be herself" (24). As her self-awareness increases, she discovers that she is "passive," enjoys "watch[ing] other people," and manifests an apparent "lack of will" (132, 178). Bunter, for whom Brynhild feels a deep sympathy, likewise manifests a "detached interest" (105) in the "show" of life, does not relish surfaces or "how things look" (217). Bunter is characterized by the same passivity of will Brynhild has initially attributed to only to women. That such a difference in the experience of will is a difference of human species, not of sex or class, is reinforced when Bunter relates in some detail the story of his second marriage. "She seduced me," the passive, responsive Bunter says of his second wife, Freda. He then proceeds to describe Freda's egotism, her desire to "show-off" before an audience (224-26), behavior similar to Rowland's.

This distinction between two kinds of will is illuminated by Schopenhauer's ideas about this faculty. In *The World as Will and Idea* Schopenhauer stresses, in accord with the Oriental influences upon his thought, the difference between the world of phenomena as *Maya* (illusion) and the world within ourselves as reality. To pass through "the single narrow door to the truth," he explains, "we must learn to understand nature from ourselves, not conversely ourselves from nature."[4] The difference is a matter of will. For Schopenhauer, who is not completely consistent in his use of the term, Will is an unconscious, blind, incessant impulse; it is the inner nature of everything that lives, the "endless striving" behind all human desires (1:213, 364; cf. *Brynhild* 43). It is objectified in bodily actions (cf. *Brynhild* 49), which to some extent conceal, even as they reveal, the true identity of Will "as the thing in itself" constituting "the inner, true, and indestructible nature of man" (2:411). In this sense, accordingly, we do not move the will (as in Cartesian thought); rather, Will is greater than and primary to intellect. Awareness of the reality of this will emerges piecemeal and *a posteriori*, as our intellect assesses our actions and reactions (2:421). To fail to recognize this underlying, internal truth about this unitary Will is to live on the surface (*Maya*) of life and to be deluded by a sense of personal distinctness separate from and better than that of others (1:455), who seem less real in comparison to oneself.   Hence the origin of so much misery in the world, Schopenhauer concludes.   Believing, either consciously or unconsciously, that "the essence of success is personality, that is to say individual distraction" (87), Rowland, Cloote, and Freda manifest the egotism and impulsiveness of the blind Will at its worst.   In the Schopenhauerian context of Wells's novel, the consequences of their behavior are at once ludicrous and tragic.

Good action, In Schopenhauer's view, requires liberation, insofar as it is possible, from the perception of and attachment to the world as phenomena, or "show." Through self-knowledge, insofar as it is attainable, we can approach awareness of the noumenal reality within phenomenal particularity and multiplicity. Through conscious disinterest in the surface of existence one can arrest egotism, suppress individuality, at least to some extent. Through this more passive disposition the disinterested person recognizes that all beings lie "as near to him as his own person lies to the egoist" (1:489): "all true and pure love is sympathy, and all love which is not sympathy is selfishness. *Eros* is selfishness, *agape* is sympathy" (1:485). The passive "state of voluntary renunciation, resignation, true indifference and perfect will-lessness" (1:490) characterizes the ideal human disposition. This is the condition approximated— Wells does not fully endorse the Schopenhauerian implications of the passive will—by Bunter and Brynhild, whose mutual awareness of "universal desire" and "universal frustration" unites them in a "secret collaboration" (134, 266). In response to the "unsatisfied cravings" of life (218), they mutually resign themselves to their uncertain destinies.

Schopenhauer eventually argues for a contemplative detachment from the world, for an ultimate negation and withdrawal whereby (somehow) Will turns upon itself (3:430-31). Wells apparently knew this feature of the philosopher's thought, for the narrative voice of the novel speaks of Brynhild's "new half-mystical self-devotion to the physical rebirth of our world" (301). The novel emphasizes the physical world finally in a way distinct from Schopenhauer. For Wells, Schopenhauer's willful egoist and will-less saint typify two species of the human race. Both manifest something like a Collective Will—Schopenhauer speaks similarly when he defines Will as the faculty constituting the inner nature of everything. For Wells, only those with a passive will are constructively attuned. Attunement means serving instrumentally (not necessarily by intent or conscious resignation) in the evolution of humanity.

Brynhild and Bunter are two representatives of a different and emergent species of mankind. They renounce the surface of life and perceive the interior reality of existence. They experience a Collective Will within themselves. Neither rationally understands, indeed hardly recognizes "the supreme mystery" (50) which they serve, any more than does Rowland, who uses the phrase to describe his own role in life and who also believes rightly, for the wrong reasons, that "the noumenon is forever unknown" (91). The noumenon may be Nothing, and it certainly is not a deity in Wells's novel. Whatever it is, Brynhild intuits something of its reality during her pregnancy as the "juices in her blood that had taken possession of her, and filled her with this deep irrational satisfaction, had a very imperious suggestion about them being real" (300). The human will, as it participates in something like a Collective Will, remains mysterious.

But for Wells, in contrast to Schopenhauer, the force of Will does not appear to be aimless. If Wells shares the philosopher's view of the world as illusion, suffering, and frustration (218), he does not endorse Schopenhauer's final pessimism. In Wells's view, the split between noumenon (interior) and phenomena (exterior) is not eternal. As suggested by his appropriation of Christian millennial tradition and his application of the technique of the splintering frame, Wells believes in the possibility of ringing in the kingdom (as it were) through the slow, evolutionary translation of interior ideality into external actuality. So Brynhild (through her children) and Bunter (through his writings) do not resist the yielding of their wills to fate as they give birth to internal truth made manifest in the material world.

Such optimism in *Brynhild*, one should remark, is very modest. Even in the final sentence of the novel proper—"If indeed there was in human experience as yet any such thing as reality" (300)—the simply stated *as yet* hardly balances the overall implied dubiety of the other words. The fragility of this optimism is evident as well in Bunter's expression of a desperate hope that "somehow, some day we will get the better of this predestinate world" (268). Brynhild and Bunter receive intuitive *a posteriori* intimations of their place in some seemingly vague scheme, but they never consciously fathom the mystery in which they are playing crucial roles. (This point is reinforced in the narrative by a satiric presentation of a game of charades, during a weekend party, during which the participants know only the letter they represent, not the word to which they contribute [119-20]). Brynhild's and Bunter's intimations of this mystery, as the narrative voice tells us, is "half-mystical."

3

Before specifically considering the structure of *Brynhild*, it is useful to relate Schopenhauer's understanding of art to Maori symbolism. For Schopenhauer, art should not exist for its own sake but should express the noumenal mystery informing the will. Ideally, the artist contemplates this reality behind phenomena, and his or her art conveys knowledge of it through Platonic ideas, through essential forms or archetypes supplanting a reader's experience of individuality. Art, in this sense, communicates "aesthetic" knowledge, something "felt" intuitively, rather than contemplated rationally, of the mystery of existence (1:271; 3:180).

Similar concepts apparently inform Maori symbolism. In her study, Ettie A. Rout indicates that the New Zealand Maori artist rejects the notion of "Art for Art's sake" and strives to render an "expression of ideas and principles" true to human experience.[5] This same view underlies Wells's approach to art, as is most evident in his well-known controversy with Henry James. Wells went still further. "If the novel is to follow life it must be various and discursive," he announced; "life is diversity and entertainment, not completeness and satisfaction."[6] Lack of satisfaction, for Schopenhauer as well, is the chief attribute of life; and this lack is necessarily reflected in the work of the genuine artist. Similarly, the crude-looking designs of the Maori artist convey an impression of incompleteness. But just as the archetype in Schopenhauerian art approximately objectifies the mysterious hidden reality (Will) behind phenomena, each sacred symbol of the Maori artist provides the "foundation of the pattern, and a key to its inner meaning; but its inner meaning was to be secret, except to certain members of the nobility entrusted with the preservation of this inner meaning as Sacred Knowledge (cf. the Mysteries of Egyptian priests and others)" (Rout 199; cf. 205, 213).

Such notions, or very similar ones, emerge in *Brynhild*. They in fact dictate the satiric treatment of Rowland Palace in the novel. As a member of the upper class, Rowland maintains that he is "one of the great company that served the supreme mystery" (50). In a certain sense he is correct, at least insofar as, in Schopenhauerian terms, everyone is blindly driven by Will. Nevertheless, by asserting his will as ego and by substituting the "show" of life for his art, Rowland is in bad faith in his duty to serve the supreme mystery. In fact, he makes his phenomenal self its own end, hence displacing his service to noumenal reality; and he hires Cloote to be, as it were, the priest of the self. Wells has great fun with Cloote, who sees himself as Rowland's Aaron, his John the Baptist (95). Priestlike Cloote exhibits a magical and "strange hypnotic manner" (159, 289), appears to write hieroglyphics (278), and uses such expressions as "*Saecula Saeculorum* " (281; cf. 47). Cloote's activity as a public relations man parodies the sacred priestly duty of the artist.

Whereas Rowland worships himself, Alfred Bunter seeks to hide his identity. Art is sacred to Bunter, whose work (like Schopenhauerian and Maorian art) expresses ideas intimating a reality beneath the phenomena of life. In contrast to the exhibition of artificial restraint and order in Rowland's work (5, 64), Bunter's art conveys a "rude vigor" (62), an impulsiveness, uncertainty, unevenness, and lack of finish reflecting the reality (Collective Will) he intuitively senses to exist within the phenomenal world. These same features apply to *Brynhild* as a work of art.

4

Brynhild gives the appearance of an elaborate fragment. It opens at seventeen minutes past three in the morning, covers less than a year, and closes before the issues raised are resolved. The entire novel gives a surface impression of an overdone prologue; and it is, in this sense, understandable that some reviewers complained vehemently about the seemingly abrupt ending of the novel. Wells violates fictional convention in this instance, leaving the reader dissatisfied and, we might add, as "expectant" as is pregnant Brynhild. As an example of Wells's splintering frame technique, this very discontent potentially stimulates thought that potentially involves the reader in the Schopenhauerian concerns of the novel, particularly the experience of the frustration generated by ceaseless human desires.

Even the seemingly tacked-on, two-page "Envoy" resolves little. It commences by dismissing itself—"Sufficient unto the novel is the story thereof"

(301)—then proceeds in a resigned, even disinterested tone to deflate any romantic notions the reader might hold concerning Brynhild and Bunter, whose child she carries. We are told that Brynhild remains married to Rowland, their continued incompatibility a mere fact, and that she once more later in life met Bunter "with an entirely unromantic friendliness—and no revelations" (302). And Wells's novel denies revelations to the reader conditioned by tidy narrative endings and by fictional conventions in general, at least as Wells perceived them. By means of this mode of denial *Brynhild* potentially involves the reader in the narrative matter, achieves a fourth dimension (reader relativity), and evidences a form more intimated than achieved.

As Wells's reference to Maori art indicates, there is a pattern concealed, as it were, by the "decorations" of the plot of this novel. In Maori carvings "the artists frequently halved the original design," a manner similar to the truncated effect of *Brynhild*. Maori artists repeated "the halved form in different ways for friezes"; "the original design has been disguised as flowers, tendrils, feathers, etc., but the *motif* is seen readily when these composite designs are resolved to their elemental lines" (Rout 206). These motifs are, mutually in Maorian, Schopenhauerian, and Jungean terms, archetypes objectifying ultimate ideas or mysteries.

In *Brynhild* this "secret" archetype is the eddy—a backwardly-circling current of water, or whirlpool. Figuratively, an eddy refers to a turning aside or a departure from the main current of thought. It can be imaged as a spiral—a plane curve formed by a point that moves around a fixed center (Will, in Schopenhauerian thought) and that continually increases its distance from it. It is also an archetypal image repeated often in Maori carvings (as evident throughout Rout's book) as well as in the Oriental art influencing Schopenhauer. In *Brynhild* the eddy serves as an emblem of Wells's notion of the spiral of time.[7]

Both the literal and figurative meanings of eddy combine in the association of water and thought in *Brynhild*. Rowland, for instance, is said at one point to be "launched upon a wide and congenial flow of thought . . . as if the dam penning up some great reservoir of imaginations had given way" (34). The image is similarly applied to Bunter (228), and Brynhild's thoughts likewise appear to be "as deep and unfathomable as the depths of her dark eyes" (44). Rowland wishes to live in a "great flow of self-expression" (43), whereas his wife finds her thoughts to be "as shapeless . . . as things peered at in an overshadowed pool" (44).

The image of the pool, again associated with Brynhild at the end of the novel (298), is (especially when visualized with ripples) interchangeable in the book with the image of an eddy. Brynhild fears that she continually "spin[s] round and round . . . ideas," that she time and again merely "get[s] back to the same eddy" (193, 207):

> She was caught in that eddy. She was just spinning round in that eddy while the stream of life was flowing by. The eddy was flatter than it used to be but it held her just the same. And there was no prospect, no open door at least, of escape from this futile circling. (169)

Brynhild resists her experience of whirlpool-like backward-circling because she mistakenly draws an analogy between it and "the chief entertainments in the Great Fair of Life" that circulate "faster and faster" only to return "in each case to the point of departure" (169). She and Bunter deplore what they perceive as an endless recapitulation: the tyranny of determinism, predestination, the plot of history. As Bunter identifies the dilemma: "We jump out of the bed [as if to start anew] and right away we stumble over our stale selves of the day before" (209).

Both misread this experience, even as Brynhild initially misattributes difference in will to sexual distinctions—a clever Wellsian touch confuting the tendency of readers and reviewers to identify an author's view with a protagonist's. She is not, as she thinks, precisely "where she had started" (200); for, as her father explained to her when she was a child, "Everything goes round, my dear, and comes back—a little different—a very little different—but it comes back" (170). To be caught in an eddy of thought, Wells's novel suggests, is to be very slowly edified or enlightened about reality. This sense of eddy is both a modification of Schopenhauer's view of our inability to change the fundamental character of human existence and a microcosmic illustration of the evolutionary motion of the macrocosmic spiral of time. Edifying thought expands consciousness, even as the spiral image of an eddy depicts a curve increasingly expanding from its center (Will, in Schopenhauerian metaphysics).

In contrast is the linear-appearing sweep of the life lived by Rowland, Cloote, and Freda. All three hate "to be self-conscious" (3) and prefer the illusion of progress—the final chapter of *Brynhild* is ironically entitled "Mr. Rowland Palace Goes Upward and On." In turning aside from the main flow of things, Brynhild becomes increasingly self-aware. She receives, in Schopenhauerian terms, intimations of the reality behind the external ideal of human existence; she passively participates in the spiral of time, the expanding process of which splinters the frame of phenomenal (external) existence so that an internal ideal humanity might steadily emerge.

Of the several small changes in Brynhild's mind, one includes the idea of motherhood. At the start of the narrative Brynhild is presented as Rowland's surrogate mother, who sometimes feels "a deep desire to spank him hard and good" (16), as if he were a petulant child deserving reproof. Instead, she provides patient maternal support: "I'll come up with you and smooth your pillow and uncrumple your sheets and put you to sleep." (22). Suggestions of Brynhild's motherliness subtly occur several times in the course of the novel (46-47, 247-48, 258), until at its close she is carrying Bunter's child. Her maternity is itself pregnant with significance, for she is now dedicated "to the physical rebirth of [the] world" (301).

In some sense, the entire novel has been an eddy. It has, at its conclusion, circled back upon its beginning. Brynhild remains married to Rowland; her relationship with him has not changed, at least on the surface; and her primary role is still maternal. But, as she heard from her father, very small changes occur in the experience of such circling; and the eddylike development—the splintered frame—of this novel shows, what Brynhild herself barely comprehends, that such recapitulation is accompanied by a slow expansion.

Beneath the illusion of the appearance of her return, Brynhild's role and her relationship with Rowland are, like her body and mind, not quite the same as they were less than a year before. They have "evolved."

Bunter, too, must start over by giving up his assumed identity and by returning to his past. Indeed, his position at the end of the novel places him at the very same point where his story commenced: his troublesome relationship with his second wife. The "Envoy" alludes obliquely to subsequent vague changes in him, albeit on the surface his later resumption of a writer's identity appears to be basically the same as it was previously (save for the beard). More importantly, however, Bunter contributes to the eddylike structure of the narrative. He serves as a very modified version of the "entrancing Perseus" figure who, in conventional fiction, "restores meaning to life" for a heroine. Pertinently, Brynhild wonders:

> All fiction is full of these fluttering Persei, they are as common there as white butterflies on an early day in summer. They take the initiative. They overcome all your scruples. They do everything for you. It is very misleading to the young. Brynhild could not persuade herself that in real life she has ever so much as glimpsed a specimen. (172)

Certainly Bunter is no Perseus of this sort.

Yet, oddly, he does play a somewhat modified version of this typical role. As Brynhild's fellow spirit and as the father of her child, Bunter has contributed to the expansion of more than her body. He has also encouraged the expansion of her mind. In a sense, he has aided Brynhild's detection of the possibility of an *internal* release or escape. In performing this function, Bunter fulfills his conventional role in a covert and revised manner. And this modification of his typical role is akin to the eddy-effect of the change in Brynhild's maternal identity. Both recapitulate the most mundane events of life and fiction, but like episodes or personality types within the spiral of time (objectified in the eddy image), they do so with small, hardly noticeable changes in the conventions of life and of fiction.

The overall eddy-effect of *Brynhild* is represented in another feature of its narrative design. Whereas the conventional narrative line of this novel is presented satirically, the pool-like, swollen contemplative sections, reporting Brynhild's thoughts and Bunter's account of his life, are presented straightforwardly. These latter segments are eddies insofar as they are contemplative backward-circlings contrasting to the rush of events presented in the linear narrative recounting the apparent societal progress of Rowland and Cloote. These eddies start out small: at first less than three pages of Brynhild's self-reflection (22-24), later nearly five pages of thought disrupting the account of the party at Valliant Chevrell (105-9), then an entire chapter (157-200). By the end of the book, this slowly expanding eddy-effect—similar to the repetition of halved Maori sacred symbols in the decorative components of any overall design—includes the entire story, which enlarges in meaning through the technique of the splintering frame and, in the process, circles backwardly upon itself.

The archetypal image of the eddy,[8] predominant among Maori sacred symbols, is the "complete and interesting" pattern beneath the "decorations" and the "imaginative indications" referred to at the end of *Brynhild*. The image of the eddy objectifies the structure of the narrative, a form appropriate to its modified Schopenhauerian concepts, especially the notion of Will as the mysterious generating center of all life. Moreover, the eddylike structure of *Brynhild* satisfies Wells's notion of the novel as various, discursive, and incomplete—like life, in Wells's view. The structure of this work is a transitional form providing no firm sense of completion or satisfaction for the characters or for the readers, both of whom are led toward a Schopenhauerian experience of frustration. This structure remains as elusive as the transient ripples of an eddy appearing out of nowhere and disappearing into nowhere— apparently there in motion before our eyes, but never permanent or quite defined; somewhat *edifying* in their rhythmic expansiveness, but always half-mystically beyond comprehension. Like an eddy, in a figurative sense, *Brynhild* turns aside or departs from the main current of fictional conventions, as Wells saw them. Splintering its frame by means of this departure, the novel opens outwardly from within to include the reader in the eddy of its thought.

5

Apropos of Dolores manifests Wells's continuing interest in the application of modified Schopenhauerian ideas to his aesthetic theory, but nowhere to the extent evident in *Brynhild*. Rather, in *Apropos of Dolores* Wells's technique of the splintering frame is primarily expressed in terms of concepts adapted from Oswald Spengler's *The Decline of the West* (1918), the authorized English translation of which appeared in 1926. Spengler's work exerted a substantial influence on many thinkers and writers of the 1920s and 1930s. It reformulated concepts of decadence prevalent during the later nineteenth century, in such works as Max Nordau's extremely popular *Degeneration* (1895), a book reflecting attitudes similar to those in Wells's earliest fiction. . . .

There can be little doubt that Wells disagreed with Spengler on certain issues. He did not share Spengler's assessment of Gothic architecture as the epitome of Western egotism. He also rejected Spengler's theory of cyclic rise and decline; for Wells held a notion of time that subsumes such cycles within an evolutionary spiral that integrates all phenomenal patterns. Spengler may in fact be the target of a reference (made by Wells three years before *Dolores* appeared) to some unidentified historian who analogized civilizations and individuals in terms of birth and death. Moreover, the *implied* pessimism of Spengler's theory, however much it may have unconsciously appealed to Wells, was not harmonious with Wells's expressed hopefulness during the 1930s. But, typically, although Wells took exception to many of Spengler's ideas, he would have characteristically appropriated whatever he found useful in these ideas. In fact, parallels apparently exist between Wells's and Spengler's views of cyclical patterns in the history of empires. An affinity between their views is likewise suggested when the narrator of *The Anatomy of Frustration* humorously wonders whether Steele has tried "to out-Spengler Spengler."[9]

A similar query appears in *Dolores* when Stephen Wilbeck, the narrator, asks whether what he is thinking is somewhat "more arbitrary than Spenglerism?"[10] Yes and no, apparently; for he believes that even if his interpretations are like some historian's hoot, facts indeed begin to emerge in a piecemeal manner (177). Earlier Wilbeck observed that mankind endures historians like Spengler because at the worst they experiment in propositions and theories (169). And Wilbeck certainly endures Spengler and other like theorists. He is unable to resist their vulgarities, as he puts it, because he values their hodgepodge of analogies, generalizations, assertions, and facts as fodder for the superior synthesis forming in his own mind, where he discovers enough ideas "to fit out a dozen Spenglers" (172, 177-78). While he mocks socio-historical books such as Spengler's, he in fact also adopts a method for bringing subconscious ideas to the surface (189). . . .

The key word in Wilbeck's report here is *adopting*, which in the context of his narrative refers to a new species of thought evolving from *within* an older mode of thought. This concept informs both the presence of Spenglerian concepts and the aesthetic principle informing *Dolores*. With a Spenglerian distinction in mind, Wells fashioned this novel as an expression of an emerging new culture, an expression that indicts fiction of the Jamesian kind—evidencing a penchant for art-for-art's-sake ornament—as representative of a declining civilization. In a modification of Spengler's distinction between Culture and Civilization Wells found another philosophic basis for the art he was already practicing. As a result, however much it is unconventional to say so, *Dolores* may well be Wells's grandest literary achievement, especially in the application of his splintering-frame technique.

Apropos of Dolores is presented as a journal recording the various personal and philosophical thoughts of Stephen Wilbeck, a book publisher who increasingly views his egocentric wife, Dolores, as the embodiment of those forces in life that prevent humanity from attaining happiness. During most of his account, Wilbeck engages in leisurely activities and thinks, or deals with embarrassments caused by Dolores and thinks. Reminiscent of a motif in *Brynhild*, Wilbeck begins to suspect that he and Dolores represent two different species of the human race: she is *homo regardant*; he is *homo rampant* (174-75). His alienation from his wife peaks during a furious argument, when Dolores accuses him of incest with his daughter (Lettice) from his first marriage. Seized by a fit during this argument, Dolores cries out for her pain medication, which Wilbeck gives her. She dies from an overdose, and in his journal her husband confesses his uncertainty concerning whether he is responsible for her death. Eventually Wilbeck hypothesizes about his and humanity's complicity in this probable crime. Wilbeck's journal—Wells's novel—reaches an indefinite end, as Wilbeck interweaves memory and prediction concerning human existence.

Wilbeck comes to believe that he and his wife represent antagonistic historical, psychological, and evolutionary forces. At the level of history, Dolores typifies the civilization stage of Western culture, as defined by Spengler. According to Spengler, every Culture, independent of every other Culture, undergoes the organic cycle of birth, growth, decay, and death. *Culture* is the term Spengler uses to refer to the vital, creative phase of this cycle; *Civilization*, the inevitable subsequent stage, is the term he uses to refer to the rigid, cold declining phase of this cycle. A Culture attains its apex when it "has actualized the full sum of its possibilities in the shape of peoples, languages, dogmas, arts, states, sciences"; then "the Culture suddenly hardens, it mortifies, its blood congeals, its force breaks down, and it becomes Civilization."[11]

A princess by a previous marriage and formerly a bright woman accustomed to gallant men of the world, Dolores represents the traditional values of Western civilization (146, 154). Wilbeck identifies her the established historical patterns (175), particularly as manifested in the Spenglerian morphology of history. Typical of the civilization phase and the species she symbolizes, Dolores clings to the past and cannot envision the future; speaking with refinement and condescension, she never forgets, lacks flexibility, and is bereft of originality (89, 95, 145, 158). She is increasingly aggressive and, as her name suggests, inordinately unhappy (11, 44). In short, she personifies the human discontent prevalent in the civilization stage defined by Spengler. Having passed the creative (cultural) phase of her life, she now feels aimless (72). Just as Civilization, in a Spenglerian sense, émphasizes cause and effect, materialism and fads (1:103-4), so too Dolores self-consciously assigns blame for her melancholy, desires only what is elegant, and uses material objects (such as jewelry and automobiles) as a means of asserting social status (14, 40, 97, 105). Wilbeck's impression that Dolores tends to transform her lovers into technicians (152) reinforces her representation of Civilization, which in Spengler's view converts the creative instinct of its prior cultural stage into systematic behavior emphasizing the mechanical. Dolores's rigidity, coldness, adherence to forms, and preoccupation with the past emerge from her fear of decline. Her mindless desire for attention arises, Wilbeck surmises, from a profound unconscious fear of extinction, even of the possibility that she may in some sense be dead already (73-74, 158). Dolores's sense of personal tragedy derives, as it does in Western civilization as defined by Spengler (1:130), from an intense denial of time.

In contrast to Dolores and like Brynhild, Wilbeck represents the creative cultural phase of a different and emergent civilization. A member of the proletariat rather than of the nobility typified by Dolores, Wilbeck is free from petrified traditions and in the manner of *homo rampant* enjoys unstructured leisure activities (84). Whereas Dolores is egocentric, aimless, and uncreative, her husband is inspired by humanism and imagination. He justifies himself as a disseminator of creative ideas, as someone who has consciously chosen to serve and participate in the better new world (Culture) that "struggles to exist" within the old world (Civilization) that is "crumbling away" (38-39; cf. 69). Of his relationship with Dolores, he likewise concludes that they are deeply different. Whereas she belongs to an old world headed for destruction through various kinds of excess, he (as best as he can understand his life) seems to belong to a new world which may or may not successfully emerge from the devastating collapse of the older world represented by Dolores (228). As a spokesman for this new culture, Wilbeck revises an earlier Wellsian idea when he advances the Spenglerian notion that the present version of civilization, rent by war and senile traditions, is unsalvageable (278).

If Dolores's old-world mentality stresses memory, the past, tragedy,

materialism, and causality, Wilbeck's routinely forgets, looks to the future, enjoys an innate hopefulness, intuits a transcendental dimension in life, and speaks of the mystical core of being (27, 35, 48, 49, 67, 285), all characteristics of the Spenglerian definition of Culture. Dolores's incessant complaints that her husband is like a small, obstinate child who plays at mending the world as if it were a toy (45, 114, 154, 163, 193) likewise identifies Wilbeck as a representative of Spengler's concept of Culture. As Spengler explains, "a Culture is born in the moment when a great soul awakens out of the proto-spirituality of ever-childish humanity, and detaches itself, a form from the formless, a bounded and mortal thing from the boundless and enduring" (1:106).
. . .

6

The shape of Wilbeck's narrative conforms to Spengler's conception of cultural art. Not in conscious, rational control of his account, Wilbeck writes instinctively in a style that rhythmically fluctuates with his moods. The diary format of his unsystematic report mirrors his unstructured, leisured activities and thinking. Significantly, Wilbeck's occasion of deepest insight comes when he is a little intoxicated and writes in his sleep (176, 178), a Poe-esque occasion when undirected ideas surface from the depths of his unconscious. Both his thoughts and his journal arise from these formless depths, and like the new Culture Wilbeck believes he represents, each "struggles to exist," to surface as an expression of revisionary consciousness, to splinter from within the frame of the established historical and aesthetic conventions of Civilization. . . .

Wilbeck's manner, a surrogate for Wells's own *cultural* artistry, may on the surface seem chaotic, impulsive, inconsistent, and formless, even syntactically rampant; but underneath there seems to be a latent interior form, which Wilbeck intuits. Wilbeck anticipates the possibility that his thoughts, however discursive at present, may somehow contribute to an emergent structure for a new world with new traditions, including artistic conventions. At the level of experience, rather than of consciousness, he senses the truth of Spengler's notion that every artist "has something in him which, by force of inward necessity, never emerges into consciousness, but dominates *a priori* the form-language of his work" (1:345).

This *something* is Destiny, a cohesive, underlying force, "a revelation of the metaphysical order, a mysterious 'must,'" which in art always remains "inaccessible to art-reason" (1:221, 345). By Destiny Spengler means transcendent Will—in other words, a prime-word for *something* that we firmly know through inward conviction but that we are always unable to comprehend (1:300). Pertinently, Wilbeck speaks of an ultimate reality—"something not ourselves," but "intricate and inexplicable"—that operates behind the veil of our present experiences (285). Here Spengler's concept of Will coalesces with Schopenhauer's; and this composite notion informs Wells's belief in an emergent collective mind.

The protagonist of *Apropos of Dolores* is named Wilbeck because he beckons to this Will, serves as a mouthpiece of this Will (*bec* [Fr.], beak, mouth). At one point observing that human brains have seized control over our former ape-identity (212), Wilbeck gradually realizes that he is essentially a passive agent before this force. If, in Schopenhauerian terms, Wilbeck is not to resist this force and become frustrated (28-30), then ideally he should voluntarily and actively comply with it. And this is vaguely what he hopes he is doing when he accepts his role as a servant of and participant in the superior new world that seems to be emerging. He hopes that, as a voluntary agent of human Destiny, he ultimately contributes to the ordering of new ideas in mankind's progress (a kind of spiral evolution) towards a common mind (38, 213, 282). Although he is unable to attain full consciousness of this force, Wilbeck demonstrates a Spenglerian *cultural* response to his keen intuition of the influence of Destiny/Will. He accordingly confesses at the end of his narrative that finally his thoughts are mystical (285) . . . Whatever is Schopenhauerian in Wilbeck is subsumed in his performance as the Spenglerian artist in whom the "soul, like the soul of a Culture, is something potential that may actualize itself" (1:102).

NOTES

1. *Brynhild* (New York: Scribner's Sons, 1937), p. 23. Subsequent page references to this novel appear parenthetically in the discussion.

2. *Experiment in Autobiography* (New York: Macmillan, 1934), p. 656; *Anatomy of Frustration: A Modern Synthesis* (New York: Macmillan, 1936), pp. 12, 75; *You Can't Be Too Careful* (New York: Putnam's Sons, 1942), p. 288; *The Outline of History* (New York: Macmillan, 1927), p. 995. On the profound impact of Schopenhauer on the notion of compassion in *fin de siècle* fiction, see my *Fictional Structure and Ethics: The Turn-of-the-Century English Novel* (Athens: University of Georgia Press, 1990).

3. Robert Bloom, *Anatomies of Egotism: A Reading of the Last Novels of H. G. Wells* (Lincoln: University of Nebraska Press, 1977), p. 98.

4. Schopenhauer, *The World as Will and Idea*, trans. R. B. Haldane and J. Kemp (London: Kegan Paul, Trench, Trübner, 1891), 2:406. Subsequent page references to this novel appear parenthetically in the discussion.

5. Ettie A. Rout, *Maori Symbolism* (London: Kegan Paul, Trench, Trübner, 1926), p. xxx. Rout acknowledges indebtedness to Wells's *The Outline of History*, and Wells pays tribute to her in *You Can't Be Too Careful*, p. 112.

6. *The Works of H. G. Wells* (New York: Scribner's Sons, 1924-27), 13:454.

7. Other influences upon Wells's image of the spiral of time are noted in my *The Splintering Frame: The Later Fiction of H. G. Wells* (Victoria: University of Victoria English Literary Studies, 1984), pp. 32-33.

8. See the discussion of mandala symbolism in Carl Gustav Jung's *The Archetypes and the Collective Unconscious*, trans. R. F. C. Hull (Princeton: Princeton University Press, 1968).

9. *The Anatomy of Frustration*, p. 75. Concerning other observations made in the above paragraph, see Wells's *The Bulpington of Blup* (London: Hutchinson, 1932), p. 369; *The New American: The New World* (London: Cresset, 1935), p. 7; *The Holy Terror* (London: Michael Joseph, 1939), p. 73; and W. Warren Wager's *H. G. Wells and the World State* (New Haven: Yale University Press, 1961), p. 142.

10. *Apropos of Dolores* (New York: Scribner's Sons, 1938), p. 177. Subsequent

page references to this novel appear parenthetically in the discussion.

11. Oswald Spengler, *The Decline of the West*, trans. Charles Francis Atkinson (New York: Knopf, 1957), 1:106. Subsequent page references to this work appear parenthetically in the discussion.

Afterword:
The Contemporary Novel

H. G. Wells

 f the novel is to be recognised as something more than a relaxation, it has also, I think, to be kept free from the restrictions imposed upon it by the fierce pedantries of those who would define a general form for it. Every art nowadays must steer its way between the rocks of trivial and degrading standards and the whirlpool of arbitrary and irrational criticism. Whenever criticism of any sort becomes specialised and professional, whenever a class of adjudicators is brought into existence, those adjudicators are apt to become as a class distrustful of their immediate impressions, and anxious for methods of comparison between work and work, they begin to emulate the classifications and exact measurements of a science, and to set up ideals and rules as data for such classification[s] and measurements. They develop an alleged sense of technic, which is too often no more than the attempt to exact a labouriousness of method, or to insist upon peculiarities of method which impress the professional critic not so much as being merits as being meritorious.

This sort of thing has gone very far with the critical discussion both of the novel and the play. You have all heard that impressive dictum that some particular theatrical display, although moving, interesting, and continually entertaining from start to finish, was for occult technical reasons "not a play," and the same way you are continually having your appreciation of fiction dashed by the mysterious parallel condemnation, that the story you like "isn't a novel." The novel has been treated as though its form was as well-defined as the sonnet.
. . .

[The claim, for instance, that] the novel ought to be long enough for [a reader] to take up after dinner and finish before his whiskey at eleven . . . [is] obviously a half-forgotten echo of Edgar Allan Poe's discussion of the short story. Edgar Allan Poe was very definite upon the point that the short story should be finished at a sitting. But the novel and the short story are two entirely different things, and the train of reasoning that made the American master limit the short story to about an hour of reading as a maximum, does not apply to the longer work. A short story is, or should be, a simple thing; it aims at producing one single, vivid effect; it has to seize the attention at the outset, and never relaxing, gather it together more and more until the climax is reached. The limits of the human capacity to attend closely therefore set a limit to it; it must explode and finish before interruption occurs or fatigue sets in.

But the novel I hold to be a discursive thing; it is not a single interest, but a woven tapestry of interests; one is drawn on first by this affection and curiosity, and then by that; it is something to return to; and I do not see that we can possibly set any limit to its extent. The discursive value of the novel among written works of art is in characterisation, and the charm of a well-conceived character lies, not in knowing its destiny, but in watching its proceedings.

For my own part, I will confess that I find all the novels of [Charles] Dickens, long as they are, too short for me. I am sorry they do not flow into one another more than they do . . . Following on the days of Dickens, the novel began to contract, to subordinate characterisation to story and description to drama; considerations of a sordid nature, I am told, had to do with that; something about a guinea and a half and six shillings with which we will not concern ourselves—but I rejoice to see many signs to-day that that phase of narrowing and restriction is over, and that there is every encouragement for a return towards a laxer, more spacious form of novel-writing . . . a return to the lax freedom of form, the rambling discursiveness, the right to roam, of the earlier English novel, of [Laurence Sterne's] *Tristram Shandy* and of [Henry Fielding's] *Tom Jones.. . . .*

[This recovery also] derives a stimulus from such bold and original enterprises as that of Monsieur [Romain] Roland in his *Jean Christophe* . . . I name *Jean Christophe* as a sort of archetype in this connection, because it is just at present very much in our thoughts by reason of the admirable translation Mr. [Gilbert] Cannan is giving us; but there is a greater predecessor to this comprehensive and spectacular treatment of a single mind and its impressions and ideas, or of one or two associated minds, that comes to us now via Mr. [Arnold] Bennett and Mr. Cannan from France. The great original of all this work is the colossal last unfinished book of [Gustave] Flaubert, *Bouvard et Pécuchet* . . . It is not extensively read in this country; it is not yet, I believe, translated into English; but there it is—and if it is new to the reader I make him this present of the secret of a book that is a precious wilderness of wonderful reading.

But if Flaubert is really the Continental emanicipator of the novel from the restrictions of form, the master to whom we of the English persuasion, we of the discursive school, must for ever recur is he whom I will maintain against all comers to be the subtlest and greatest artist—I lay stress upon that word artist— that Great Britain has ever produced in all that is essentially the novel, Laurence Sterne.

Supplementary Readings:
1956–1994

Amis, Kingsley. *New Maps of Hell: A Survey of Science-Fiction.* New York: Harcourt, Brace, 1960.

Ash, Brian. *Faces of the Future: The Lessons of Science Fiction.* New York: Taplinger, 1975.

Asker, D. B. D. "H. G. Wells and Regressive Evolution." *Dutch Quarterly Review of Anglo-American Letters* 12 (1982): 15-29.

Batchelor, John. *The Edwardian Novelists.* New York: St. Martin's Press, 1982.

_____. *H. G. Wells.* Cambridge: Harvard University Press, 1985.

Bergonzi, Bernard. *The Situation of the Novel.* London: Macmillan, 1970.

_____. *The Turn of the Century: Essays on Victorian and Modern English Literature.* London: Macmillan, 1973.

_____ (ed.). *H. G. Wells: A Collection of Critical Essays.* Englewood Cliffs, N. J.: Prentice-Hall, 1975.

Bloom, Robert. *Anatomies of Egotism: A Reading of the Last Novels of H. G. Wells.* Lincoln: University of Nebraska Press, 1977.

Borrello, Alfred. *H. G. Wells, Author in Agony.* Carbondale: Southern Illinois University Press, 1972.

Bowen, Roger. "Science, Myth, and Fiction in H. G. Wells's *Island of Dr. Moreau.*" *Studies in the Novel* 8 (1975): 318-35.

Buckley, Jerome Hamilton. *Season of Youth: The Bildungsroman from Dickens to Golding.* Cambridge: Harvard University Press, 1974.

Coren, Michael. *The Invisible Man: The Life and Liberties of H. G. Wells.* New York: Random House, 1993.

Costa, Richard Hauer. "Edwardian Intimations of the Shape of Fiction to Come: Mr. Britling/Job Huss as Wellsian Central Intelligence." *English Literature in Transition* 18 (1975): 229-42.

_____. *H. G. Wells.* Boston, Twayne, 1985.

Dessner, Lawrence Jay. "H. G. Wells, *Mr. Polly*, and the Uses of Art." *English Literature in Transition* 16 (1973): 121-34.

Dickson, Lovat. *H. G. Wells: His Turbulent Life and Times.* New York: Atheneum, 1969.

Draper, Michael. *H. G. Wells.* London: Macmillan, 1987.

Gill, Stephen M. *Scientific Romances of H. G. Wells: A Critical Study.* Cornwall, Ont.: Vesta, 1975.

Glover, Willis B. "Religious Orientations of H. G. Wells: A Case Study in Scientific Humanism." *Harvard Theological Review* 65 (1972): 117-35.

Haining, Peter (ed.). *The H. G. Wells Scrapbook.* New York: Clarkson N. Potter, 1979.

Hammond, John R. *An H. G. Wells Companion: A Guide to the Novels, Romances and Short Stories.* London: Macmillan, 1979.

_____. *H. G. Wells: Interviews and Recollections.* London: Macmillan, 1980.

_____. *Herbert George Wells: An Annotated Bibliography of His Works.* New York: Garland, 1977.

Haynes, Roslynn D. *H. G. Wells: Discoverer of the Future.* New York: New York University Press, 1980.

Herbert, Lucille. "*Tono-Bungay* : Tradition and Experiment." *Modern Language Review* 33 (1972): 140-55.

Hillegas, Mark R. *The Future as Nightmare: H. G. Wells and the Anti-Utopians.* New York: Oxford University Press, 1967.

Hughes, David Y. "Bergonzi and After in the Criticism of Wells's SF." *Science-Fiction Studies* 3 (1976): 165-74.

Hume, Kathryn. "Eat or Be Eaten: H. G. Wells's *Time Machine.*" *Philological Quarterly* 69 (1990): 233-51.

_____. "The Hidden Dynamics of *The War of the Worlds.*" *Philological Quarterly* 62 (1983): 279-92.

Hunter, Jefferson. *Edwardian Fiction.* Cambridge: Harvard University Press, 1982.

Huntington, John. *The Logic of Fantasy: Science Fiction and H. G. Wells.* New York: Columbia University Press, 1982.

_____ (ed.). *Critical Essays on H. G. Wells.* Boston: G. K. Hall, 1991.

Hyde, William J. "The Socialism of H. G. Wells." *Journal of the History of Ideas* 17 (1956): 217-34.

Hynes, Samuel. *The Edwardian Turn of Mind.* Princeton: Princeton University Press, 1968.

Jacobs, Robert G. "H. G. Wells, Joseph Conrad, and the Relative Universe." *Conradiana* 1 (1968): 51-55.

Kagarlitsky, Julius. "H. G. Wells in Russia." *Soviet Literature* 9 (1966): 150-55.

_____. *The Life and Thought of H. G. Wells.* London: Sedgwick & Jackson, 1966.

Ketterer, David. *New Worlds for Old: The Apocalyptic Imagination, Science Fiction, and American Literature.* Garden City, N. Y.: Anchor Books, 1964.

Lodge, David. *Language of Fiction.* New York: Columbia University Press, 1966.

_____. *The Novelist at the Crossroads and Other Essays.* Ithaca: Cornell University Press, 1971.

MacKenzie, Norman and Jeanne. *The Fabians.* New York: Simon & Schuster, 1977.

_____. *The Time Traveller: The Life of H. G. Wells*. London: Weidenfeld & Nicolson, 1973.

McConnell, Frank. *The Science Fiction of H. G. Wells*. New York: Oxford University Press, 1981.

Morton, Peter R. "Biological Degeneration: A Motif in H. G. Wells and Other Late Victorian Utopianists." *Southern Review* 9 (1976): 93-112.

Müllenbrock, Heinz-Joachim. "Nationalismus und Internationalismus im Werk von H. G. Wells." *Neuren Sprachen* 18 (1969): 478-97.

Murray, Brian. *H. G. Wells*. New York: Continuum, 1990.

Newell, Kenneth B. *Structure in Four Novels by H. G. Wells*. The Hague: Mouton, 1968.

Parrinder, Patrick. *H. G. Wells*. Edinburgh: Oliver & Boyd, 1970.

_____ (ed.). *H. G. Wells: The Critical Heritage*. London: Routledge & Kegan Paul, 1972.

Philmus, Robert M. *Into the Unknown: The Evolution of Science Fiction from Francis Godwin to H. G. Wells*. Berkeley and Los Angeles: University of California Press, 1970.

_____. "Revisions of His Past: H. G. Wells's *Anatomy of Frustration*." *Texas Studies in Literature and Language* 20 (1978): 249-66.

_____. "The Time Machine; Or, The Fourth Dimension as Prophecy." *Publications of the Modern Language Association* 84 (1969): 530-35.

Pritchett, V. S. "Wells Marches On." *New Statesman* 72 (23 September 1966): 433-34.

Raknem, Ingvald. *H. G. Wells and His Critics*. London: Allen & Unwin, 1962.

Ray, Gordon N. *H. G. Wells and Rebecca West*. London: Macmillan, 1974.

Rose, Jonathan. *The Edwardian Temperament, 1895-1919*. Athens: Ohio University Press, 1986.

Scheick, William J. *The Ethos of Romance at the Turn of the Century*. Austin: University of Texas Press, 1994.

_____. *Fictional Structure and Ethics: The Turn-of-the-Century English Novel*. Athens: University of Georgia Press, 1990.

_____ and J. Randolph Cox. *H. G. Wells: A Reference Guide*. Boston: G. K. Hall, 1988.

Schultz, Bruno. *Die Utopie in der Angloamerikanischen Literatur: Interpretationen*. Düsseldorf: Bagel, 1984.

Smith, David C. *H. G. Wells, Desperately Mortal: A Biography*. New Haven: Yale University Press, 1986.

Stevenson, Lionel. *The History of the English Novel: Yesterday and After*. New York: Barnes & Noble, 1967.

Suvin, Darko. *Metamorphoses of Science Fiction: On the Poetics and History of a Literary Genre*. New Haven: Yale University Press, 1979.

Timko, Michael. "H. G. Wells Dramatic Criticism for the *Pall Mall Gazette*." *Library* 17 (1962): 138-45.

Wagar, Warren W. "H. G. Wells and the Scientific Imagination." *Virginia Quarterly Review* 65 (1989): 390-400.

_____. *H. G. Wells and the World State*. New Haven: Yale University Press, 1961.

West, Anthony. *H. G. Wells: Aspects of a Life*. London: Hutchinson, 1984.
Williamson, Jack. *H. G. Wells: Critic of Progress*. Baltimore: Mirage Press, 1973.
Young, Kenneth. *H. G. Wells*. London: Longmans, Green, 1974.

Index

About the Editor

WILLIAM J. SCHEICK is J. R. Millikan Professor of English and American Literature at the University of Texas at Austin. He was formerly the editor of *Texas Studies in Language and Literature* and has served on a number of editorial boards. He has published some 15 books and more than 140 articles.

ISBN 0-313-28859-3